Sustainability and Private Law

Sustainability and Private Law

Bram Akkermans and Gijs van Dijck (Eds.)

eleven
international publishing

Published, sold and distributed by Eleven International Publishing
P.O. Box 85576
2508 CG The Hague
The Netherlands
Tel.: +31 70 33 070 33
Fax: +31 70 33 070 30
email: sales@elevenpub.nl
www.elevenpub.com

Sold and distributed in USA and Canada
Independent Publishers Group
814 N. Franklin Street
Chicago, IL 60610, USA
Order Placement: +1 800 888 4741
Fax: +1 312 337 5985
orders@ipgbook.com
www.ipgbook.com

Eleven International Publishing is an imprint of Boom uitgevers Den Haag.

ISBN 978-94-6236-986-3
ISBN 978-94-6094-441-3 (e-book)

Table of Contents

1 Introduction

Bram Akkermans and Gijs van Dijck

Sustainability is a broad and often undefined concept. For some it refers to ecological aspects such as climate change and global warming. For others, it also includes work on democracy and good governance.[1] The 17 UN Sustainable Development Goals refer to all of these aspects. Sustainable development is commonly understood as the process by which we achieve sustainability.

In her influential report, Brundtland defined sustainable development as 'development that meets the needs of the present without compromising the ability of future generations to meet their own needs'.[2] Sustainability thus presents itself as an organisational principle that allows factoring future generations into decision-making processes. The principle does not merely apply to states and governments, but to everyone. Sustainability, therefore, comes with a call to all of us to contribute towards creating a sustainable society.

In many fields, such as economics, philosophy and religious studies, there is substantial attention for sustainability.[3] Legal scholars have traditionally focused on environmental law, but hardly on the more general topic of sustainability.[4] Slowly, however, as there is more attention to climate change, labour circumstances and income inequality, more lawyers begin to deal with these issues. A good example of this is perhaps the work on corporate social responsibility (CSR).[5] There, for example, companies often take on obligations to improve circumstances of workers, or to reduce environmental impact of production processes.

This book explores the role of private law (and whether it has one in the first place) in relation to sustainability: Can private law contribute towards achieving sustainability? It focuses on the more traditional fields of private law, including property law, business law, tort law, and contract law. The book is exploratory, as the question what private law should

1 See J. Blewit, *Understanding Sustainable Development* (London/New York: Routhledge (second edition), 2015), p. 7 (Blewitt 2015).

2 WCED, *Our Common Future* (Oxford: Oxford University Press, 1987) p. 43.

3 See, *inter alia*, K. Raworth, *Doughnut Economics* (London: Random House, 2017), Pope Francis, Laudatio Si'. *On the care for our common home* (Vatican, 2015).

4 See F. Capra and U. Mattei, *The Ecology of Law. Toward a Legal System in Tune with Nature and Community* (Oakland: Berrett-Koehler Publishers Inc, 2015), U. Mattei and A. Quarta, *The Turning Point in Private Law* (Northampton:Edward Elgar, 2018).

5 See, for example, Anna Beckers, *Enforcing corporate social responsibility codes: on global self-regulation and national private law*. (Oxford: Hart Publishing, 2015), Mark Kawakami, *Flawed strategies to reducing labor exploitations: Reassessing the role of private actors in the global supply chain* (Maastricht: Datawyse / Universitaire Pers Maastricht, 2017).

contribute towards sustainability and sustainable development first requires an analysis of the role private law may play.

The Structure of this Book

The research in this book is the result of collaboration in the Maastricht European Private Law Institute (M-EPLI). At this institute, we attempt to reflect on common research themes and to contribute to them from our expertise. After exploring the allocation of regulatory competences, we collectively turned our attention to one of the largest challenges of our time.[6] Over a series of intensive meetings, M-EPLI researchers discussed what they understand to be sustainability, what the contribution from their field could be and how this could be combined in a volume. Like the 17 UN Sustainable Development Goals, a wide variety of angles can be observed in the various contributions.

In this book, Jaap Hage and Agustin Parise each take on more general questions about the role of private law and the movement towards sustainability in private law. Hage asks himself the question of the role of private law. Parise signals a general trend in moving towards a new ecological paradigm in private law.

Bram Akkermans and Jill Robbie offer reflections from property law. Akkermans takes a more general focus on property law and attempts to provide it with new fundamental values. Robbie takes the perspective of land reform in Scotland and focuses on what working on doctrinal property law can mean to achieve sustainability.

Michael Faure and Yayun Shen and Gijs van Dijck provide insights from tort law. Faure and Yayun take environmental liability and investigate how tort law can be employed to work towards sustainability. Van Dijck takes a similar perspective but focuses on how tort law can be used to address environmental harm.

Kim Berg and Mark Kawakami reflect on the role of company law in working towards sustainable solutions. CSR plays an important role in their investigations. William Bull, finally, offers insights from the perspectives of optional instruments in European private law. He focuses on the way in which optional private law can empower private parties to move towards their own sustainable solutions.

The book concludes with a chapter written by the editors in which we try to discover common themes and common issues and in which we attempt to raise questions for further research. With that, we hope to contribute towards bringing more attention to sustainability in private law research.

---

6 Bram Akkermans, Jaap Hage, Nicole Kornet and Jan Smits (Eds.), *Who Does What. On the allocation of regulatory competences in European Private Law* (Antwerp: Intersentia, 2015).

2 Law and Sustainability

Jaap Hage

2.1 Introduction

Many institutions suffer from serious problems. Recent examples are:
- the system in which pollution of the environment is only limited to a small extent,
- the continuing emission of greenhouse gasses which leads to global warming,
- the way in which bankers are rewarded, which stimulates them to conduct short-term policies that can easily lead to crises in the financial system,
- the economic inequality between more and less developed countries, which leads to large, scale migration and refugee crises, and so on.

These problems question the institutions that give rise to them, and raise the issue whether these institutions can continue to exist in their present form. Are our institutions sustainable? Sustainability has become a hot issue.

Because societal institutions often find their basis in legal arrangements, such as environmental law, international trade law and the freedom of contract, there is an obvious relation between law and sustainability. It is possible to elaborate on this relation with an eye to many different issues, and other contributions in this volume illustrate this. However, in this particular contribution I want to address the issue whether law should promote sustainability in general.

At first sight this may seem a superfluous question. Is it not obvious that law should promote sustainability? Should we not focus on more important questions such as which kinds of sustainability law should promote first and what means law should use to do so? In this contribution I will not only try to answer the question whether law should promote sustainability, I will also try to show that this general question does not have an obvious affirmative answer, and that the more detailed questions – however important they are – should not be answered without paying attention to the more general question.

The answers to important questions surprisingly often depend on what count as good reasons in answering these questions. This is a rather abstract methodological question, but a crucially important one. The first two steps in my argument, which together take up more than half of my argument, are therefore methodological. The idea that a discussion about the desirability of law promoting sustainability is superfluous may be inspired by a way of looking at legal science that is influenced by the agonistic aspect of legal procedures.

I will argue in section 2 that this agonistic perspective is not unavoidable in legal science and actually should be avoided.

Whether law should promote sustainability is a question about what the content of law should be. How are such questions to be answered? Should we use some procedure, such as democracy, to find the right answer, or should we take a more substantive approach, such as the strategy to minimise poverty, or pollution of our environment?[1] These questions are addressed in section 3.

Then we will redirect our attention from methodological issues to sustainability. At first sight it may seem clear what sustainability is, but on closer inspection, much of the clarity vanishes. In section 4 we will take a closer look at sustainability and we will find that some forms of sustainability are more attractive than others. After this section it should have become clear why we need an answer to the more general question about the desirability of sustainability, next to answers to the question how sustainability should be promoted.

Section 5 aims to answer the main research question of this contribution. However, it will turn out that large parts of the answer were already given in the 'preliminary' discussions that paved the way for what seemed to be the main question.

This contribution is concluded in section 6.

2.2 Two Ways to Justify Laws

An argument why law should promote sustainability may seem superfluous, because 'everybody' is already convinced that sustainability is important and valuable and that therefore law should promote it. Such a view, that an argument is superfluous because everybody is already convinced may be especially attractive to lawyers, because it sits well with the way in which lawyers often look at argumentation and justification, namely that they are necessary to convince, but superfluous if agreement already exists. Let me explain this.

There are two main ways in which a claim that law should fulfil a particular function, such as promoting sustainability, can be justified.[2] One starts from a set of premises, which are assumed to be true and are adopted as a kind of axioms of the arguments. It shows

1 More in abstract, a substantive approach adopts a standard to evaluate law, while a procedural approach adopts a procedure to establish a standard.

2 A more extensive account of the different approaches to justification can be found in Jaap Hage, 'The Justification of Value Judgments. Theoretical Foundations for Arguments about the Best Level to Regulate European Private Law', in Bram Akkermans, Jaap Hage, Nicole Kornet and Jan Smits (eds.), *Who Does What? On the allocation of regulatory competences in European Private Law*, Cambridge: Intersentia 2015, p. 15-56.

how the conclusion about the function of law follows from these axioms. Because the axioms are taken to be true and because the argument is logically valid, the conclusion must also be true. For example, it is assumed that law must promote welfare, including the welfare of future generations, and that sustainability contributes to this welfare. From these two premises it follows that law must promote sustainability.

The other starts from the conclusion and derives this conclusion from some premises, which are provisionally adopted. The argument is presented to the auditory that must be convinced of the conclusion. If the auditory accepts the provisional premises and if the argument is logically valid, the auditory will normally – that is: if it is logical – be convinced of the conclusion. If it is not convinced, the auditory must point out which premise(s) it does not (yet) accept. If this happens the procedure repeats itself with an argument to convince the auditory of the disputed premise(s). For example, if the auditory does not accept that law should promote sustainability, the proponent of sustainability gives the two premises and the auditory must indicate which one (or even both) of the premises it does not accept. Then the procedure repeats itself for the non-accepted premise(s). The procedure ends as soon as the auditory accepts all the required premises, or the proponent cannot produce suitable premises anymore. In the first case the conclusion has been justified to the auditory; in the second case the conclusion was not justified.

This second way is agonistic in the sense that it is based on a disagreement between the proponent of the conclusion and the auditory, which is, at least in first instance, not convinced. The argumentative procedure must continue until either the proponent gives up, or the auditory accepts a set of premises from which the conclusion ultimately follows. A court procedure exhibits many traits of such an agonistic procedure. In a typical civil procedure the one party tries to convince the other party, where the court functions as an arbiter that guides over the rules of the argumentative procedure. In a procedure in which other interests than merely private ones are involved, both parties (if there is more than one) try to convince the court. Lawyers, who are often tempted to look at argumentation as a tool to be used in court procedures, may feel especially attracted to this second way to justify claims about law.

A major difference between the first and the second way is that the second way aims at conviction and agreement, while the first way aims at truth. In many contexts agreement may be more important than truth. This is especially the case when there is no truth to be had, or at least people believe this to be the case. Morality may be a case in point. Many people believe that moral judgments ultimately reflect the personal convictions of the persons that hold them and that there is no independent moral truth about which people disagree. Still people sometimes sincerely disagree about moral issues, and this disagreement may lead to conflicts that need to be pacified. A search for the moral 'truth' only continues the conflict, and what is needed is a peaceful way to reach agreement.

Some believe that the same holds for law, especially in so-called 'hard cases'. In hard cases there is no one right answer, and therefore we need a procedure that can lead to a peaceful settlement of disagreement, rather than to the elusive 'right answer'. That is why procedures are crucially important in law. It is also a good reason for lawyers to use argumentative procedures that aim at conviction and agreement, rather than try to find the legal truth.

Is the question whether law should promote sustainability a question where agreement is more important than truth? Of course the answer depends on whether there is truth to be had. Is there a true answer to the question? If not, agreement may be the best aim to pursue, if only because the better aim of truth is not available. However, I will argue that a true answer is available, although it may be very hard to find. That does not show that it is not important anymore to strive for conviction and agreement. However, if truth is possible, not any agreement will suffice. It must be an agreement that might be true for all we know.[3] Mere agreement that law should promote sustainability should not satisfy us as reason why more argumentation is superfluous, and therefore I will continue my argument.

2.3 How to Determine the Content of Law?

2.3.1 The Procedural Approach

Lawyers are fond of the *Trias Politica*, in particular the version that was popularised by Montesquieu (*De l'esprit des lois*). The state has to fulfil three functions in relation to the law: it must create laws, it must execute them, and it must apply them in adjudication. The idea of the *Trias Politica* is that different state organs must be charged with fulfilling these three functions. In particular it means that the judiciary must apply the law, and that the legislator must make law. This division between applying and making law, however difficult it may be to maintain it in legal practice, still underlies much legal thinking. Lawyers as such are often considered to have no role in making law; that is a matter of the legislator and therefore of politics.

This 'therefore' is based on a view that was popularised by Rousseau (*Du contrat social*), namely that a people should be autonomous in the sense that it rules itself. A people should be free and it can only be free if it lives by rules that it has set itself for itself. Political organs of the state, such as parliament, should therefore play a crucial role in legislation, and lawyers as such have at most an advisory role in that connection. The law should reflect

3 This is argued more elaborately in Jaap Hage, 'Anything goes: An Apology for Parallel Distributed Legal Science' in *Informal Logic*, vol. 36 (2016) no. 3, DOI: http://dx.doi.org/10.22329/il.v36i3.4719.

the will of the people as such, the *volonté général*, and it is the function of politics to establish that will.

This view, according to which laws reflect the will of the people, leads to a procedural way of determining the content of law. Somehow we must find a way to determine what the people want and the discovered will should be turned into law. Modern states often use a two-step procedure to accomplish this: elections determine the composition of parliaments, and parliaments determine the content of the law. Of course there are many variations on this theme, but the basic idea is the same: the content of the law should be determined procedurally, on the basis of the will of the people, and not substantively, on the basis of some presupposed standard(s).

2.3.2 *The Substantive Approach and the Role of Democracy*

The alternative for a procedural approach is a substantive approach: the content of the law should be good, and those laws should be adopted that are inherently good, or which bring about good results. At first sight, the will of the people – or anybody else's – is irrelevant in this connection. The only thing that counts is whether the laws are good. What the people want does not matter. If the people want good laws, those laws should be adopted because they are good, not because the people want them. If the people want bad laws, those laws should not be adopted because they are bad, even though the people want them.

On closer inspection, things turn out to be more complicated. If laws should be adopted for the reason that they are good laws, there is need for a procedure to find out which laws are good. Many believe that human beings, certainly when they are adults, are the best judges of what is good for them. Therefore the will of the people is important in establishing what the law should be. Not because the will of the people determines what is good, but because the will of the people is a good epistemic device to find out what is good.

Perhaps the will of the people is even more important, even on a substantive approach. If we should adopt laws for the reason that they are good, we need a criterion to determine what makes a law a good law. Such a criterion may refer to the will of the people, for instance because laws are better when they are stable and efficacious[4] and because laws that find support in the will of the people tend to be more stable and efficacious. In that case, the will of the people and democratic procedures are not merely relevant as epistemic devices, but they are (co-)determinative of the goodness of laws.

Whether the will of the people – and in line with this will – democratic procedures are relevant on a substantive approach to law depends on the criterion that is used to determine whether laws are good. Does this criterion, directly or indirectly, refer to the will of the

4 Cf. Lon L. Fuller, *The morality of law*, revised edition, New Haven: Yale University Press 1963, chapter II.

people? Is the will of the people a reliable indicator of which laws will be good according to this criterion? These are the questions that need to be answered in order to find out whether democracy should play a role in a substantive approach to law.

2.3.3 *Intermezzo: A Democratic 'Rechtsstaat'*

At this stage, some lawyers may protest that my argument is highly theoretical and that the actual practice in most Western countries has a mix of a procedural and a substantive approach to law, which goes under the name of 'democratic *Rechtsstaat*.'[5] In such a democratic *Rechtsstaat* law-making is a democratic procedure, but the power of the legislator is limited by a constitutional framework that safeguards rights of legal subjects. The existence and prevalence of this institution seems to disprove the opposition between procedural and substantive approaches to law: 'real' law is both procedural and substantive.

This appearance is deceptive, however. A democratic *Rechtsstaat* is popular because it combines the attractiveness of democratic procedures with protection of rights, which are deemed so fundamental that they deserve protection against undesirable outcomes of the democratic procedure. However, this is compatible with a substantive, rather than a will-based, justification of democratic procedures. A democratic *Rechtsstaat* may be deemed good because both the protection of fundamental rights and respect for the will of the people are considered to be substantively good. On this explanation of the popularity of the democratic *Rechtsstaat*, this popularity does not prove that the opposition between will and substantive goodness is misguided, but rather that a substantive view of good law is compatible with a – limited – role for democratic procedures.

2.3.4 *Substantive Criteria for Good Laws*

> "Consider the following story:
> Julie and Mark are brother and sister. They are traveling together in France on summer vacation from college. One night they are staying alone in a cabin near the beach. They decide that it would be interesting and fun if they tried making love. At the very least, it would be a new experience for each of them. Julie was already taking birth control pills, but Mark uses a condom too, just to be safe. They both enjoy making love, but they decide never to do it again. They keep that night as a special secret, which makes them feel even closer to each other.

5 I use the German expression '*Rechtsstaat*' rather than its English counterpart 'rule of law', because the notion of a *Rechtsstaat* emphasises, more than the notion of the rule of law, substantive limitations on state powers, for instance in the form of fundamental or human rights.

Do you think it is acceptable for two consenting adults, who happen to be siblings, to make love?"

This brief story was used by social psychologist Jonathan Haidt to investigate the role of reason in making moral judgments.[6] Haidt found that most people thought the described behaviour of Julie and Mark to be unacceptable, even though they had trouble justifying their judgments. Haidt explained this outcome by postulating that moral decision-making is typically *not* the outcome of rational thinking, but rather a matter of feelings. The reasons people adduce for their judgements, if they can find any, are not what made them give their judgements, but they are rationalisations afterwards. The reasons may be good or bad, but they are not the reasons that made people form their judgments. Haidt's findings are supported by much more research in moral psychology.[7]

From this research we can conclude that moral intuitions are not a reliable guide to correct moral judgements.[8] Intuitive judgements often stand in need to be corrected by moral reasoning. Therefore it is not a wise strategy to test evaluative theories, including theories on what makes for good law, against our moral judgments. Kant (*Grundlegung zur Metaphysik der Sitten*) was correct when he claimed that reason should provide us with the standard for moral rightness. Analogously we should look at reason to find a standard for good laws. However, otherwise than what Kant would have us to believe, reason by itself cannot provide standards for behaviour. Reason needs input to generate output, and this input consists in human emotions. For example, reason cannot determine that we should eat, but given that we feel bad when hungry (a kind of emotion) reason can determine that we should eat in order to avoid hunger.

This was already emphasised by Hume (*Treatise on Human Nature*) who claimed that reason is merely a servant of what he called the 'passions'. The same idea was elaborated by Bentham (*An Introduction to the Principles of Morals and Legislation*) and the utilitarian school of ethics that built upon his foundational work.[9] According to classical utilitarianism,

6 Jonathan Haidt, *The happiness hypothesis. Putting ancient wisdom and philosophy to the test of modern science*, London: Random House 2006, p. 20/1, with references to reports on the original experiments.

7 Cf. Walter Sinnott-Armstrong (ed.), *Moral Psychology, volume 2: The Cognitive Science of Morality: Intuition and Diversity*, Cambridge: MIT Press 2008, p. xiii/xiv.

8 If moral intuitions are not a reliable guide to correct moral decisions, this does not mean that they do not co-determine which moral decisions are correct. Moral intuitions may function as the input to a process of generating a coherent set of beliefs, including moral beliefs, and the moral beliefs in the set may be considered correct because of their role in the coherent set. However, there is no guarantee that the intuitions that are input to a process of justification are also a reliable guide to determine the outcome of this process. For more details on this role of moral intuitions, see Jaap Hage, 'Recht en utilisme. Een pleidooi voor het utilisme als richtlijn voor de wetgever' in *Law and Method* 2015, DOI 10.5553/REM/.000011, or www.jaaphage.nl/pdf/Recht%20en%20utilisme.pdf.

9 See Julia Driver, *Consequentialism*, London: Routledge 2012, Joshua Greene, *Moral Tribes. Emotion, Reason and the Gap between Us and Them*, London: Atlantic Books 2013.

(legislative) acts should be evaluated with an eye to their impact on happiness: a law is better, the more happiness it generates. This standard does not provide us with very substantial clues for the evaluation of laws, but it has one major advantage: it makes the translation from the evaluative to the empirical. The question to how much happiness a law leads may be very hard to answer, but it is an empirical question. Given the utilitarian standard, it is a matter of hard facts whether a law is good, and what are the best possible laws.

A second advantage of this utilitarian standard is that it takes the views – or rather the feelings – of individual persons seriously. According to classical utilitarianism, everybody's happiness counts equally in determining what the best laws are.

I cannot argue extensively for the use of the utilitarian standard to evaluate legislation here[10] and will assume without much argument that the maximisation of happiness should function as standard for substantive evaluation of laws. Application of this utilitarian standard may lead to procedural conclusions such as the conclusion that laws should be determined democratically. Whether it actually leads to that conclusion depends on the facts: does democratic adoption of laws maximise happiness? This is not the place to speculate on the answer.

2.3.5 *Democracy or Utilitarianism?*

Laws can be evaluated procedurally and substantively. The most obvious procedural standard is whether a law came about democratically. For the sake of argument I adopted utilitarianism as the substantive standard. The question that needs to be answered now is whether laws should be evaluated procedurally or substantively. More concretely: should we ask whether a law was made in a democratic fashion, or should we look whether the law leads to more, and preferably the maximum amount of, happiness? The answer to this question is complicated by the fact that a democratic procedure may contribute to the maximisation of happiness.

Rather than attempting to fully answer the question, I will argue that in our actual practices we seem to adopt procedural approaches, including democracy, for the reason that they lead to substantively good results. The obvious illustration of this point is that we hesitate to let young people make important decisions without supervision. Both in private law (juridical acts) and in public law (franchise) society gives minors powers that are more limited than those of adults. Since minors do not have less will than adults, this practice is hard to justify from a purely procedural perspective. The reason – which is broadly recognised – to give minors less powers is that they are not yet capable of exercising

10 A more extensive argument can be found in Jaap Hage, 'Recht en utilisme'.

these powers in the interests of themselves or society at large. This is a substantive argument: a procedure – the performance of juridical acts, including voting – that gives much influence to what a person wants, is only endorsed if there is good reason to assume that it will lead to substantively good results. Apparently society adopts procedures, including democracy, because of their good results. This makes democracy dependent on its good results, and the goodness of these results depends on the adopted standard, in this case utilitarianism.

Democracy and utilitarianism are not alternatives for each other, because there may be good utilitarian reasons to adopt democracy. However, if such reasons turn out to be lacking it is more likely that society prefers a substantive evaluation of laws to a purely procedural one. For that reason I will adopt a substantive standard, the maximisation of happiness, to answer the question whether law should promote sustainability.

2.4 Sustainability

Should law promote sustainability? On the utilitarian standard, the answer depends on two factors. The first is how much happiness the promotion of sustainability leads to, and the second is how much happiness alternatives for sustainability lead to. Both questions are not answerable unless we obtain more precise insight in what sustainability precisely is. If we do not know that, the question of how much happiness sustainability leads to has no well-defined answer, and neither has the question what the alternatives are.

What is sustainability? In chapter 2 of the Report of the World Commission on Environment and Development 'Development and International Economic Co-Operation: Environment' sustainable development is defined as '… development that meets the needs of the present without compromising the ability of future generations to meet their own needs'.[11] This authoritative definition focuses on development, but not only developments can be sustainable. A particular practice such as allowing unlimited emission of greenhouse gasses or paying bankers by giving them bonuses depending on the price of their company's shares may also be more or less sustainable. A slight modification of the above definition of sustainable development leads to the following formulation:

A practice or development is sustainable if and only if it meets the needs of the present without compromising the ability of future generations to meet their own needs.

Regrettably this definition of sustainability merely moves the vagueness from the term 'sustainable' to the terms 'need' and 'compromise'. However, it has the advantage of making one particular aspect of sustainability clear; it has to do with the relation between the present and future generations. In the following I will ignore the vagueness of 'compromise' and focus on the nature of needs and on the relation between generations.

11 www.channelingreality.com/Documents/Brundtland_Searchable.pdf (last visited on 31 March 2017).

2.5 Needs and Happiness

The definition of sustainability focuses on the needs of both the present and future generations. When the Report elaborates on needs it does not define them, but mentions employment, food, energy, housing, water supply, sanitation and health care. This list is strongly focused on survival, and not on happiness or well-being, although the Reports refer (in section III.3) to 'needs for survival and well-being'. It seems clear that a human being on the brink of dying is typically not well, but it does not follow that a person whose needs for survival are met also has his needs for well-being met. Moreover, there are circumstances in which death may make an end to serious suffering and would *in that limited sense* lead to an increase in well-being. From a utilitarian perspective the emphasis on survival is not necessarily wrong, but nevertheless lop-sided.

This issue can easily be solved by replacing the notion of a need, or its interpretation, by the notion of happiness. The following definition of sustainability would result:

> A practice or development is sustainable if and only if it optimises the happiness of the present generation of sentient beings without compromising the ability of future sentient beings to optimise their own happiness.

From a utilitarian perspective this new definition is better than the former one, which focuses on needs. However, to make the definition suitable for happiness, it was necessary to introduce three complications. First it refers to happiness, which is perhaps less concrete than the notion of needs.[12] Second, it mentions whose happiness is taken into account, and it does so in the most inclusive way by counting in all sentient beings, and not – for instance – only human beings.[13] And third it refers to the optimisation, rather than the maximisation, of happiness. The reason is that maximisation does not imply a lower boundary, and the maximum of happiness may be very unhappy indeed. In that case optimisation may mean ending the strive for happiness, as in euthanasia.

In this contribution I will not pay much attention to the nature of happiness, on its causes, or on the possibility to measure it. Instead I refer the interested reader to the large and vastly increasing amount of literature on these topics.[14] In the next section I will address

12 The word 'need' has a ring of objectivity. Whether something is a need, rather than a mere desire, seems not to be a matter of taste. However, it is far from easy to distinguish between 'real' needs and mere desires.

13 This broadening of the scope of the happiness principle may lead to results that are more surprising than the requirement to treat higher animals with sufficient care. Many kinds of animals that might have been happy have been exterminated by humans. It cannot be completely excluded that a world that maximises happiness and biodiversity would be one without Homo Sapiens.

14 Good starting points are:
- the Wikipedia-site on happiness (https://en.wikipedia.org/wiki/Happiness),

the topic that seems most relevant to sustainability, the question whose happiness should be taken into account.

In this section I will say a little more on the ability of a generation to maximise its own happiness. If sustainability is worthy to be promoted by law, it should not merely enable future sentient being to maximise their own happiness, but it should make future sentient beings sufficiently happy. It is not easy to determine what amount of happiness is required in this connection. A minimum condition would be that the beings in question would prefer to continue living if they have given sufficient thought to the question whether they want to continue living. Obviously this test can only apply to beings that are capable of thinking about this question. Equally obviously, it needs specification of what counts as 'sufficient thought' on whether a being wants to continue living.

A much more demanding test would be that future sentient beings would be at least as happy as the present sentient beings. If this test were to be adopted, a sustainable social arrangement would have to lead to a continuous increase of happiness over time. This seems to be too demanding and most likely we need a standard that is in between the desire to survive-test mentioned in the previous paragraph and the continuous increase-test mentioned in this paragraph. What this proper test would be like is a matter for future research.

2.6 Future Generations

The most attractive, and at the same time the most troublesome aspect of sustainability is that it deals with the future. This aspect is attractive because sustainability does not merely look at present interests, but also at the interests of future sentient beings. In this sense it is broad-minded and good, at least at first sight. It is also problematic, because on closer inspection it is not at all obvious that present sentient beings should take the interests of future sentient beings into account.

- the lemma on happiness in the *Stanford Encyclopedia of Philosophy* (https://plato.stanford.edu/entries/happiness/),
- Richard Layard, *Happiness. Lessons from a New Science*, London: Penguin 2005,
- the *Journal of Happiness Studies* (www.springer.com/social+sciences/wellbeing+%26+quality-of-life/journal/10902) and
- *The World Database of Happiness* (http://worlddatabaseofhappiness.eur.nl/).

2.6.1 Explanation of Our Care for the Future

Let us first consider the seeming attractiveness of care for the future. To make the argument easier, I will from now on only focus on human beings, because they are the only present sentient beings that we know of who can consciously make plans for the remote future.[15]

Taking care of the future is a trait with survival value, because it makes generating and raising offspring possible. That explains why human beings take their own future into account when they plan their behaviour. Taking care of one's offspring has survival value for one's genes,[16] and that explains that humans take care of the future of their children and the following generations of offspring. Moreover, taking care of one's group members, including future members of one's social group, contributes to the survival and procreation of the members of the group which explains that care for the future is not confined to care for one's own offspring.[17]

All of this does not only explain why humans take care for their own future and for future generations. It also explains their intuitive reactions when the questions are raised whether a person should think of the future and whether we should take the interests of future generations into account. However, explanation is not the same thing as justification. The question whether it is rational to take care of one's own future is not answered by (almost) everybody's natural inclination to do so. The same holds for our natural inclination to take care of future generations: it may motivate our behaviour, but that does not prove that it is rational to do so. So here we find a reason not to rely on our spontaneous feeling and intuitive judgements in deciding whether sustainability is a good thing that deserves to be protected by law. A more rational approach is to maximise happiness, and to take our feelings and intuitions into account in discovering what makes us happy.

2.6.2 The Rationality of Care for the Future

When we only focus on the present generation of humans, the happiness of future generations only plays a role to the extent that it has impact on our present happiness. Our present happiness is not influenced by the happiness of future generations, but only by

15 There are plenty of other animals that in a sense make plans for the future, but these plans are either for the near future or not made consciously. See Frans van der Helm, *Dieren met toekomstplannen*, Amsterdam: Amsterdam University Press 2016. Perhaps the future will bring artificially intelligent systems which can experience happiness and which care about future generations. If that is the case, their happiness should be taken into account.

16 The idea that the selection that is relevant for evolution occurs on the level of genes, rather than on the level of species is the central theme of Richard Dawkins, *The Selfish Gene*, Oxford: Oxford University Press 1976.

17 This argument about group-level selection is controversial amongst biologists. For an illuminating discussion, see Jonathan Haidt, *The Righteous Mind. Why good people are divided by politics and religion*, London: Penguin 2012, p. 270-274.

our expectations about that happiness. However, these expectations are influenced by the fact that we know that happiness-promoting policies are more interested in our expectations than in the fulfilment thereof. In other words, we may become distrustful about policies that seem to promote future happiness, because we know that these policies really aim at raising our expectations about future happiness. To take this distrust away, the policies must at least create the impression that they are sincerely aimed at promoting future happiness. Perhaps the best way to do so is to really promote future happiness.

It is questionable whether a utilitarian policy should only focus on the feelings and intuitions of the present generation. We have already seen that the maximisation of happiness is not necessarily confined to the happiness of human beings. If all happiness counts, then also the happiness of non-human beings. The limitation to sentient beings is only justified on the assumption that non-sentient beings do not experience happiness or unhappiness. So if not only humans are counted but all sentient beings, why limit the utilitarian calculus to actual sentient beings and not take future happiness into account as well? Discussions of this topic often invoke moral intuitions,[18] but we have seen that those are not a sign of rationality.

The only rational argument that I can presently think of is that if we should count the happiness of other sentient beings than the one who does the counting, and if we should not only count present happiness but also the future happiness of beings which already exist, we should purely for reasons of consistency also count the happiness of beings which do not exist yet.[19] Of course, there is uncertainty about the existence of future beings and about what will make them happy, but that is not a reason to discount their happiness, but only a reason why our judgment on what to do is uncertain.

We should therefore conclude that it is rational to take care for future generations and to count in their happiness to the same degree as we count in the happiness of present sentient beings. If we take the task of law to be to maximise happiness, as we should, this means that law should promote future happiness, including that of future generations, as well as present happiness. This means that law should promote sustainability in the revised version that was proposed in section 5.

2.7 Conclusion

The purpose of this paper was not to indicate how law can contribute to sustainability but to establish whether law should do so and what kind of sustainability, if any, deserves

18 E.g. Julia Driver, *Consequentialism*, London: Routledge 2012, p. 82/3.

19 The *locus classicus* for arguments along this line is Derek Parfit, *Reasons and Persons*, Oxford: Clarendon Press 1984.

support from the law. To answer these question it was necessary first to establish whether the content of law should be determined procedurally or substantially. It was argued that these two do not exclude each other, but that the substantive determination is the more important because the value of procedural determination of law's content has only instrumental value.

Second, without much argumentation the step was taken from sustainability to happiness. The value of sustaining things is also merely instrumental for happiness, and not everything should be sustained.

The fundamental discussion of what contributes to happiness was also circumvented in this contribution, and the focus was on the happiness of future generations. It was briefly argued that it is rational, because consistent, to pay as much attention to the happiness of future generations as to the present generation. The final conclusion was therefore that *law should promote practices or developments that optimise the happiness of the present generation of sentient beings without compromising the ability of future sentient beings to optimise their own happiness.*

What does this mean in practice? A lack of relevant knowledge makes it difficult to give answers that are more than truisms. Much more research is necessary, both on the psychology, sociology and economics of happiness, and on the way in which law can contribute to the maximisation of happiness. The theory of decision-making under uncertainty – there is much we do not know, especially when the future is concerned – will most likely play an important role in this connection, as will the theory of default reasoning. Clearly, not all of the necessary research is legal research, but some of it is, because law is an important influence in society. Lawyers should be ashamed that they have until quite recently paid more attention to the exegesis of authoritative texts than to research how law can contribute to the happiness of the present and of future generations of sentient beings.[20] This should change, and it is an important task for policy makers and legal educators to set this change in motion.

20 More elaborate on this topic is Jaap Hage, 'Weg met de hermeneutiek in het recht', in E.T. Feteris e.a. (red.), *Gewogen oordelen. Essays over argumentatie en recht,* Den Haag: BJu 2012, p. 41-54. An English-language version of this article will be published by Springer in 2020 and an advanced draft is available on www.jaaphage.nl/html/The_limited_function_of_hermeneutics_in_law.html.

3 Preliminary Reflections on Paradigms, Ownership, and Ecology

*Agustín Parise**

3.1 Introduction

Society at large plays a role in securing the sustainability of the environment, yet owners of property must play a specific role. Sustainability does not fall within the exclusive competence of public law, being welcomed by private law, hence by the law of property. Several governmental and non-governmental organisations have warned of the jeopardy involved in the relationship between holders of rights and the environment. Those claims have reached the legislatures, where significant efforts have canalised towards the prevention of further depletion of natural resources. For example, the Constitution of Slovenia of 1991 welcomes the regulation of restrictions to the right of ownership to ensure the economic, social, and ecological function of property.[1] In America, the Constitution of Colombia states also since 1991 that property is limited by an ecological function.[2] Further, the 2015 Argentine Civil and Commercial Code includes limitations to individual rights over things in order to protect the sustainability of ecosystems;[3] while a Brazilian high court understood in 2012 that there are ecological concerns that prevent owners from destroying natural resources that benefit society.[4] Similar situations may be faced with hydraulic fracturing

---

* The content of this paper has been published – with the exception of section 3.4 – with minor changes in the PhD dissertation of the author, entitled *Ownership Paradigms in American Civil Law Jurisdictions: Manifestations of the Shifts in the Legislation of Louisiana, Chile, and Argentina (16th-20th Centuries)* (Brill 2017).

1 See art 67 of the Constitution of the Republic of Slovenia, available in English at www.dz-rs.si. See also Suzana Kraljić and Vesna Rijavec, 'Slovenia', *International Encyclopedia Laws: Family and Succession Law* 7 (2014) § 498.

2 See art 58 of the Constitution of Colombia, available in English at www.constituteproject.org/constitution/Colombia_2005.pdf. See also Helena Alviar Garcia, 'Looking beyond the Constitution: the social and ecological function of property', in Rosalind Dixon and Tom Ginsburg (eds), *Comparative Constitutional Law in Latin America* (Edward Elgar 2017) 158.

3 See arts 14 and 240 of the Argentine Civil and Commercial Code, available at http://servicios.infoleg.gob.ar/infolegInternet/anexos/235000-239999/235975/norma.htm#8. See also Aníbal J Falbo and José Alberto Esain, 'El Código Civil y Comercial y el ambiente' (2015) RCCyC (17 August) 19; and Carlos A. Rodríguez, 'Derecho ambiental y Código Civil y Comercial' (2015) La Ley Actualidad (2 June) 1.

4 Nicholas S Bryner, 'Public Interests and Private Land: The Ecological Function of Property in Brazil' (2016) 34 Va Envtl LJ 122. On the Brazilian court, see Nicholas S Bryner, 'Brazil's Green Court: Environmental

in South Africa, with gas drilling in the Netherlands, with mining in China, or with surface mining in the USA. These new claims stretch beyond the tenets of the social function paradigm of ownership. Societies and ownership paradigms evolve: is it time to speak of a new paradigm? Has an ecological function paradigm taken the stage? Looking into shifts in paradigms helps understand the changes that private law is experiencing when facing the challenges triggered by the need to reach sustainability.

These questions call for preliminary reflections on paradigms, ownership, and ecology. Paradigms are valuable tools to understand the law. Looking at paradigms within the realm of law welcomes the study of *how*, at a certain time and place, legal orderings are affected by social interaction.[5] Paradigms, in the legal realm, can deal with an overarching legal doctrine or dogma, as combined with the prevailing ideologies in a certain society.[6] Ownership entails a historical evolution that cannot be overlooked;[7] and, together with other property-law institutions, they are key elements of culture and civilizations: architectural pillars for society.[8] Ecology is understood in this paper as 'the science of the interactions of living creatures [including, naturally, human beings] with one another and the abiotic conditions within their environments.'[9] Owners of property are fundamental *creatures* in their respective environments and are able to invite many external or abiotic conditions that are not always beneficial.

This paper is divided into three parts. First, the paper explains the role of paradigms in the study and understanding of the law. That part also offers techniques to identify paradigm shifts. Second, the paper addresses, as an illustration of the shifts in paradigms, two paradigms of ownership that developed since the nineteenth century in American Civil Law Jurisdictions.[10] Finally, the paper points to an Ecological Function of Ownership

---

Law in the Superior Tribunal de Justiça (High Court of Brazil)' (2012) 29 Pace Environmental Law Review 470.

5 Ubaldus de Vries, 'Kuhn and Legal Research: A Reflexive Paradigmatic View on Legal Research' (2013) 3:1 Recht en Methode in onderzoek en onderwijs 7, 12.

6 Enrique P Haba, 'Ciencias del derecho, La controversia de paradigmas en la Teoría del Derecho contemporánea' in Manuel Ossorio y Florit et al (eds), *Enciclopedia Jurídica Omeba*, vol 7 appendix (Driskill 1996) 122.

7 Raymundo M Salvat, *Tratado de Derecho Civil Argentino: Derechos Reales*, vol 2 (5th edn, Tipográfica Ed Argentina 1962) 6.

8 Eduardo Cordero Quinzacara, 'De la propiedad a las propiedades. La evolución de la concepción liberal de la propiedad' (2008) 31 Revista de Derecho de la Pontificia Universidad Católica de Valparaíso 493, 494.

9 Malte Faber and Reiner Manstetten, *Philosophical Basics of Ecology and Economy* (Dale Adams tr, Routledge 2009) 19.

10 In this paper American Civil Law Jurisdictions consist of former Spanish territories that currently comprise jurisdictions from the Americas where the Continental European system of law prevails in private law. These also consist of mixed jurisdictions (*e.g.*, Louisiana), which are excellent objects for the study of transplantation and circulation of ideas and paradigms. Pure common law jurisdictions are not American Civil Law Jurisdictions. The latter likewise exclude American territories that are traditionally assimilated as having been dependents of European jurisdictions beyond Spain.

Paradigm (EFOP) that is taking the stage even beyond American Civil Law Jurisdictions. Recent developments have demonstrated that a paradigm shift is taking place.

3.2 Unveiling the Value of Legal Paradigms

This paper focuses on specific types of paradigms, namely the ownership paradigms. Already in 2000, CH van Rhee and JHM van Erp highlighted that comparative legal historical studies on property law can result in illuminating exercises.[11] It has been claimed that 'one can hardly find a more significant and fascinating field of comparative study than the law of property;'[12] and yet comparative property law studies are still relatively neglected.[13] In Europe, property law is no longer taught with a purely local or vernacular approach,[14] yet if compared with other areas of the law, such as contract law, the literature of comparative property law is somehow scarce.[15]

Ownership is mainly a matter of mentality,[16] and understanding the mentality of a certain time and place helps in grasping the full extent of a right. Boundaries between the interests of different actors (*eg*, State, owners) are troublesome.[17] Property-law institutions provide fertile ground for problems when boundaries overlap.[18] Those problems attract the attention of scholars beyond the law, welcoming studies by economists, sociologists, political scientists, and even theologians.[19] Hence, problematising ownership often results in raising questions that deal with the role of the different actors. As this paper aims to show, ownership indeed evolves around the interplay of the different actors. Looking at paradigm shifts helps integrate aspects that are often analysed individually or as watertight compartments. As previously mentioned, studies on ownership should examine legal

---

11 CH van Rhee and JHM van Erp, 'Introduction to the Special Issue on Property Law' (2003) 3-2003 European Review of Private Law 279, 281. In the Americas, for example, Ezequiel Abásolo suggested the comparative legal historical study of ownership. See Ezequiel Abásolo, 'Las actuales reflexiones latinoamericanas sobre historia jurídica, iluminadas por la experiencia disciplinar argentina de la primera mitad del siglo XX' Forum Historiae Iuris (07. Mai 2009). www.forhistiur.de/2009-05-abasolo/ at § 23.

12 John Henry Merryman, 'Ownership and Estate (Variations on a Theme by Lawson)' (1974) 48 Tul L Rev 916.

13 JHM van Erp, 'Comparative Property Law' in Mathias Reimann and Reinhard Zimmermann (eds), *The Oxford Handbook of Comparative Law* (Oxford University Press 2008) 1048.

14 JHM van Erp, 'From Euratom Property Law to European Union Property Law: A Concise Overview of the Development Towards a European Property Law' in Luigi Moccia (ed), *The Making of European Private Law: Why, How, What, Who* (Sellier European Law Publishers 2013) 159.

15 JHM van Erp, 'A Comparative Analysis of Mortgage Law: Searching for Principles' in María Elena Sánchez Jordán and Antonio Gambaro, *Land Law in Comparative Perspective* (Kluwer Law International 2002) 69.

16 The expression was shared by Abelardo Levaggi while dictating a course on the history of property law at the University of Buenos Aires in August 2001.

17 Charles A Reich, 'The New Property' (1964) 73 Yale L J 733.

18 José Castán Tobeñas, *La propiedad y sus problemas actuales* (2nd edn, Reus 1963) 7.

19 *Ibid.*

aspects, yet also, amongst others, social, economic, political, cultural, and ideological aspects,[20] all of them across time and space, and all resulting in a broader understanding of the emerging background.

Ownership Paradigms consist of the abstract understanding of what constitutes the right of ownership and what this right comprises. That abstract understanding finds consensus amongst jurists, provides model problems and solutions, and changes according to time and space. Ownership Paradigms should be considered tools to assess the conditions of the right of ownership, and the way actors perceive societies and trigger law change and application. Ownership Paradigms are affected by the prevailing ideologies in a certain society, and are shaped after the interplay of things (movable or immovable) with individual actors (*eg*, owners, State, Church) and society at large. When these three elements interact, one of them tends to prevail while the other two do not fully disappear, shaping an ownership paradigm, and resulting in the abovementioned abstract understanding.

3.2.1 Conceptualisation

The conceptualisation of Ownership Paradigms used in this paper derives from the more generic understandings of scientific paradigms used by philosophers of science and of legal paradigms used by jurists. A paradigm, as defined by *The Oxford English Dictionary*, is 'a conceptual or methodological model underlying the theories and practices of a science or discipline at a particular time; (hence) a generally accepted world view.'[21]

Thomas S Kuhn offered groundbreaking, and currently seminal, ideas on scientific paradigms in his work *The Structure of Scientific Revolutions* (1962).[22] According to Kuhn, a scientific paradigm – referred to by part of the literature as model, *Leitbild*, or archetype[23] – is an achievement that is 'sufficiently unprecedented to attract an enduring group of adherents away from competing modes of scientific activity'[24] and 'sufficiently open-ended to leave all sorts of problems for the redefined group of practitioners to resolve.'[25] A scientific

20 Rosa Congost, 'La "gran obra" de la propiedad. Los motivos de un debate' in Rosa Congost and José Miguel Lana (eds), *Campos cerrados, debates abiertos: análisis histórico y propiedad de la tierra en Europa (siglos XVI-XIX)* (Universidad pública de Navarra 2007) 22.

21 'paradigm, n' OED Online. April 2018. Oxford University Press. www.oed.com/view/Entry/137329?redirectedFrom=paradigm.

22 Thomas S Kuhn, *The Structure of Scientific Revolutions* (2nd edn, enlarged, The University of Chicago Press 1970). Thomas Samuel Kuhn introduced several modifications and clarifications to his 1962 work, mainly in his *Postscript-1969*. See Haba (n 6) 122; and Carlos Ramos Núñez, *Codificación, Tecnología y Postmodernidad* (Ara Editores 1996) 23. See the recent approach to the work of Kuhn in MC Mirow, 'Rerum Novarum: New Things and Recent Paradigms of Property Law' (2016) 47 The University of the Pacific Law Review 183, 183-186.

23 Ramos Núñez (n 22) 23.

24 Kuhn (n 22) 10.

25 *Ibid.*

revolution results in the generation of a consensual model that modifies the historical perspective of a certain scientific community;[26] and acquiring scientific paradigm status reflects indeed maturity in the development of a scientific field.[27] The American philosopher of science understood that scientific paradigms are 'universally recognised scientific achievements that for a time provide model problems and solutions to a community of practitioners.'[28] A scientific paradigm invites consensus on a certain assumption that enables the devising of a problem and of arguments and solutions to deal with that problem.[29] These scientific paradigms provide tools for the observation of a body of knowledge,[30] being informative of the type of research questions that must be posed and on how answers should be interpreted.[31]

Legal paradigms are welcomed by the legal narrative. Some scholars used the work of Kuhn as a means to understand legal disciplines,[32] while others claimed that the Kuhnian model did not apply to social sciences, such as law.[33] As mentioned, looking at paradigms within the realm of law, however, welcomes the study of *how*, at a certain time and place, legal orderings are affected by social interaction.[34] Paradigms, in the legal realm, can deal with an overarching legal doctrine or dogma, as combined with the prevailing ideologies in a certain society.[35] In a narrower sense, legal paradigms can consist of, amongst other things, laws, customs, court decisions, and doctrinal writings that provide solutions to specific problems (*eg*, ownership) at specific times and places, and that have gained recognition amongst jurists.[36] Accordingly, a legal paradigm can be defined as a value or concept that is shared by a legal community at a certain time and place.[37] Jean Louise Cohen further stated that legal paradigms are 'an integrated set of cognitive and normative background assumptions about the relationship the law should establish between the state and society, and the form legal regulation must take.'[38] Other literature highlighted that legal paradigms are useful tools to assess the conditions of certain matters that are subject to regulation.[39] Legal paradigms, indeed, can refer to the implicit images that actors might

26 Ramos Núñez (n 22) 23.
27 Kuhn (n 22) 11.
28 *Ibid.* viii. See also Haba (n 6) 122.
29 de Vries (n 5) 8.
30 *Ibid.*, 9.
31 *Ibid.*
32 Thomas Schultz, *Transnational Legality: Stateless Law and International Arbitration* (Oxford University Press 2014) 64.
33 See the examples mentioned in de Vries (n 5) 11.
34 *Ibid.*, 12.
35 Haba (n 6) 122.
36 *Ibid.*, 123.
37 Peter Boulot, 'A New Legal Paradigm: Towards a Jurisprudence Based on Ecological Sovereignty' (2012) 8 Macquarie Journal of International and Comparative Environmental Law 1, 10.
38 Jean L Cohen, *Regulating Intimacy: A New Legal Paradigm* (Princeton University Press 2002) 143.
39 de Vries (n 5) 7.

have of their own societies and that guide the law-making and application processes.[40] Finally, comparative law literature recurred to legal paradigms, defining them as 'the manner in which legal systems address problems in specific (cultural) ways to attain (functionally equivalent) solutions.'[41]

The legal literature previously referred to paradigms of ownership,[42] yet no leading definition seems to have been proposed. As mentioned before, in this paper, Ownership Paradigms consist of the abstract understanding of what constitutes the right of ownership and what this right comprises. That abstract understanding finds consensus amongst jurists, provides model problems and solutions, and changes according to time and space.

3.2.2 *Techniques to Trace Shifts*

It is impossible to speak of a single paradigm of ownership that crosses through time and space. Jurisdictions, at different times, experienced different Ownership Paradigms. Much can be learned by looking at *how* solutions to problems were developed in different places at different times.[43] Ownership is linked to the role of different actors within society and to the evolution of social organisation, hence exceeding the exclusive realm of legal studies, and ultimately making manifest the existing structure at a certain time and place.[44]

Studies have focused on *what* motivated shifts[45] in Ownership Paradigms, for example in American Civil Law Jurisdictions.[46] Scholars must abstract the different conceptions (*eg*, ownership) across their evolution, focusing on essential features that turn conceptions immutable and non-essential features that explain their shifts.[47] Legal institutions are

40 Jürgen Habermas, 'Paradigms of Law' (1996) 17 Cardozo Law Review 771.

41 Ralf Michaels, 'Comparative Law' in Jürgen Basedow et al (eds), *Max Planck Encyclopedia of European Private Law*, vol I (Oxford University Press 2012) 298.

42 See, amongst the copious literature, the references in Antonio Gambaro, 'Property Rights in Comparative Perspective: Why Property Is So Ancient and Durable' (2011) 26 Tulane European and Civil Law Forum 205.

43 James Gordley, *Foundations of Private Law: Property, Tort, Contract, Unjust Enrichment* (reprint, Oxford University Press 2007) 3.

44 Juan Francisco Delgado de Miguel (coord), *Instituciones de Derecho Privado: Reales*, vol II (Civitas 2002) 57.

45 A paradigm shift, as defined by *The Oxford English Dictionary*, is 'a conceptual or methodological change in the theory or practice of a particular science or discipline; (in extended sense) a major change in technology, outlook, etc.' See n 21.

46 See generally Agustín Parise, *Ownership Paradigms in American Civil Law Jurisdictions: Manifestations of the Shifts in the Legislation of Louisiana, Chile, and Argentina (16th-20th Centuries)* (Brill 2017).

47 Randall Lesaffer, 'Law and History: Law between Past and Present' in Bart van Klink and Sanne Taekema (eds), *Law and Method: Interdisciplinary Research into Law* (Mohr Siebeck 2011) 141.

subject to mutation[48] – and being creations of humanity – are transformed together with societies, with political structures, and with mentalities.[49] Legal institutions, including those of property law, such as ownership, are in constant evolution and transformation, either at a slow or at a fast pace.[50] Resilience is a characteristic of property law institutions,[51] since these tend to change according to time and space: they are far from being eternal.[52]

Paradigms never fade overnight, yet the main points of inflection can be spotted.[53] A shift or scientific revolution will break with a previous paradigm and place a new one that will be likewise accepted.[54] Therefore, an established assumption will be replaced when a paradigm shift occurs.[55] These revolutions and shifts evolve around the idea of reaching equilibrium. The normativity and social condition of legal institutions may attain equilibrium, yet if they dissociate due to the emergence of anomalies, mutation will take place and society will interpret or apply the legal institution (*eg*, ownership) in a different way. Ultimately, if the dissociation continues, a reform will take place, and the legal institution will need to be reformed.[56] As societies and mentalities evolve, anomalies evolve. These anomalies sometimes may not be explained by prevailing paradigms, showing weaknesses that will ultimately demand new paradigms to emerge.[57] Anomalies are deemed to resist problematisation within the limits offered by existing paradigms.[58]

A number of research paths can assist in identifying the shifts in Ownership Paradigms. Qualitative methodologies used by social sciences can assist in the further exploration and development of shifts in Ownership Paradigms. Further, these exercises can use comparative case studies and process-tracing techniques, while also benefiting from traditional historical techniques to analyse sources and from the functionalist approach to the comparative study of law.

---

48 Abelardo Levaggi, *Manual de Historia del Derecho Argentino (Castellano-Indiano/Nacional)*, vol I (2nd edn, Depalma 1996) 6; and Rosa Congost, *Tierras, leyes, historia: estudios sobre "la gran obra de la propiedad"* (Crítica 2007) 40.

49 Jean-Louis Halpérin, *Histoire du droit des biens* (Économica DL 2008) 2.

50 Levaggi (n 48) 3.

51 Luigi Moccia, 'Réflexions sur l'idée de propriété' (2011) 1-2011 Revue internationale de droit comparé 7, 36.

52 Halpérin (n 49) 2.

53 See, for example, the reference to the paradigm shift in Germany from codification to constitution in Knut Wolfgang Nörr, 'From Codification to Constitution: On the Changes of Paradigm in German Legal History of the Twentieth Century' (1992) 60 Tijdschrift voor Rechtsgeschiedenis 145, especially 149.

54 Ramos Núñez (n 22) 23. Kuhn claimed that 'scientific revolutions, and the successive transition from one paradigm to another via revolution is the usual developmental pattern of mature science.' Kuhn (n 22) 12.

55 de Vries (n 5) 7.

56 Levaggi (n 48) 3.

57 Schultz (n 32) 63-64.

58 de Vries (n 5) 10.

Case studies are not foreign to the law curricula, where they are used in the process of helping students bridge the divide that exists between practice and foundational studies.[59] This method – not free from criticism – is extensively followed across different disciplines,[60] and studies on shifts in paradigms may likewise find benefits in its application. Case studies, differently from other methods, provide detailed perspectives into existing mechanisms, interests of actors, and limitations they face at specific moments.[61] Case studies must evolve around objects of research that are limited in both time and space, while they should also welcome meaningful abstractions.[62] A case study could be defined as a means to systematically look into an institution (*eg*, ownership) aiming to its description, exploration, and explanation.[63] The comparative case studies may be exploratory, and as such, the assemblage of sources could be undertaken before defining clearly all research questions.[64] Accordingly, a study would depart from an overarching research idea that would be translated into a set of research questions as the exploration develops. A comparative case study would mainly follow an exploratory approach, in which the phenomenon of shifts of Ownership Paradigms is to be studied, exploring which are the elements that are of importance to motivate this phenomenon.

Case studies can be used to understand the interaction of relevant facts that are characteristic of an institution (*eg*, ownership).[65] Consisting of studies of institutions in single instances, case studies can then shed light on broader arguments.[66] They ultimately may assist in the development of theory, such as one explaining shifts in Ownership Paradigms.[67] Generalisations are difficult when working with case studies, since the resulting research has to demonstrate that the selected cases are representative of other cases where similar occurrences may take place.[68] However, case study methodologists claim that a hypothesis may be generalised if it explains a hard case or a case that seemed unlikely to be explained.[69]

59 Bruce L Berg, *Qualitative Research Methods for the Social Sciences* (7th edn, Pearson Education 2010) 318.
60 *Ibid.*, 317.
61 Bob Hancké, *Intelligent Research Design: A Guide for Beginning Researchers in the Social Sciences* (Oxford University Press 2009) 61.
62 *Ibid.*, 62.
63 Berg (n 59) 317.
64 *Ibid.*, 327.
65 *Ibid.*, 318.
66 Hancké (n 61) 62.
67 Berg (n 59) 321.
68 Hancké (n 61) 61.
69 Andrew Bennett and Jeffrey T Checkel, 'Process Tracing: From Philosophical Roots to Best Practices' in Andrew Bennett and Jeffrey T Checkel (eds), *Process Tracing in the Social Sciences: From Metaphor to Analytic Tool* (Cambridge University Press 2015) 13.

Process-tracing techniques are to be used – within the comparative case study – to link conditions with outcomes.[70] Alexander L George stated that process tracing was the identification of evidence that was available in case studies and that could be used to elaborate inferences about historical explanations.[71] Process tracing, therefore, offers intermediate steps in processes, enabling the elaboration of inferences about hypotheses on *how* processes occur and to determine *if* and *how* processes generate the outcome of interest.[72] The snapshots provided by process tracing may result in avoiding a full narrative when moving from cause to outcome, however.[73] Process tracing is closely linked to historical explanations, and Clayton Roberts used it to define important steps that lead to the causation of an outcome.[74] Process-tracing case studies build on the observation that most social science arguments and theories are condensed representations of causal links (if A, then B follows).[75] That technique may assist in the elaboration of a generalisable theoretical explanation to be extracted from the evidence found in the causal mechanisms that are identified in the specific cases and that can be ultimately generalised.[76] Process tracing can result in generalisations, and the solution in a specific case can be used to explain or understand similar situations.[77]

The application of traditional historical techniques to the analysis of sources can also be of benefit when studying shifts in paradigms. Sources deal both with internal and with external comparative legal history elements, since law should be regarded *in totum*.[78] An approach from causes to effects should help in identifying the 'genetic' history of the institution and of the shifts in, for example, Ownership Paradigms.[79] Moving in a regressive way, from the present to the past, may lead researchers to lose their path,[80] leading to mistakes.[81] The historical flow of events suggests a progressive and chronological approach to the study. The progressive method, within process tracing, is therefore of value, being

70 Frank Schimmelfennig, 'Efficient Process Tracing: Analyzing the Causal Mechanisms of European Integration' in Andrew Bennett and Jeffrey T Checkel (eds), *Process Tracing in the Social Sciences: From Metaphor to Analytic Tool* (Cambridge University Press 2015) 101.
71 Bennett and Checkel (n 69) 4-5.
72 *Ibid.*, 6.
73 Schimmelfennig (n 70) 125.
74 Bennett and Checkel (n 69) 8.
75 Hancké (n 61) 66.
76 Derek Beach and Rasmus Brun Pedersen, *Process-Tracing Methods: Foundations and Guidelines.* (University of Michigan Press 2013) 1, 3, 11. A causal mechanism is 'a complex system which produces that behavior by of [sic] the interaction of a number of parts according to direct causal laws.' Stuart S Glennan, 'Mechanisms and the Nature of Causation' (1996) 44:1 Erkenntnis 49, 52. See also Bennett and Checkel (n 69) 9.
77 Hancké (n 61) 67-68.
78 Carlos O Bunge, *Historia del Derecho Argentino*, vol I (Facultad de Derecho y Ciencias Sociales 1912-1913) xxxii.
79 See the reference to the interaction of genetic method and cause-effect in *Ibid.*
80 Levaggi (n 48) 9.
81 *Ibid.*

suitable since it addresses, amongst other things, the historicity and the changes in the meaning of terms and words.[82]

Empirical legal research has been recognised as a tool for law[83] when wanting to understand *how law works in the real world*[84] and when aiming to enrich doctrinal studies with systematic studies that aim to unveil the active interplay between law and society.[85] Empirical legal research helps recognise patterns or themes, and enables the exploration of shifts and problems.[86] Therefore, the analysis that follows from the application of such methods could assist scholars and policy makers to fully grasp reality and act consequently.[87] The possibility to trace shifts in paradigms could be augmented by means of empirical legal research.

A functionalist approach to understand shifts in paradigms is also recommended, since different jurisdictions may refer to the same phenomena in different ways.[88] This type of approach, promoted by Konrad Zweigert and Hein Kötz,[89] understands that law reacts to social problems that are faced and shared by all societies alike:[90] a systemic totality.[91] That shared function enables the comparison across legal institutions (*eg*, ownership) even if facing divergent doctrinal structures.[92] It deals with what legal institutions *do* instead of what they *claim* to do.[93] The functionalist approach has been applied successfully to property law institutions.[94] Those who advocate for a functionalist approach deem it the

82 *Ibid.*

83 On empirical legal research, see Julieta Marotta, *Access to Justice and Legal Empowerment of Victims of Domestic Violence through Legal Organisations in the City of Buenos Aires: A Qualitative Empirical Legal Study*, UNU-MERIT/MGSoG Dissertation Series No 186 (Maastricht University 2017), especially 7. This paragraph builds on the elaboration of Julieta Marotta in the above-mentioned work.

84 See Nuffield Foundation, Nuffield Inquiry on Empirical Legal Research. Law in the Real World, www.nuffieldfoundation.org/nuffield-inquiry-empirical-legalresearch-law-real-world.

85 See Paddy Hillyard, 'Law's Empire: Socio-Legal Empirical Research in the Twenty-First Century' (2007) 34 Journal of Law and Society 266.

86 See Lisa Webley, 'Qualitative Approaches to Empirical Legal Research' in Peter Cane and Herbert M Kritzer (eds), *The Oxford Handbook of Empirical Legal Research* (Oxford University Press 2010) 929.

87 See Lee Epstein and Andrew D Martin, *An Introduction to Empirical Legal Research* (Oxford University Press 2014) 4.

88 See, amongst the copious literature, the study in Ralf Michaels, 'The Functional Method of Comparative Law' in Mathias Reimann and Reinhard Zimmermann (eds), *The Oxford Handbook of Comparative Law* (Oxford University Press 2008).

89 Konrad Zweigert and Hein Kötz, *Einführung in die Rechtsvergleichung auf dem Gebiete des Privatrechts*, vol I (2nd edn, Mohr 1984).

90 Michaels (n 41) 297; and A Esin Örücü, 'Methodology of Comparative Law' in Jan M Smits (ed), *Elgar Encyclopedia of Comparative Law* (Edward Elgar Publishing Limited 2006) 444.

91 Jaakko Husa, 'Functional Method in Comparative Law – Much Ado About Nothing? (2013) 2 European Property Law Journal 4, 6.

92 Michaels (n 41) 297-298.

93 Oliver Brand, 'Conceptual Comparisons: Towards a Coherent Methodology of Comparative Legal Studies' (2007) 32 Brooklyn Journal of International Law 405, 409.

94 Bram Akkermans, 'The Use of the Functional Method in European Union Property Law' (2013) 2 European Property Law Journal 95, 110.

only fruitful means to understand reality, while those who advocate against its use deem it the epitome of negative elements in comparative studies.[95] When looking into the realm of comparative property law, van Erp stated that

> The functional [approach] works both ways: it focuses on convergences and divergences at the same time. The latter aspect is sometimes forgotten and it is particularly this aspect which is highly important for property law. From a functional perspective the various layers of property law in the EU [yet also beyond] can be examined on the basis of how they solve comparable problems in a comparable way.[96]

Functionalist studies are interested in the transplantation of institutions.[97] Those approaches deal with the circulation of ideas and the flow of paradigms, identifying differences and similarities, and providing channels amongst jurisdictions.

It should be noted that shifts in paradigms can be sensed by means of events that affect at least one of the sources of law. For example, legislative enactments – within the understanding of process tracing – could be regarded as elements to establish causal mechanisms. Time and space constraints in a project may make impossible a comprehensive study of all sources of law (*eg*, customs, doctrine, jurisprudence).[98] Related studies could look at different sources of law autonomously or collectively. Readers should be mindful that studies should likewise consider the normative framework, the application of law, and the doctrinal assessment.[99] Therefore, a comprehensive approach requires attention to the three aspects,[100] because other human acts may indeed show potential problems.[101]

---

95 Michaels (n 88) 340; and Husa (n 91) 21.

96 JHM van Erp, 'The Functional Comparative Method in European Property Law – C. Godt Some Comments'. (2013) 2 European Property Law Journal 90, 93.

97 Brand (n 93) 410.

98 Other works advocated for a study of only a selection of problems or matters dealing with ownership, avoiding an *in totum* approach. Cordero Quinzacara (n 8) 495.

99 See generally Helmut Coing, *Aufgaben des Rechtshistorikers, Sitzungsberichte der Wissenschaftlichen Gesellschaft an der Johann Wolfgang Goethe-Universität Frankfurt am Main*, vol 13:5 (Steiner 1976). See also Abelardo Levaggi, 'Consideraciones sobre la enseñanza de la historia del derecho' (1990) 27 Revista de Historia del Derecho "Ricardo Levene" 159, 160.

100 Levaggi (n 99) 160.

101 Eduardo Martiré, *Consideraciones Metodológicas sobre la Historia del Derecho* (Editorial Perrot 1977) 20; Rafael Altamira y Crevea, *Historia de la Propiedad Comunal* (J López Camacho 1890) 27; Bunge (n 78) xxxiii; Abelardo Levaggi, 'Consideraciones sobre investigación en historia del derecho' (2009) 1:1 Revista del Instituto Latino Americano de Historia de [sic] Derecho 154, 154-155; and Levaggi (n 48) 12, 15.

3.3 OWNERSHIP PARADIGMS[102]

Ownership Paradigms shift, and there are indications that a new paradigm is taking the stage, being referred to in this paper as the EFOP. The twentieth century reflected a change in the paradigm of ownership. The liberal paradigm of ownership that had taken the stage during the nineteenth century was replaced by one that advocated for the social function of ownership, where the state could intervene and assure that the holder used the object according to the benefit of society. The idea of a social function is being replaced by one that refers to ownership as fulfilling an ecological function, where there is a duty to secure sustainability.[103]

3.3.1 *Liberal*

The nineteenth century experienced a change in the Ownership Paradigm in American Civil Law Jurisdictions. These jurisdictions indeed incorporated provisions on ownership within their civil codes. Even when codification started and was developed in Europe, the New World was not foreign to the phenomenon, being fertile ground for codification endeavours. The Modern Period welcomed the development of a liberal paradigm of ownership, which replaced an allocation paradigm that included, amongst other characteristics, a decomposition of ownership in *directum* and *utile*.[104] American Civil Law Jurisdictions gradually shifted to that new liberal paradigm, and consequently made manifest its adoption in local nineteenth-century civil codes.[105] That century has been

102 It should be noted that this section of the paper builds on the conclusions to chapters 4 and 5 of Parise (n 46). Therefore, further references for the assertions made should be found in the above-mentioned work.

103 See, for example, Bryner, 'Public Interests and Private Land' (n 4); Richard A Barnes, 'The Capacity of Property Rights to Accommodate Social-Ecological Resilience' (2013) 18:1 Ecology and Society art 6, available at http://dx.doi.org/10.5751/ES-05292-180106; and Boulot (n 37).

104 Abelardo Levaggi, 'El proceso de transformación del régimen de la propiedad según la codificación iberoamericana del siglo XIX' in Eugénio dos Santos (ed), *Actas do XII Congresso Internacional de AHILA*, vol V (Faculdade de Letras da Universidade do Porto 2001) 413. See on the understanding of *dominium duplex* during the sixteenth century, amongst the copious literature, the interesting approach in Paolo Grossi, 'La categoria del dominio utile e gli *homines novi* del quadrivio cinquecentesco' in Paolo Grossi, *Il dominio e le cose: percezioni medievali e moderne dei diritti reali* (Giuffrè 1992). For more information on *dominium duplex*, see Paolo Grossi, 'La proprietà e le proprietà nell'officina dello storico' in Paolo Grossi, *Il dominio e le cose: percezioni medievali e moderne dei diritti reali* (Giuffrè 1992) 637-648; Paolo Grossi, 'Ideologia e tecnica in una definizione giuridica (la definizione obertina di Feudo dai Glossatori a Cujas)" in Paolo Grossi, *Il dominio e le cose: percezioni medievali e moderne dei diritti reali* (Giuffrè 1992); and Robert Feenstra, '*Dominium utile* est chimaera: Nouvelles réflexions sur le concept de propriété dans le droit savant (à propos d'un ouvrage récent)' (1998) 66 Tijdschrift voor Rechtsgeschiedenis 381. On a current approximation to *dominium duplex*, see Dirk Heirbaut, 'Feudal Law: the Real *Ius Commune* of Property in Europe, or: Should We Reintroduce *Duplex Dominium*?' (2003) 3-2003 European Review of Private Law 301.

105 Levaggi (n 104) 413.

deemed 'the codification century of civil law'[106] and all private law tended to revolve around the new codes.[107] No full grasp of ownership can be attained when the codification phenomenon is not fully understood. That scenario helps explaining why tracing changes mainly in those texts may help explain the shifts in Ownership Paradigms. These new texts embraced the liberal ideal of an absolute, unique, and perpetual real right of ownership, subject to the will of a single owner, but limited by some conditions determined by law that related to social responsibilities.[108]

Ownership as incorporated in first-generation civil codes[109] was, in American Civil Law Jurisdictions, an absolute right that followed the tenets of the liberal paradigm. Civil codes provided the centre for private law provisions and encapsulated the seminal property law institutions. Codification developed within social and legal contexts that were replicated throughout different parts of the Americas. There was a circulation of legal ideas and a flow of paradigms that linked jurisdictions within the continent. Different political and social backgrounds provided different scenarios for codification, however. There are common legal bases and temporal parallels amongst jurisdictions, yet each jurisdiction merits its own study.[110]

Several points attest to the existence of the liberal paradigm. First, that nineteenth-century codification took place within a Pan-American context that sought the adoption of codes. Second, that codified provisions offered a framework for ownership. That right was considered absolute across jurisdictions and was in accordance with the tenets encapsulated in the *Code Napoléon*. The wording of the articles in many codes often benefited from material or formal sources that could be traced back to Europe. Third, that jurisdictions shared a similar understanding of ownership. The pollination of texts demonstrates that interest was not limited to Europe, and that when drafting in the Americas jurists also looked at vernacular sources. Fourth, that codification was not static, and that ownership kept evolving in American Civil Law Jurisdictions. As a corollary, it

106 Julio César Rivera, 'The Scope and Structure of Civil codes. Relations with Commercial Law, Family Law, Consumer Law and Private International Law. A Comparative Approach' in Julio César Rivera (ed), *The Scope and Structure of Civil Codes* (Springer 2013) 7.

107 It should be noted that in some jurisdictions, such as Louisiana, the code persists in being the centre even during the twenty-first century. See Agustín Parise, 'Private Law in Louisiana: An Account of Civil Codes, Heritage, and Law Reform' in Julio César Rivera (ed), *The Scope and Structure of Civil Codes* (Springer 2013) 453.

108 Levaggi (n 104) 419.

109 On generations of codes see, Agustín Parise, 'Civil Law Codification in Latin America: Understanding First and Second Generation Codes' in J Michael Milo et al (eds), *Tradition, Codification and Unification: Comparative-Historical Essays on Developments in Civil Law* (Intersentia 2014); and Agustín Parise, 'Harmonization of Private Law in Latin America and the Emergence of Third-Generation Codes' in Stefan Vogenauer and Rodrigo Momberg (eds), *The Future of Contract Law in Latin America: The Principles of Latin American Contract Law* (Hart 2017).

110 Víctor Tau Anzoátegui, *La Codificación en la Argentina (1810-1870): Mentalidad Social e Ideas Jurídicas.* (2nd edn, revised, Librería Histórica – Emilio J Perrot 2008) 16.

can be claimed that there was a Pan-American understanding of ownership in first-generation codes. That understanding can be traced back to European codes and to American elaborations. Accordingly, ownership cannot be regarded as merely a European construct, because local developments played a role in its shaping, being shared across American Civil Law Jurisdictions. It must be noted, finally, that codification was not limited to normative transfers in the Americas, it also extended to intellectual challenges regarding creation and adaptation.[111]

3.3.2 Social Function

The twentieth century experienced a change in the Ownership Paradigm in American Civil Law Jurisdictions. The liberal paradigm of ownership was gradually replaced by one that advocated for the social function of property. The social function paradigm spread across the continent, and motivated corresponding changes in the wording of constitutions and civil codes, while it also included changes in the interpretation by courts and in the development of special legislation that advocated for the new approach to ownership. The idea of a social function, though popular amongst jurists in Continental Europe and in most American Civil Law Jurisdictions, seems not to be fully explored yet within the English-language legal discourse.[112]

Private law experienced a socialisation process in the period 1890-1930,[113] since the liberal paradigm had offered few limitations to the right of ownership. Gradual changes

111 See Agustín Parise, 'Libraries of Civil Codes as Mirrors of Normative Transfers from Europe to the Americas: The Experiences of Lorimier in Quebec (1871-1890) and Varela in Argentina (1873-1875)' in Thomas Duve (ed), *Entanglements in Legal History: Conceptual Approaches, Global Perspectives on Legal History* (Max Planck Institute for European Legal History, Open Access Publication, Frankfurt am Main, 2014, p. 315-384. http://dx.doi.org/10.12946/gplh1) 353-354.

112 See, for example, Thomas T Ankersent and Thomas Ruppert, '*Tierra y Libertad*: The Social Function Doctrine and Land Reform in Latin America' (2006) 19 Tulane Environmental Law Journal 69, 119; and Nestor M Davidson, 'Sketches for a Hamiltonian Vernacular as a Social Function of Property' (2011) 80 Fordham Law Review 1053, 1069. On recent reactions to the liberal paradigm, in the English-language narrative, see, for example, Joseph W Singer, 'Property and Social Relations: From title to Entitlement' in GE van Maanen and AJ van der Walt (eds), *Property Law on the Threshold of the 21st Century: Proceedings of an International Colloquium 'Property Law on the Threshold of the 21st Century', 28-30 August 1995, Maastricht* (Maklu 1996); and Gregory S Alexander, 'The Social-Obligation Norm in American Property Law' (2009) 94 Cornell Law Review 745. On the developments in Continental Europe, from an USA perspective, see MC Mirow, 'The Social-Obligation Norm of Property: Duguit, Hayem, and Others' (2010) 22 Florida Journal of International Law 191. It should be noted that volume 80 of the *Fordham Law Review* (2011) offered a notable English-language collection of papers on the social function paradigm. The papers included in that volume were published in Argentina, offering a Spanish translation that added an interesting perspective to the existing Spanish literature. See Daniel Bonilla Maldonado (coord), *La Función Social de la Propiedad* (Eudeba 2013).

113 Jean-Louis Halpérin, *Histoire du droit privé français depuis 1804* (Presses Universitaires de France 1996) 186.

started to occur in society regarding the extent of that right, and the social function paradigm started to develop across the Western Hemisphere. That approach entailed a less 'egoistic' understanding of ownership.[114] Changes had occurred in the social and economic structures of different jurisdictions, with massive migrations into cities and the effects of the Industrial Revolution.[115] Accordingly, the crude individualistic paradigm started to be challenged as a reaction to the social problems that were developing across the Western Hemisphere.[116]

Several points attest to the existence of the social function paradigm. First, that many changes took place regarding ownership, starting during the second half of the nineteenth century, and experiencing a peak in the period 1890-1930. Second, that the new ideas developed both in Europe and in the Americas, and found reception that was not limited to English, French, German, and Spanish legal literature, and even extended to the writings of the Church. Third, that the new ideas were also welcomed within constitutional texts, both of Europe and of the Americas. Society demanded a departure from the liberal paradigm that had prevailed during the nineteenth century, and that legislatures were open to the reception of a new understanding of ownership. There was a *contagion* of constitutions that welcomed the new paradigm, and that was triggered after the Mexican (1917) and Weimar (1919) constitutions. Fourth, the new ideas were welcomed within civil codes as part of the doctrine of abuse of rights that served as a channel for the reception of the new ideas. A pollination of that doctrine was experienced in the Old World and in the New World, at similar time-periods. Fifth, that special legislation developed outside the civil codes and welcomed the new ideas. Legislatures addressed social needs, such as land reform, colonisation of lands, and regulation of tenancy contracts. Those enactments succeeded in reaching a paradigm shift, even in jurisdictions where constitutional texts or civil codes were not subject to substantive changes.

American Civil Law Jurisdictions indeed abandoned the liberal paradigm and incorporated the tenets of the social function paradigm within their legal frameworks. The degree of departure from the previous paradigm differed according to the different jurisdictions, some being more conservative than others. A group of jurisdictions welcomed the new paradigm expressly in their enactments, even referring to the term *social function*, while other jurisdictions weakened the absolute character of ownership by adopting doctrines and principles that had an indirect impact on that fundamental pillar of property law.

---

114 Beatriz Areán, *Curso de Derechos Reales: Privilegios y Derecho de Retención* (3rd edn, Abeledo-Perrot 1994) 188.

115 Cordero Quinzacara (n 8) 503.

116 Gumersindo de Azcárate, *Ensayo sobre la historia del derecho de propiedad y su estado actual en Europa*, vol III (Imprenta de la Revista de Legislación 1879-1883) 357-453.

3.4 ECOLOGICAL FUNCTION OF OWNERSHIP PARADIGM

The social function paradigm spread across continents, and some jurisdictions are currently encountering a new paradigm.[117] The EFOP, being that new paradigm, refers to ownership as fulfilling an ecological function, where there is a duty to secure sustainability.[118] Limitations to ownership have indeed proliferated since the final decades of the twentieth century because of environmental controls.[119] It has been correctly stated, already in 2002 by Myrl L Duncan, that 'land ownership disconnected from community is a logical impossibility.'[120] Building on the definition of ecology, the new paradigm calls for a new look into the interactions of living creatures within their environments: that new look will help in making life possible for current and future generations.[121] Awareness of the role of humans as creatures in an environment enables reconciliation between ownership and ecology.[122]

A main challenge of sustainability relates to reaching a development that is grounded in ecology, social equity, cultural diversity, and democratic participation.[123] A new paradigm therefore calls for 'public good associated with environmental protection,'[124] in words of Nicholas S Bryner.

---

117 The literature is copious, since the topic can be approached from property law and other fields alike. Titles that follow are only illustrative, since they offer indications on a change that is required due to the interplay of property law and the environment. See the early approach in Donald McGillivray and John Wightman, 'Private Rights, Public Interests and the Environment' in T Hayward and J O'Neill (eds), *Justice, Property and the Environment: Social and Legal Perspectives* (Ashgate 1997); and the more recent approach in Fritjof Capra and Ugo Mattei, *The Ecology of Law: Toward a Legal System in Tune with Nature and Community* (Berrett-Koehler Publishers 2015). For a recent overview from Europe, see Gerd Winter (ed), *Property and Environmental Protection in Europe* (Europa Law Publishing 2016). For an approach from the US, see Jonathan Cannon, 'Environmentalism and the Supreme Court: A Cultural Analysis' (2006) 33 Ecology Law Quarterly 363. For an approach from Latin-American, see María Cristina Puente Salinas, *Perdidos entre las leyes y los árboles. Propiedad y posesión en un bosque protector ecuatoriano* (Flasco 2008), especially chapters 4 and 5. As already mentioned, the new ideas can be approached from different fields. See, for example, an approach from architecture in Carlos Felipe Velasco Fuentes, *Shifting the Ownership Paradigm in the Built Environment: A Regenerative Approach to Ownership and Appropriation*, Master Thesis in Architecture, University of British Columbia (2016).

118 See, for example, Bryner, 'Public Interests and Private Land' (n 4).

119 Terry W Frazier, 'Protecting Ecological Integrity within the Balancing Function of Property Law' (1998) 28 Environmental Law 53.

120 Myrl L Duncan, 'Reconceiving the bundle of sticks: land as a community-based resource In Memoriam: Professor Curtis J. Berger' (2002) 32 Environmental Law 773.

121 Renata Raupp Gomes et al, 'A função ecológica da propriedade na perspectiva dos direitos de terceira dimensão: um necessário resgate da fraternidade' (2016) 21 Revista Novos Estudos Jurídicos – Eletrônica 1222.

122 Frazier (n 119) 103.

123 Mariano H Novelli, 'Bases jurídicas de la educación para el desarrollo sostenible en el Mercosur' (2008) 6:11 Academia 183, 187.

124 Bryner, 'Public Interests and Private Land' (n 4) 149.

The literature referred to the attention that must be devoted to ecology and the environment within the property law context.[125] A first example relates to Garrett Hardin and the *tragedy of the commons.*[126] He alerted already in the 1960s that there was no correct allocation of ownership if an exhaustion of common resources (*eg*, forestry) occurred. That *tragedy* called for the correct allocation of ownership, since a complete environmental degradation could be triggered. However, the *tragedy* does not prevent owners from causing more environmental threats, also referred as externalities (*eg*, cutting native flora and replacing with fast-growing species). The new paradigm now calls for a step further, hence extending the scope of the *tragedy* to secure that abiotic conditions do not affect the ecological function of ownership. A second example relates to the *payment for eco-system services.*[127] Common resources enable ecological functions for which society members do not pay. A payment system representing the ecological functions and services of the particular resource is needed when aiming to secure the correct incentives.[128] The new paradigm again calls for a step further, extending the scope of the *payment for eco-system services* to ensure a way to sustain the ecological function of ownership.

The EFOP is novel because regardless of acknowledged precedents (*eg*, *tragedy of the commons, payment for eco-system services*) never before has environment occupied the paramount position within the paradigms of ownership. Only now, it is possible to speak of a new paradigm. Only now, the environment prevails over the individual and social character of ownership.

This new paradigm enables environmental and ownership limitations, stretching beyond the tenets of the social function paradigm, and gaining paradigm status itself.[129] The reception of the EFOP by jurisdictions can take place in different ways, reacting to different policy changes and addressing diverse aspects of social responsibility and environmental law. Aspects of the new paradigm may be encapsulated within fundamental laws or constitutions, possibly following guiding precepts welcomed in international documents. Constitutions include references to the social responsibility that derives from the duty to conserve the land (*eg*, Slovenia, 1991).[130] Codes, in civil law jurisdictions, also

---

125 This paragraph builds on ideas shared by Michael G Faure with the author in an email dated 10 October 2016 (on file with the author of this paper).

126 See generally Garrett Hardin, 'The Tragedy of the Commons' (1968) 162:3859 Science 1243.

127 See generally Robert Costanza et al, 'The value of the world's ecosystem services and natural capital' (1997) 387 Nature 253. See the more recent Robert Costanza et al, 'Changes in the global value of ecosystem services' (2014) 26 Global Environmental Change 152-158.

128 On eco-systems services see, Jonathan Silvertown, 'Have Ecosystem Services Been Oversold?' (2015) 30:11 Trends in Ecology & Evolution 641. Several developments related to these services took place in Latin America, see Patricia Balvanera et al, 'Ecosystem services research in Latin America: The state of the art' (2012) 2 Ecosystem Services 56.

129 Gonzalo Perez Pejcic, 'Primer Ensayo sobre la función ambiental de la propiedad' (2014) 92 Lecciones y Ensayos 129, 131 and 157. See also Bryner, 'Public Interests and Private Land' (n 4).

130 See n 1.

welcome ideas that enrol within the EFOP (*eg*, Brazil, 2002).[131] Jurisdictions likewise incorporated aspects of the ecological function of ownership within special legislation (*eg*, Sweden, 1998).[132] Common law jurisdictions may welcome change by means of legislation, and acknowledge the paradigm in court decisions. Further, *green* courts have been developed in jurisdictions to deal with environmental protection (*eg*, India, 2010).[133] Court decisions and changes in the law may likewise take place in other legal systems. Scholars point to the need to secure a healthy environment, hence introducing limitations to the right of ownership.[134]

The understanding of the new paradigm will benefit from an interdisciplinary approach, since inputs from several academic fields provide innovative perspectives, and ultimately because the EFOP will affect several academic fields, including politics and environmental sciences. An interdisciplinary approach should be integrated to the already mentioned techniques,[135] where experts will contribute from their fields. For example, the interaction of jurists with researchers on ecological economics, an area that encompasses the relationship between ownership of property and the environment, will be enriching to fully grasp the traits of the new paradigm. Further, costs and financial responsibility are important aspects when assessing the interplay of the environment and property law. These aspects are core for the interdisciplinary scope of the new paradigm, and studies should invite participation from experts in law and economics, corporate social responsibility, and environmental law. Studies would therefore explore those important aspects in the new paradigm.

3.5 Closing Remarks

Paradigms evolve, and Ownership Paradigms are no exception. This paper offered some preliminary reflections on the interplay of paradigms, ownership, and ecology. Shifts were noted when looking at ownership in American Civil Law Jurisdictions and global challenges dealing with ecology were presented by means of the EFOP. A look into shifts in paradigms helps understand the changes that private law is experiencing when facing the need to

131 See art 1228 of the Brazilian Civil Code, available at www.planalto.gov.br/ccivil_03/leis/2002/L10406compilada.htm.

132 See art 1 of the Swedish Environmental Code, available in English at www.government.se/legal-documents/2000/08/ds-200061/.

133 Domenico Amirante, 'Environmental Courts in Comparative Perspective: Preliminary Reflections on the National Green Tribunal of India' (2012) 29 Environmental Law Review 441.

134 See, for example, Sebastián Moscoso Sepúlveda and Silvia Alejandra Padilla Quintero, 'Función social y ecológica de la propiedad en los Parques Nacionales Naturales de Colombia' (2016) 4 Revista Global Iure 65, 74.

135 See section 3.2.2.

reach sustainability. After all, changes have to take place in order for all living creatures to coexist in the current global environment.

This paper first addressed the role of paradigms in the study and understanding of the law. The focus was devoted to the different paradigms of ownership. As mentioned before, Ownership Paradigms consist of the abstract understanding of what constitutes the right of ownership and what this right comprises. That abstract understanding finds consensus amongst jurists, provides model problems and solutions, and changes according to time and space. Further, that first part of the paper offered a number of research paths that can assist in identifying shifts in paradigms. Hence, references were made to the use of, amongst others, case studies, process-tracing techniques, and empirical legal research.

The paper then looked into the shifts in Ownership Paradigms in American Civil Law Jurisdictions starting in the nineteenth-century. That approach was used as an illustration of the shifts in paradigms. The liberal paradigm took the stage first. Jurisdictions incorporated provisions on ownership within their civil codes. As mentioned before, the new texts embraced the liberal ideal of an absolute, unique, and perpetual real right of ownership, subject to the will of a single owner. The social function paradigm followed. The social function paradigm spread across the continent, and motivated corresponding changes in the wording of constitutions and civil codes, while it also included changes in the interpretation by courts and in the development of special legislation. That approach entailed a less 'egoistic' understanding of ownership. Paradigms indeed shifted, and accommodated ownership to the needs of actors in society.

The paper finally pointed to the EFOP, stretching beyond American Civil Law Jurisdictions. Recent developments have pointed towards a paradigm shift. Ownership has to fulfil an ecological function, where there is a duty to secure sustainability. An interdisciplinary approach will help to fully discover and understand the way owners need to behave, being living creatures in an environment. Society acknowledges that preserving the environment is a key element for the survival of humankind. Knowledge on the EFOP and the previous Ownership Paradigms may trigger policy proposals that may bring legal solutions to global problems. This might have an impact on practical terms by means of the development of policy models that may be more readily transferable, targeting jurisdictions likely to embrace the approach through law reform; and may result in a move towards solutions, providing a platform for major law reform. Further, academic studies could develop new theories on the property law implications of the EFOP and its impact on other areas of the law. Future studies, above all, should deal with the Ownership Paradigms in different jurisdictions.

No comprehensive study has been done on the EFOP, even though the environment has a fundamental impact on the daily lives of people in all societies. An inclusive approach would bring together learnings from different legal systems and would need to address the following questions: What is the role of property owners in securing the sustainability of the environment? How far can owners go in the exploitation of their property? When should the State intervene on ownership to guarantee the protection of the environment? When is social responsibility triggered when dealing with ownership? A look into different jurisdictions will offer scholars and society information to understand the elements of the EFOP.

It is time to start to explore, since actors and society need to know how abiotic conditions may affect things in the environment. It is time to move forward. Time indeed 'seems [to be] an increasingly precious commodity'[136] in a context dealing with ecology. A paradigm shift is on its way.

136 Paul Babie, 'Property, Negligence, and the Intergenerational Inequity of Climate Change' Research Paper No 2016-42, The University of Adelaide 5.

4 Sustainable Property Law

Towards a Revaluation of Our System of Property Law

*Bram Akkermans**

4.1 Introduction

At the beginning of the previous century, one of the oldest colleges at the University of Oxford, New College Oxford, was confronted with a problem with the oak beams in the dining hall, which needed to be replaced. The fellows of the college were posed with a problem on how to solve this. One of the junior fellows raised the idea to see if there were any oak trees on the many pieces of land held in ownership by the college since its foundation. The college Forrester was summoned to the college and stated upon his arrival that he had been waiting for a request of this sort. As it turns out, at the founding of the college in 1379, young oak trees had been planted to supply the college with new wood if this would ever be necessary in the future. So it happened and the new oak beams in the dining hall at New College Oxford can be viewed for over 100 years already.[1]

The foresight of the founders of the college shows a design of an institution that is meant to stay for a very long time. The design does not only foresee in the needs of the generation that would use the building, but also incorporates the many generations that would follow. In our modern day terminology, we could conclude that the design of New College Oxford is a sustainable design.

Sustainability, and sustainable development as a method, come to that, has been receiving more and more attention in the last years.[2] Sustainability concerns the ideas of preservation and protection. Many proponents of sustainability refer to a photo of the planet earth, taken by an astronaut on board of the Apollo 8 spaceship, and a photo of the earth as a globe from 1972.[3] These photos show, according to the proponents of sustain-

* This contribution is based, but is a revised and extended version, on my TPR inaugural lecture, held at the Catholic University of Leuven on 16 March 2018. A (Dutch language) version of that lecture is published in *Tijdschrift voor Privaatrecht* (2018), 1437-1470.

1 www.atlasobscura.com/places/oak-beams-new-college-oxford.

2 See John Blewitt, Understanding Sustainable Development, 2e editie (Londen, New York: Routledge, 2015), p. 6 *et seq.*

3 See John Blewitt, Understanding Sustainable Development, 2e editie (Londen, New York: Routledge, 2015), p. 7. The photo's bear the titles Earthrise (1968) and Blue Marble (1972).

ability, that the earth is not limitless and that humanity must treat her with care to enable future generations to enjoy her as well.

Sustainability does not only concern ecological sustainability, but also the way in which we live together, choose our government and governance structures, and share or do not share our wealth with each other. In 2015 the United Nations established, after a very long negotiation process, 17 Sustainable Development Goals (SDGs). These goals deal with, apart from ecological sustainability, democratic governance and economic progress for everyone. They deal, in other words, with wellbeing for everyone. Although these UN SDGs do not have formal legally binding power, all member countries to the UN are expected to give effect to the SDGs by reforming current policy and the making of new policy and legislation.[4]

As can be seen from the example of New College Oxford, sustainability has been considered for hundreds of years already. These are therefore not new initiatives, but the attention they receive is new. At the same time a situation has arisen that requires immediate attention for the sustainability problem. Think, in this context, about natural phenomena such as increasing sea levels and global warming, large forest fires and mudstreams in the United States of America and Australia, but also the Dutch problems arising from the extraction of natural gas.

How, in other words, have we come to this? In the past decades there has been a lot of attention from natural scientists and economists for this question. Most research points to the ideas of Neo-liberal economics, introduced as a political model by Margaret Thatcher and Ronald Reagan in the 1980s. In Neo-liberal thinking, which builds on 19th century *laisser faire* thinking in economics, the economy is seen as a balance of offer and acceptance, in which we all participate as rational actors with the aim to enrich ourselves and each other. The market is leading in this and government interference or other supportive measures are not to be taken. Profitability and economic growth are the central driving forces.[5]

Private law plays an instrumental role here as primary supplier of the building blocks of economic development. The freedom of ownership, free circulation of goods and the freedom of contract enable us to give value to a thing, that you may consider to be your own and that you may freely transfer for a value in conformity with the market value of that thing.[6] In this perspective, rules of property law are transactional rules that – together – form a coherent and especially efficient system. To put it simply: a natural person accrues

4 These are principles of 'soft law' and – according to some are also principles of international customary law. See John Blewitt, Understanding Sustainable Development, 2e editie (Londen, New York: Routledge, 2015), p. 14, 68.

5 Kate Raworth, Doughnut Economics (Londen: Random House, 2017), p. 62-63, 68 et seq.

6 The term `thing' is used here in the meaning of a physical object that can be the subject matter of a property right.

as many things in ownership as possible to enrich himself and to freely and exclusively dispose over these.

It is this – capitalist – system that natural scientists and economists point to as the cause of problems. Extraction and profit have reigned too strongly in past decades. Natural phenomena such as global warming due to the burning of fossil fuels, but also the financial crisis of 2008 are, so these critics state, a direct consequence of the way in which we deal with our things.

A short example to illustrate this. In the period prior to the financial crisis banks became publicly traded companies. The consequence of this was that the main objective of the bank was no longer only to provide good services to its client, but also to grow and make more profit for shareholders and investors. In the 1990s banks succeeded in these new targets and managed to attain up to a factor 20 growth levels.[7] At a certain moment, however, the market for the granting of loans became saturated, and growth levels stabilised and, with that, also turnover and profits. Banks, led by large stock exchange listed banks on Wall Street, began to cut loans into pieces and repackage these to be able to sell these to investors as derivatives. With that, journalist Marjorie Kelly shows in her most recent book 'Owning our Future' an investment market in products was created that disconnected itself from the real world. A market that became so disconnected that at the beginning of this century a package of loans or mortgages traded on Wall Street no longer automatically represented an actual piece of land. The result of the bursting of the bubble that resulted from this is known and many banks, not only in the US, became insolvent or almost became insolvent as a result of these practices. Private law was, once more, instrumental in this. The loan, a contract, and the mortgage, a limited property right, are the basis of these types of transactions. The result, however, is very disproportional: shareholders were protected, but landowners and homeowners lost their land and house.[8]

In the past years a lot of new initiatives have been created that partly provide an answer to the problem of excessive profits and growth targets and that all – in some way – proceed on the basis of sustainability. Examples of this are offered by the sharing economy, with sharing-car company Cambio in Germany and Belgium, housing sharing platform AirBnB and transport platform Uber, circular building and cooperative initiatives of governments, companies and citizens. Also here, private law continues to supply the building blocks on the basis of which these innovative platforms can do their work. For the most part this is the law of contract and not the law of property. In fact, the law of property is pushed to

7 See Marjorie Kelly, Owning our Future. The Emerging Ownership Revolution (Oakland: Berrett-Koehler Publishers Inc, 2012), p. 53 *et seq.*

8 Marjorie Kelly, Owning our Future. The Emerging Ownership Revolution (Oakland: Berrett-Koehler Publishers Inc, 2012), p. 67-70, 78-82, 85 *et seq.*

the background by these sharing initiatives in favour of contract law, more than was already the case in the last 30 years.

Sharing, after all, implies the 'leasing' of things and not the ownership thereof. In most cases the business model in the sharing economy is the offering of a service on the basis of a right of ownership. Sustainability lies specifically in the idea that the thing is used more often, for example a car that is used more than two cars that stand still all day when their owners are at work. The idea behind this is that producers would produce more sustainable products if their profit does not come from a one-off transfer of ownership, but through a business model where one thing keeps delivering periodic income. The concept of ownership for a consumer becomes superfluous in such an approach.[9]

This is an undesirable development to me, as it does not automatically serve sustainability. After all, the producer can also claim a higher monthly payment if he replaces the current thing with a nicer, better, more extensive model. Before we, in other words, throw out a part of our law of property, it makes sense to explore the possibilities of a sustainable property law. In order to do that we must (1) look at the role and purpose of private law, (2) at sustainability and property law and (3) see if this can lead to concrete solutions. In order to do this I bring existing literature together that will form the ingredients for formulating a proposal for the revaluation of our law of property into a sustainable law of property.

4.2 The Purpose of Property Law

In our current system property law is at the service of personal development. After the abolishment of the feudal system, with enlightened ideas on a new society, the right of ownership finally became available for everyone. The system of private ownership and free circulation of goods made it possible to accrue wealth. In this way land, back then the most valuable object one could have, was no longer in the hands of a small elite. With the Industrial Revolution after that movable objects, besides land, also became of importance. The underlying principle was that through mass production of things everyone could accrue wealth on their own.

When there was ownership of a thing, the owner was free to dispose over that thing in any way he wished. The lawyers who drafted the French civil code based themselves in this respect on the work of Bartolus, who in his turn gave definition to the Roman law concept of ownership. Bartolus described the right of ownership as the right to dispose

9 See, for example, Judith Merkies, The End of Ownership, European Voice 6 maart 2012, www.politico.eu/article/the-end-of-ownership/.

over an object in the most complete manner.[10] The French 19th century author Demolombe writes affirmatively, for example, on the question whether the owner of a painting also has the power to set fire to that painting. This liberalist philosophy, which should be placed in a time of great thinkers such as Robert Pothier and John Locke, uses an instrumentalist approach: the law of property is a means to achieve a purpose, the accrual of wealth. In other words, a utilitarian philosophy. Some thinkers even went further on the basis of Locke's theory and developed a libertarian theory of ownership in which the right of ownership is a pre-political right, a right that everyone has before legislation is created.[11] There exists, in other words, a link between political philosophy and ownership.

With the rise of economic theories in the 19th and 20th centuries a second link between law and society was made. Not only on the basis of political philosophy, but also on the basis of economic thinking – which in its turn also finds its basis in philosophy of, for example, Adam Smith – the law of property became instrumental once more to the realisation of a purpose: welfare and economic growth.

In 1947 in Mont Pèlerin in Switzerland three economists met to lay the foundations of what would become Neo-liberal thinking. These economists, among which were Friedrich Hayek and Milton Friedman, argued – inspired by market economist Adam Smith – for a free market economy with as little government interference as possible. Economic growth, expressed in the Gross Domestic Product (GDP), became the leading objective. Private law, especially the right of ownership, became the means to achieve this. Ownership became, more than ever, a status symbol for welfare, freedom and especially the incentive to trade. Law and economic scholars such as Ronald Coase and Richard Posner brought the attention to the law of property as a system of transactions.[12] The transferability and actual transfer of property rights became the leading method of analysis. In 2018, the most famous proponent of such an analysis is Henry Smith from Harvard Law School.[13] He makes an analysis of the transactional aspects of property law, which he names the operating system. In Smith's analysis, the operating system revolves around the costs that are concerned with a transaction. Essentially the rule applies that if the proceeds are higher than the costs, the transaction can take place and should actually be encouraged. This applies to the rules of transfer of property rights, but also for the number and content of the catalogue of property rights.

10 Feenstra, Romeinsrechtelijke grondslagen van het privaatrecht (Leiden: Brill Uitgevers, 1990), p. 40, see also Bram Akkermans and William Swadling in Sjef van Erp and Bram Akkermans (Eds.), Text, Cases and Materials on Property Law, Ius Commune Casebooks for the Common Law Of Europe (Oxford: Hart Publishing, 2012), p. 217-218.

11 Gregory Alexander en Eduardo Peñalver, An Introduction to Property Theory (Cambridge: Cambridge University Press, 2012), p. 35 et seq.

12 See R.H. Coase, "The Problem of Social Cost", 3 J. Law & Economics 1960, 7 = doi. org/10.1086/674872; R. Posner, Economic Analysis of Law (Boston: Little Brown 1973).

13 H. Smith, "Property as the Law of Things", 125 Harvard Law Review 2012, 1692ff.

Opposed to Smith's law and economics analysis is a group of progressive property lawyers who base themselves not on economic, but on philosophical foundations. They are concerned with the purpose of the law of property in our society. Their analyses do not only have a descriptive aim, as with law and economics research, but also often have a normative aim by providing content to the purpose property law plays in our society. Singer, for example, brings out attention to equality and democracy as constitutional aims and shows how the rules of property law, such as the rules on the distribution and redistribution of ownership of land, can play a role in improving living conditions for everyone. If equality is the purpose, Singer argues, then the rules of property law must be placed in a constitutional perspective.

Singer uses the famous Kelo case to illustrate this. In this case a group of citizens objected to the expropriation of their neighbourhood.[14] The city of New London in the state of Connecticut wanted to take this neighbourhood to persuade pharmacist Pfizer to establish itself there. Expropriation (or taking in US terminology) in the private and not public interest. The American Supreme Court ruled that it was permissible to take this land with a private purpose if the taking was for the benefit of the development, read growth, of the local economy. Singer argues that this decision was wrong because it only concerns the transaction, i.e. the transfer of ownership of the land from private citizens, through the government, to a private party that will ensure economic growth, but also the question how society considers the ownership of land. Having ownership of land is not only about the right to exclude others and extract value from the land for yourself, but also about exercising your right of ownership in the context of other land owners.[15] Community, in other words, also provides content to the way in which the right of ownership is exercised or, in case of Kelo, respected.

It is especially Alexander, also an American scholar, who emphasises the positive duties that go with the right of ownership. Alexander takes his inspiration from German constitutional property law and mostly South American theories on the social function of ownership.[16] For his own theory Alexander looks back to Aristotle and Thomas of Aquinas and states that the purpose of property law is not only to give exclusivity and welfare, but also to create wellbeing for everyone, individuals and the community. Alexander distinguishes himself with this from other, more economically inspired approaches, because he

14 See also Gregory Alexander's discussion of the Kelo decision in relation to his human flourishing theory. Gregory Alexander, Property and Human Flourishing (Oxford: Oxford University Press, 2018), p. 225 *et seq*.

15 Joseph Singer, Property as the Law of Democracy, 63 Duke Law Journal 1287 (2014), p. 1323.

16 These South American theories are based on the work of the French lawyer Léon Duguit. See Léon Duguit, Les transformations générales du droit privé depuis le code Napoléon 21, 2e editie (Parijs: Félix Alcan, 1912). See on this, Matthew Mirrow, The Social Obligation Norm of Property: Duguit, Hayem, and Others, 22 Florida Journal of International Law (2010), p. 191.

widens the purpose of property law to also include within the right of ownership the rights of others and the interest of the community.[17]

Differences of opinion therefore exist about what is the purpose of property law. The mainstream, more private-law-inspired thought is to see the right of ownership as an individualist right, for which accrual of value, increase in wealth and individual welfare are the starting points.[18] A diverging and more progressive thought that wins in power is more public-law-inspired and brings besides the private law point of view an additional context of wellbeing and equality that influences that.

In relation to sustainability this is a very interesting discussion. Sustainable development goals deal with wellbeing of ourselves and those around us. We are, I submit, therefore before a fundamental choice: do we keep clinging to a pure private law inspired understanding of ownership and property law or are we prepared to incorporate these or a part of these SDGs in our property law? With climate change, the finiteness of fossil fuels and the increasing inequality in the world, but also considering the obligations we put on ourselves to achieve the UN SDGs, a choice for the second option seems inevitable.

4.3 PRIVATE LAW AND SUSTAINABILITY

Sustainability generally refers to ecosystems that are able to continuously remain divers and productive. Think in this respect about forests that maintain themselves for centuries already without any human interference. But sustainability not only concerns ecological sustainability, but also the way in which we treat the earth. The 17 UN SDG do therefore not only relate to these (1) ecological objectives, such as healthy drinking water, clean energy and stopping climate change, but also on (2) governance aspects, in which equality and democracy are leading, and (3) economic aspects, in which sustainable economic growth from which everyone should benefit is central.

The UN agreements call on all of us to contribute to these objectives: governments, the private sector, societal organisations and even citizens. The starting point is that we cannot do this all through our governments and that everyone must work on this together. The law of property, and not the law of contract or tort, will have to deliver most of the building blocks for this. After all, our understanding of ownership, of land but also ownership of companies by the shareholders, is crucial in the way in which we have designed our society.

17 Gregory Alexander, Property's Ends: The Publicness of Private Law Values, Cornell Law School Research paper No 14-13 (2014), Gregory Alexander, Property and Human Flourishing (Oxford: Oxford University Press, 2018).

18 See, in this sense, Teun Struycken, De numerus clausus in het goederenrecht (Deventer: Kluwer, 2007), p. 236.

In the context of sustainable development of private law, scholars have pointed to three important aspects in the last years: (1) the importance of the commons, (2) the circular economy and circular construction and (3) the sharing economy in which services are more important than ownership.

In relation to the commons this work only concerns the way in which these are governed, but especially the idea that in former times, before the French Revolution and the large European codifications, a lot of land was held in common ownership. Natural scientist Fritjof Capra and legal scholar Ugo Mattei put the emphasis in their book 'The Ecology of Law' on how the Neo-liberal thinking already mentioned has led to privatisation of what was common before. Ugo Mattei uses the example of the provision of water in Naples, Italy. There, in the 1980s, the water company was privatised, with disastrous results in the quality of the drinking water and the prices for users. When the Italian parliament declared water into a commons, Mattei led a movement to make the Neapolitan water company public once more. Not by expropriation, but by changing the mission statement of the company as an activist shareholder from profit into general and public service.[19]

Commons, in which the right of ownership is shared by a large group, or even by everyone, has been gaining in popularity in the last years. In the 21st century this does not refer to joint ownership of the means of production, such as in a communist system, but entails cooperation between citizens and governments to achieve, mostly sustainable, objectives.

A short example of such an initiative. In a neighbourhood a group of citizens is constructing a baking-house, a communal wood fired oven, which together with a windmill on the same premises will provide space and opportunity for everyone to bake their own bread.[20] A communal oven was very normal in the Middle Ages in many communities. There was a great danger for destruction by fire for the often wooden houses and a stone building with an oven provided safety and economies of scale.[21] In 2018 this initiative is about something different: this is about the community and the feeling of belonging to a community and of course about the sustainable use of energy. On a baking day easily 25 people will bake bread in an oven that only needs to be heated once.

This citizens initiative fits very well in a global trend. Journalist Marjorie Kelly provides other examples such as common windmills, cooperative living solutions and large companies that are co-owned by their employees.[22] The development of the commons actually

19 Fritjof Capra and Ugo Mattei, The Ecology of Law. Toward a Legal System in Tune with Nature and Community (Oakland: Berrett-Koehler Publishers Inc, 2015), p. 164-167.

20 See http://molenmeterik.nl/wp/uitbreiding-molen/

21 Also known as *four banal*, see François de Boutaric, Traité des droits seigneuriaux et des matières feodales (Toulouse: Jean-François Forest, 1767). p. 379 (available at https://archive.org/embed/traitdesdroitsse00bout).

22 Marjorie Kelly, Owning our Future. The Emerging Ownership Revolution (Oakland: Berrett-Koehler Publishers Inc, 2012), p. 147 *et seq.*

goes much further than that. Think in this respect about open source software, the digital commons, and YouTube and Wikipedia, to which everyone can provide his or her own creative contribution.[23]

A second aspect of sustainability in private law relates to the circular economy. The Ellen MacArthur Foundation describes the circular economy as a closed system in which products and services are exchanged. This system is designed to reduce waste and prevent pollution, use products and materials and keep using them and to let natural systems recover and thrive.[24] In The Netherlands Monica Chao-Duivis recently paid attention to the private law aspects of the circular economy.[25] This especially concerns the rules of accession, dealing with the question what is one unity of objects and who owns these. Creating more flexibility in the traditionally very strict rules provides the possibility to replace whole facades of houses by new versions with higher isolation values or to place solar panels on a building with several property relations resting on it.[26] A facade or solar panel can then be owned by another, making room for joined initiatives such as collective solar panels in a neighbourhood, or leasing of a facade to a house that fits the highest isolation standards.

A lot of attention for this is generated by architect Thomas Rau. Rau is known for his initiatives in the area of circular construction, especially the 'Alliander' building that is accompanied by a materials passport: an overview of all materials that are used in the construction and that can – that is how the building is designed – be reused when the building is demolished.[27] A more recent initiative is the 'madaster': an attempt to come to a cadastral registration of materials.[28] In his book 'Material Matters' Rau, together with Sabine Oberhuber, proposes to move towards a special lease rights (*beklemrecht* in Dutch) instead of ownership. The idea behind this is that the materials are in use and not in ownership and that in that way can return to the owner who may reuse them or reshape them into other sustainable materials.[29]

Arie Mes and Hendrik Ploeger in their advice to the Dutch Notarial Professional organisation (KNB) put the emphasis on rules of accession and argue in favour of more

23 See Felix Stadler, Digital Commons: A dictionary entry. http://felix.openflows.com/node/137.
24 See www.ellenmacarthurfoundation.org/circular-economy/overview/concept.
25 Monica Chao-Duivis, Privaatrechtelijke aspecten van de circulaire economie in het bijzonder circulair bouwen. Deel 1 (Tijdschrift voor Bouwrecht 9 (2017/139) Deel 2 (Tijdschrift voor Bouwrecht 10 (2017/154), Deel 3 (Tijdschrift voor Bouwrecht 1 (2018/1).
26 See Monica Chao-Duivis, Privaatrechtelijke aspecten van de circulaire economie in het bijzonder circulair bouwen. Deel 2, Tijdschrift voor Bouwrecht 10 (2017), p. 1036, Pernille van der Plank, Natrekking door Onroerende Zaken (Deventer: Kluwer, 2016), p. 126 *et seq.*
27 See www.rau.eu/portfolio/liander/
28 www.madaster.com.
29 Thomas Rau and Sabine Oberhuber, Material Matters. Het alternatief voor onze roofbouwmaatschappij (Haarlem: Bertram en De Leeuw Uitgevers, 2016), p. 155 *et seq.*

flexibility by allowing party autonomy in this area.[30] Also Pernille van der Planck comes to similar conclusions in her book on accession.[31] More party autonomy, is the thought, makes it possible to come to new and creative solutions.

Rau's lease construction comes close to the third aspect already mentioned: the sharing economy. In the private law debate on the sharing economy mostly the contractual aspects are central. This concerns the commercial providing of services to citizens, such as car-sharing project Cambio, or from citizens to citizens through sharing platforms such as AirBNB and Uber. Instead of leaving a thing, such as a car, unused for 80% of the time, much more efficient use can be made of it by sharing it with others or to use it to provide services to others. The law of property is pushed to the background here, as the central issue is the service and not the entitlement to the thing. In fact, a lot of times the end of ownership is argued for in this context.[32] Or, when the end of ownership and property law is not called for, the right of ownership is reduced to the right of the producer or facilitator of the service. The theory is that if the business model of the producer not only concerns the one-off sale of the thing, but that it is a model where the producer receives periodic payments to the use of the thing, the producer will make more sustainable products. For example: a private-lease of a car rather than the ownership of a car. The longer the product lasts, the more income the thing will deliver to the producer. The same applies to a situation in which a lessee shares his right with others in a sharing project, possibly through AirBNB or Uber.[33]

Private law, especially property law, plays an essential role in the achieving of sustainability. However, it seems that private law practice is ahead of private law theory in this respect.[34] Property law and the right of ownership are easily set aside in favour of the law of obligations. A development that has already been going on for a century.[35]

---

30 Arie Mes, Hendrik Ploeger en Barbra Jansen, Eigendom van Onroerende zaken, met name natrekking (titels 1 en 3). Flexibele eigendomsverhoudingen in het vastgoedrecht, in Leon Verstappen (Red.), Boek 5 BW van de toekomst. Over vernieuwingen in het zakenrecht (Den Haag: KNB, 2016), p. 164.

31 Pernille van der Plank, Natrekking door Onroerende Zaken (Deventer: Kluwer, 2016), p. 126 *et seq*.

32 See Judith Merkies, The End of Owenrship, European Voice 6 maart 2012, www.politico.eu/article/the-end-of-ownership/.

33 It could be in violation of the general terms and conditions of a sharing platform, depending on what right is created on the object. It is clear that AirBnB does not allow lessors to rent their objects in violation of their own rental conditions. See Article 7.3.4 of the AirBnB General Terms and Conditions through www.airbnb.com.

34 See, in the same sense, Monica Chao-Duivis, Privaatrechtelijke aspecten van de circulaire economie in het bijzonder circulair bouwen. Deel 1 (Tijdschrift voor Bouwrecht 9 (2017/139), p. 915.

35 See on this Remi Libchaber, La recodification du droit des biens, in: Le Code civil 1804-2004 (Livre du Bicentenaire), Paris: Dalloz/Lexis Nexis Litec 2004, p. 297 *et seq*. Bram Akkermans, The Principle of Numerus Clausus in European Property Law (Antwerpen: Intersentia, 2008), p. 385 ff. Jens-thomas Füller, Eigenständiges Sachenrecht? Jus Privatum. Beitrage zum Privatrecht 104 (Tübingen: Mohr Siebeck: 2006), p. 2 *et seq*.

However, property law can play a crucial role in the achievement of sustainability and the SDGs, if we consider property law to be a flexible rather than a closed toolbox, as a dynamic rather than static system. To do that we need to provide new values to our system of property law and revalue it in a way that allows internalising the concept of sustainability. That is possible, I intend to show, without pleading for the end of property law and without going to a pure communal system.

4.4 Towards a Sustainable Property Law

4.4.1 New Philosophical and Economic Foundations

The law of property and especially the right of ownership traditionally are essential for personal development in our society. It provides freedom, a status symbol and is an incentive to accrue more wealth.[36] Founded in a liberal economic system that aims for growth and welfare, the individual in our system is the holder of subjective rights with the right of ownership as the most extensive right from the catalogue.[37] The right of ownership grants its holder exclusivity and especially the power to exclude others.[38]

The right of ownership provides, in other words, the right to take from the object on which it is created.[39] In the most simple meaning to harvest from your land, but also to fertilise your land and plant crops on it in such a manner that eventually the land will be exhausted. The behaviour of large American banks prior to the financial crisis in 2008 can also be described like this. After all, banks received rights of mortgage in their portfolio and split these into parts to trade them for as much money as possible, after which they created derivatives of these rights and, basically, even traded in derivatives that were no longer directly linked to a specific right of mortgage or a specific object.[40] The result is well

36 Monica Chao-Duivis, Privaatrechtelijke aspecten van de circulaire economie in het bijzonder circulair bouwen. Deel 2 (Tijdschrift voor Bouwrecht 9 (2017/154), p. 1041 'having a right of ownership has, for a long time, be considered essential for our society as we know it. It provides freedom, status and is considered an incentive to trade…'

37 Teun Struycken, De numerus clausus in het goederenrecht (Deventer: Wolters Kluwer, 2007), p. 236.

38 Article 5:1 Duch Civil Code, Article 544 Belgian Civil Code.

39 Marjorie Kelly calls this 'extractive ownership', Marjorie Kelly, Owning our Future. The Emerging Ownership Revolution (Oakland: Berrett-Koehler Publishers Inc, 2012), p. 11-12. See also Fritjof Capra and Ugo Mattei, The Ecology of Law. Toward a Legal System in Tune with Nature and Community (Oakland: Berrett-Koehler Publishers Inc, 2015), p. 6-7 who mention the difficulty of the closing of a parcel to the outside world by the owner.

40 Marjorie Kelly, Owning our Future. The Emerging Ownership Revolution (Oakland: Berrett-Koehler Publishers Inc, 2012), p. 78-79.

known: the bubble imploded and millions of people lost their home as a result of these very complex financial transactions.[41]

The economic model that is at the foundation of our property law is a Neo-liberal model: economic growth, expressed in the gross domestic product, is the leading principle. The state withholds itself from interference with the market as much as possible to provide free reign for the principles governing the market economy. Since the financial crisis it is clear for many that this cannot continue. Economist Kate Raworth is one of the first to offer an alternative by taking sustainability, and not economic growth as the starting point. Her model, known as doughnut economics, proceeds on the basis of a bandwidth, the doughnut, within which we executed our economy and our transactions in a sustainable manner. The minimum threshold, the hole of the doughnut, is a basis of fundamental social rights, the upper threshold the ecological ceiling.[42] Raworth's main argument is that economic growth and profit are fine, but that excessive growth and excessive profit bring more problems than they can solve.[43]

The link between our economic foundational principles and private law, the law of property in particular, is obvious. A different economic foundation can therefore provide a different method with which we use our rules of property law. Besides economics, it is also possible to use political philosophical foundations for this same purpose. If the purpose of property law is not utilitarianism, i.e. welfare and profit maximisation, but wellbeing and human flourishing for ourselves and also our community, our context and perspective dramatically change. There is no real contradiction between utilitarianism and human flourishing, but rather a difference in perspective: Gregory Alexander's theory on human flourishing does not only deal with the individual, but also with the community.[44]

Human flourishing means staying within the bandwidth in order to – at the minimum level – provide everyone with fundamental basic needs and – at the maximum level – deal with our materials in a regenerative and not extractive manner. In the terminology of journalist Marjorie Kelly already mentioned, this means a regenerative property law instead of an extractive property law: a system of doctrinal and technical rules that supplies the building blocks to create a sustainable environment.[45]

These are not ideas that are completely new to our system of property law. It is true that the right of ownership is the most extensive individualistic right – which especially

41 See www.nbcnews.com/id/42881365/ns/business-personal_finance/t/no-end-sight-foreclosure-quagmire.

42 Kate Raworth, Doughnut Economics (Londen: Random House, 2017), 51, see also her performance at Pakhuis de Zwijger via https://dezwijger.nl/programma/kate-raworths-doughnut-economics?lipi=urn%3Ali%3Apage%3Ad_flagship3_feed%3BjBVP5eojTm6wc%2FVCs4vbRQ%3D%3D.

43 Kate Raworth, Doughnut Economics (Londen: Random House, 2017), p. 53-60.

44 Gregory Alexander and Eduardo Peñalver, An Introduction to Property Theory (Cambridge: Cambridge University Press, 2012), p. 80 et seq. Community plays a crucial role in thinking about sustainability as the sustainable development goals are to be achieved together.

45 Kelly calls this regenerative ownership, but this approach applies to the full law of property.

enables the extraction from the object on which it is created – but there are several other instances in which the law of property functions in a different manner.

The most logical example of this is the duty to maintain the object of the person holding a right of usufruct. He who is usufructuary for another is expected not only to use the object, but also to preserve and maintain the object so that the value of the object remains stable.[46] Another example of the same duty can be found in the concept of *negotiorum gestio*, the fiduciary duty to take care of an object that belongs to another without any prior agreement to that.[47] The owner of the dominant land in case of a right of servitude must maintain the buildings and constructions he placed on the serviant land to be able to use his right.[48] Another example is the legal relation between apartment owners, who have a duty against each other to maintain the land and the building.[49]

The thought, in other words, that when someone is using an object of another, he does so in a sustainable manner in order to be able to return the object in the best possible condition, is already part of property law's DNA. It is a central concept in some instances, such as usufruct, or is read into property relations, such as in case of the relations between apartment owners.[50]

Not in private-law property law, but in the area of constitutional property law there has been attention for the effect of fundamental rights on property law for a while already. In our context, this mostly relates to Article 1 of the First Protocol to the European Convention for the Protection of Human Rights and Fundamental Freedoms (ECHR). In relation to this article, the European Court of Human Rights in 2002 introduced a positive obligation for the State to protect the ownership of its citizens.[51] This case dealt with the safety of a person illegally occupying a small piece of land at the bottom of a garbage belt. Due to a methane-gas explosion and the garbage and landslide that resulted because of this the man lost his house, which was nothing more than a shed. The security of the enjoyment of the right of ownership is therefore not only the responsibility of the owner, but also of the State. The right of ownership is therefore, besides a private law power, also a fundamental right that needs to be facilitated and protected by the State. The same applies of course for landowners whose land or house is endangered by rising sea levels as a result of global warming.

46 See for example Article 3:214 Dutch Civil Code, Article 578 Belgian Civil Code.
47 See Article 6:196 Dutch Civil Code.
48 Article 5:74 Dutch Civil Code.
49 Article 5:108 Dutch Civil Code.
50 See for example RB Limburg, 29 maart 2017, zaaknummer 5445461 \ CV EXPL 16-8550.
51 Öneryildiz v Turkey (2012) 18 June 2002.

4.4.2 Re-Valuation: A Positive Proprietary Obligation

It is the combination of these already existing connections that open the way for a revaluation of our property law. The new values on which a sustainable property law can be based are sustainability and sustainable development. A doughnut of values, for which the law of property provides the building blocks.

The most important value is wellbeing or human flourishing for ourselves and for our community. The idea that we use materials in a responsible manner by not consuming them, but by using them with the aim of being able to re-use them afterwards. This cannot only be an obligation that arises from the state, but must be internalised into our law of property. The private law method for this *par excellence* is the proprietary obligation, the *obligatio propter rem.* The content of this does not only flow from agreements between private parties, but also from an integral way of thinking in which public law and private law work together to realise sustainability.[52]

Gregory Alexander's work on human flourishing in property law provides a strong foundation on the basis of which this new obligation can be built.[53] In his most recent work Alexander contrasts community with the neoliberal concept of ownership.[54] Human flourishing theory is, in Alexander's view, that the 'vital purpose of property is to enable individuals to live a flourishing life'.[55] To that effect, Alexander identifies the communities we live in and holds that our membership of these communities, be it our family, religious group and even our country, bring with it a dependence on others.[56] A social thesis to promote human flourishing lies at the basis that assumes that to be a person with capabilities for human flourishing, you must be actively part of a society that enables the type of political, social and moral culture, as well as infrastructure, that allows you to flourish.[57]

From that social thesis, Alexander derives general and specific obligations that are not just for anyone, but for holders of property rights, especially owners.[58] The assumption is that when you have assets (or resources) that enable you to contribute to human flourishing

52 See Gregory Alexander, Property and Human Flourishing (Oxford, Oxford University Press, 2018), p. xv-xvi.

53 Gregory Alexander, Property and Human Flourishing (Oxford: Oxford University Press, 2018).

54 Gregory Alexander, Property and Human Flourishing (Oxford: Oxford University Press, 2018), p. 3 *et seq.*

55 Gregory Alexander, Property and Human Flourishing (Oxford: Oxford University Press, 2018), p. xiv (in general), p. 39 (on ownership in particular).

56 Gregory Alexander, Property and Human Flourishing (Oxford: Oxford University Press, 2018), p. xv (in general), p. 75 *et seq* (on communities in particular).

57 Alexander formulates this as: 'In order for me to be a certain kind of person – a free person with the basic capabilities necessary for human flourishing – I must be in, belong to, and support a certain kind of society – a society that supports a certain kind of political, social, and moral culture and that maintains a decent background material structure', Gregory Alexander, Property and Human Flourishing (Oxford: Oxford University Press, 2018), p. 55.

58 Gregory Alexander, Property and Human Flourishing (Oxford: Oxford University Press, 2018), p. 59.

there may be a duty to do so. To fulfil a general obligation may be to vote for the right political party to enact policy or to pay taxes, to fulfil a more specific obligation may entail doing something for a particular group and may be in kind rather than money.[59]

For this to materialise, Alexander holds, we need to identify the community that we are part of, and the interdependence that this community brings, before we can conceptualise the general or specific obligation that ownership in this community brings with it. What our obligation is will depend on the context that these elements provide. In Alexander's theory we are not, therefore, dealing with a one-size-fits all obligation for all owners.

In his most recent work Alexander deals with the issue of a clean environment as an infrastructural requirement for human flourishing.[60] The community that we are part of determines what type of obligation property right holders may have against each other as well as against others. Alexander identifies two types of communities: (1) those with a territorial foundation, such as our neighbourhoods, cities and even countries and (2) those with a non-territorial foundation, such as our (extended) families and even intergenerational links between family members.[61] Not everyone belongs to their community in the same way and the commitment to the community may also change over time. A child is dependent on her parents in different ways than when she grows into an adult with her own life with a family of her own. The obligations we owe to our community members are therefore, in Alexander's view, different in content and different depending on our involvement (or dependency) in our community.

Alexander does not directly address sustainability. In his analysis a clean environment is part of the infrastructure we need to enable human flourishing. A general obligation exists in his view that can be fulfilled by paying taxes to ensure the State takes care of this.[62] When Alexander deals with intergenerational communities and the question whether there are obligations we owe to future generations, he writes about an obligation not to 'milk' our resources.[63] Such obligation must, finally, be carried out 'by the state, through taxation and regulatory programs'.[64]

In the context of sustainability, I argue for action by all of us and the incorporation of an obligation of sustainability *propter rem*. Alexander's Human Flourishing theory does

59 Gregory Alexander, Property and Human Flourishing (Oxford: Oxford University Press, 2018), p. 55-58.

60 Gregory Alexander, Property and Human Flourishing (Oxford: Oxford University Press, 2018), p. 56.

61 Gregory Alexander, Property and Human Flourishing (Oxford: Oxford University Press, 2018), p. 75 *et seq* (on communities), p. 103 *et seq* (on intergenerational-communities).

62 Gregory Alexander, Property and Human Flourishing (Oxford: Oxford University Press, 2018), p. 56-57.

63 Alexander refers to 'milking' in the same way as I use the concept of exhaustion and extraction in this contribution. See Gregory Alexander, Property and Human Flourishing (Oxford: Oxford University Press, 2018), p. 117, 119-120.

64 Gregory Alexander, Property and Human Flourishing (Oxford: Oxford University Press, 2018), p. 122-123.

not go as far as this, but does offer inspiration to attempt to construct such an obligation.[65] For that to happen we need to establish (1) whether such obligation falls under the social thesis, (2) what is the community in which this obligation becomes relevant, (3) whether this gives rise to a general and/or specific obligation, and (4) to whom the obligation is owed and (5) what may be its content.

First, the inclusion of sustainability in the Human Flourishing social thesis seems uncontroversial. It is part of the political and social culture, as well as the infrastructure we need to enable human flourishing of ourselves and our communities. Although Alexander only includes a clean environment as an aspect of this, other issues of sustainability, such as equality, social justice and democracy also easily fit within the scope of this thesis.

Second, the community we belong to will greatly determine the existence and scope of the obligation that results. One community could be our fellow humans. As inhabitants of planet earth, we are all connected to each other. Especially when issues of environmental sustainability are concerned the realisation that what happens in one part of the planet, for example in terms of CO2 emissions, has an effect on other parts of the planet or even the whole planet. For example with rising sea levels as a result of global warming. At the same time, Alexander argues, most inhabitants on the planet are strangers to each other and not usually in the position that they can contribute to the development or nurturing of each other's capabilities.[66] Global citizenship, in Alexander's reasoning, does not provide enough connection to base obligations on.

The context of sustainability, especially environmental sustainability, may contribute to this reasoning in such a way that we can begin so speak of a global community. Our well-being, after all, depends us developing a sustainable society. The global realisation of our interdependence relating to these natural phenomena makes us responsible for each other's well-being. Alternatively, we can use smaller communities, such as Europe (EU citizenship is actually a valid legal concept and EU citizens are closely related to each other by rules of EU Law) or our own country.[67]

Another community that we can identify in this context are Alexander's intergenerational communities. In these, which are more individually based, we are linked to our ancestors as well as responsible for those that will come after us. Surely this also includes

65 Alexander explicitly states that the theory serves as an inspiration and not a roadmap, Gregory Alexander, Property and Human Flourishing (Oxford: Oxford University Press, 2018), p. xvii.

66 Gregory Alexander, Property and Human Flourishing (Oxford: Oxford University Press, 2018), p. 93-94.

67 In Alexander's analysis nation states are certainly a community in his theory, applying the same reasoning to the European Union in relation to EU Citizens words very well. Gregory Alexander, Property and Human Flourishing (Oxford: Oxford University Press, 2018), p. 90-92.

the way in which we deal with our planet to ensure that future generations will also be able to make use of its resources.[68]

Third, the membership of this global, European, or national, as well as intergenerational community of sustainability brings both general and specific obligations. Property owners hold resources that are essential to enable human flourishing by treating their objects in a sustainable manner. Such general obligation towards themselves as well as to others should come with their membership of their community or communities. Specific obligations can also exist for two reasons: depending on the property right, the specific obligation of sustainability may be not to exhaust the land, or not to foreclose on a sub-prime mortgage right.[69]

Fourth, these obligations are – first and foremost – owed towards the other members of the community. When it comes to the general obligation this seems obvious, but a complication arises when we ask the question who is able to enforce such obligation. Can another member of the community ask for fulfilment of such general obligation in a certain context, or is that a state matter and can we ask from the state to have a policy in place sufficient to protect this general obligation?[70] However, one may also reason a duty of care exists for every owner, natural person or corporation, to fulfil the global general obligation that they are under.[71] One or several members of the community may then certainly hold a property holder to his general obligation to treat his object in a sustainable manner. Specific obligations can exist between right-holders of property rights, for example the holder of a mother right and the holder of a daughter right. Because they are more specific they are more specifically enforceable between the parties that concern them.

Fifth and final, the content of these obligations is filled from our understanding of sustainability. As our understanding of how our current way of dealing with our planet needs to change to achieve a truly sustainable society grows, the content of the obligations that arise for holders of property rights – who have the resources to contribute to the development and therewith human flourishing of themselves and their community – will evolve and become more and more concrete.

---

68 See also Gregory Alexander, Property and Human Flourishing (Oxford: Oxford University Press, 2018), p. 122.

69 See my arguments and explanation on this below in section 5.

70 Alexander, under reference to the South African example created in Government of the Republic of South Africa v Grootboom, 2001 (1) SA 46 (CC), chooses for the latter as he holds that general obligations are to be fulfilled by paying taxes. Gregory Alexander, Property and Human Flourishing (Oxford: Oxford University Press, 2018), p. 126 at note 37.

71 This is an argument currently raised by the Dutch NGO *Mileudefensie* (environmental defence) that will attempt to hold Shell to a duty of care (in tort law) to stop producing fossil fuels. See https://milieudefensie.nl/klimaatzaakshell.

4.4.3 *An Algorithm for the Development of Sustainable Property Law*

In 2012 André van der Walt created a brilliant algorithm for the development of a property law in post-apartheid South Africa.[72] In South Africa the law of property faces an enormous challenge to create more social justice and welfare for everyone. To honour his work and his life as a world-renowned legal scholar, I reform his algorithm in an algorithm for the creation of a sustainable property law:

a. There is one system of law in which there is no distinction between public law and private law;
b. Sustainability is the starting point and organisational principle at the foundations for the development of our law and legal system. The UN SDG are the most recent expression of this and, as highest source of law, give direction to the development of our law and legal system;
c. The theoretical foundation of our property law is that of human flourishing; the doughnut economy is the foundation for economic growth and development;
d. Property law, whether it concerns legislation, common or customary law, or case law gives effect to sustainability and sustainable development;
e. Property rights, especially the right of ownership, is seen not only as an individualistic right, but also as a right with the obligation to protect and preserve for the future the object on which the right is created. This is a general as well as a specific obligation to connote to human flourishing in our communities. It is generative instead of extractive ownership;
f. Limited property rights are derived from a more encompassing right and therefore contain the same generative obligation as the right of ownership from which they derive themselves;
g. Existing property rights are respected and protected, in so far as they are not in violation with the idea of sustainability and sustainable development;
h. The legislature must make legislation that gives effect to sustainability and the UN SDG;
i. The executive creates policy to guarantee and promote sustainability and the UN SDGs;
j. The judiciary has as its tasks to interpret existing legislation and existing legal relations in such a way that they are aligned with sustainability and the UN SDGs;
k. Legislation and legal relations that do not comply with these concrete SDGs and the policy made by the executive, cannot continue to exist;
l. It is the task for us legal academics to find out how legislation can be made, changed and interpreted in the context of sustainability and the SDGs.

72 André van der Walt, Property and Constitution (Pretoria: Pretoria University Press, 2012), p. 23-24.

Regardless of the international agreements on sustainability, there are still nationally oriented and nationally designed systems of property law.[73] A certain incompatibility between the international and national level will therefore remain. The necessity to give effect to these developments seems obvious, but has so far not proven difficult. This also makes sense as our rules of private law are designed to incorporate societal change and to adapt to innovative situations. At the same time, I have tried to demonstrate, private law is also in the service of the ruling economic and philosophical thought. By tackling both of these foundations it becomes possible to bring the law of property in the service of new ideas and principles and to recalibrate our rules.

All that is perhaps a bit abstract, which is unavoidable when new theory is created. In two short examples I would like to illustrate what we could achieve using the sustainability-algorithm.

4.5 Two Short Case Studies

4.5.1 *The Right of Ownership: Land Ownership of the NAM*

Since 1959, in the north of the Netherlands, the Nederlandse Aardolie Maatschappij (NAM) drills for gas in the province of Groningen and the North Sea. Before the concession to excavate gas was granted to NAM there was a lot of debate whether this was a government task –gas was for the general use of everyone –or a corporate activity –in which private parties make a lot of profit from selling gas.[74] The privatised model was favoured and the effects of this choice are known: so much gas was extracted that earthquakes and social unrest that these brought were the consequence.[75] The ownership of the gas-fields, as well as the gas, be it in the hands of the government or not, is an extractive ownership until now. The NAM and the Dutch state generate substantial revenue with extracting gas.

This does not fit the algorithm for a sustainable property law. Human flourishing does not only mean profitability for the NAM and income for the Dutch State, but also care for the land and the minerals in there as well as for the occupants of the land. The question remains whether the 18 billion euro reserved to pay for damage caused by the drilling for gas is enough. After all, those 18 billion euro could also have been spent on preventing the damage. In the balancing of interests, in other words, the algorithm requires us to include all perspectives in our decision-making processes.

---

73 With the Paris Climate Agreement, the successor of Johannesburg (2002) and Rio (1993), market-liberalism still rules in private law. See John Blewitt Understanding Sustainable Development, 2e edition (Londen, New York: Routledge, 2015), p. 21-23, 29-30.

74 www.co2ntramine.nl/hoe-nam-macht-kreeg-nederlandse-aardgas/

75 See Rechtbank Noord-Nederland 1 maart 2018, C/19/109028 / HA ZA 15/33.

A proprietary obligation of the owner makes it a lot easier to demand from the NAM or the Dutch state to deal with their right of ownership in a different manner. If we consider such a duty as contained in the right of ownership, the doctrine of abuse of right can also be of assistance here. The use of a power that causes damage to another in a disproportional manner can be an abuse of right.[76]

4.5.2 *Limited Property Rights: Mortgages*

Another example concerns the right of hypothec (or mortgage) as a limited property right derived from a right of ownership with a positive obligation of sustainability. Human flourishing plays a direct role here too. The owner uses his right of ownership to provide security in order to be able to acquire that right of ownership: a loan is taken and at the moment of acquisition of the right of ownership a right of hypothec is created for the creditor. The owner knows that he will have to fulfil his obligations to be able to enjoy his ownership, as foreclosure and forced public sale will result and make him lose his ownership if he does not. This system has been around and has been working for centuries. What has changed in the last decades is that banks, under enormous pressure of profit maximisation by shareholders and investors, have started granting loans to people of which they knew, or at least should have known, would not be able to fulfil their payment obligations.[77]

To make matters worse, these banks have also proceeded to make derivatives from these rights of hypothec to make these as attractive as possible for re-financing of debt. Although the banks were following the rules, the effects have been disastrous. Advanced securitisation techniques have led to an investment bubble that imploded in 2008 because many were unable to fulfil their payment obligations. Banks, pushed by their shareholders and investors, foreclosed and realised their rights of hypothec in most of these cases. After all, the profit of the bank was priority and in transactions in derivatives the person that originally was granted the loan is not involved (the real economy), but the trade on the financial market is leading (the financial economy). Once more, the balancing of interests was made without taking all circumstances into account, something that the sustainability algorithm requires us to do differently.

A right of ownership that contains an obligation of wellbeing also includes such an obligation when a limited property right is derived. When realising the limited property right, here of the right of hypothec, this includes the obligation to consider the wellbeing of the person granting the right of hypothec. Joseph Singer even argues that, on the basis of theoretical insights on wellbeing in property law, that a bank should not be allowed to

76 Asser/Bartels/Van Velten 5, n. 44, 46.

77 See Marjorie Kelly, Owning our Future. The Emerging Ownership Revolution (Oakland: Berrett-Koehler Publishers Inc, 2012), p. 87-98.

foreclose on a property if they have deliberately granted a loan to someone of which they knew would not be able to repay.[78] That is not a very strange consideration in the context of sustainability: especially cooperative banks have proven to do very well in the financial crisis. These banks have mostly not been able to take part in very risky securitisation transactions, because the shareholders of such banks are also the clients. Some cooperative banks have helped their clients by allowing them to pay interest only for a period of time and so prevent execution of the right of hypothec in many cases, while other banks did nothing but foreclose on their portfolios.[79]

Human flourishing and wellbeing in other words, implies that the relation between the holder of the primary right and the holder of the limited property right remains. We should also reconsider our rules on accessority in this light and provide new life to these. The positive obligation of the owner can also bring a positive obligation for the holder of a limited property rights, such as a right of hypothec. The holder of the right of hypothec must therefore have another purpose than just profitability.

4.6 Conclusion

Sustainability and human flourishing go hand in hand. The UN sustainable development goals have as their objective to promote our wellbeing, for us as individuals as well as for our community. That will not happen at once and also not by tomorrow. However, it is clear that this deals with more than international obligations only. If we want to achieve sustainable development goals or at least make a serious effort to do so, then private law must provide its contribution.

Legal certainty and durable legal relations are traditionally the starting points in the law of property. Sustainability is not in the way of these. The objective is, so I have tried to argue, that we must become more aware of the context of our property law. Why do we have the rules that we use and why do we provide content to these in the way that we do? Liberal and Neo-liberal foundations have gained the upper hand in the last decades, in such a way that we perhaps have exceeded the aims that we wished to pursue and in the way we have been treating our planet in the process. Of course this has not all been bad, but from a sustainability perspective we have not yet been able to do much good.

More and more concrete initiatives are appearing. Neighbourhood initiatives, supported by energy companies, for clean energy such as solar, wind or heat, cooperative living communities in which only the buildings are owned by the residents, and sharing projects,

78 Also known as a sub-prime loan, see Joseph Singer, Property as the Law of Democracy, 63 Duke Law Journal 1287 (2014), p. 1301-1302.

79 Marjorie Kelly, Owning our Future. The Emerging Ownership Revolution (Oakland: Berrett-Koehler Publishers Inc, 2012), p 38, 40-45.

facilitated by platforms such as AirBnB and Uber. What is lacking is the general overarching theoretical foundation on the basis of which we do this. Personal ideals, mostly ecological in nature, often play a role, but all try to navigate in an existing system that is mostly centred around an individualistic concept of ownership. The rules of the operatating system, i.e. the rules of the acquisition and loss of ownership, are aimed to create certainty for the owner. We use the concept of unity of the object, which is under pressure so much in the circular economy, the exclusionary power of the owner, which is under pressure so much in the sharing economy, and the relatively easy rules for the execution of rights of hypothec, to create and maintain the most economically efficient system.

The idea to make the law of property superfluous by giving everything the form of a service contract is not the right way to go. Revaluation, i.e. providing our system with new values by conceptualising the proprietary obligation, brings the law of property to the centre. It gives us all the duty to consider how we deal with our things, for example our homes. With that, we provide the building blocks to – together – design a sustainable economy in which human flourishing, including economic growth and further development of new initiatives, is central. A theoretical foundation, such as I have tried to create, is only the beginning.

5 Moving Beyond Boundaries in the Pursuit of Sustainable Property Law

Jill Robbie[*]

5.1 Introduction

New Zealand scholars Prue Taylor and David Grinlinton state that it is "often the rules of property law, modified by planning and resource management regulation, that most directly govern human interaction with the natural environment."[1] Despite the importance of property law as a component in the system of regulation of our natural resources, consideration of how property law should be reformed in the transition to sustainability is a relatively fledgling topic for analysis.[2] This, perhaps, should not be surprising. Realisation of the scale and extent of the global challenges facing the Earth's resources has occurred only relatively recently whereas, at least in Europe, the tradition of property law reaches back to Antiquity. However, it is difficult to ignore that global projects aimed at tracking and evaluating the state of our natural environment are producing increasingly dire warnings about the impact of humanity on the planet as well as emphasising the magnitude of the transformation required to ensure that we live within the Earth's resources.[3] The growing awareness of environmental issues since the 1970's provides the context for the emergence of the concept of "sustainable development" as a key organising principle for governance and regulation. The phrase "sustainable development", although a highly contested concept, has been defined as "development that meets the needs of the present without compromising the ability of future generations to meet their own needs"[4] and comprises the three pillars

* My thanks to Prof Bram Akkermans, Dr Elsabe van der Sijde and Prof John Lovett for comments on previous drafts of this chapter.

1 P. Taylor and D. Grinlinton, "Property Rights and Sustainability: Towards a New Vision of Property" in D. Grinlinton and P. Taylor (eds), *Property Rights and Sustainability: The Evolution of Property Rights to Meet Ecological Challenges* (2011) p. 9.

2 See citations at fn 92 below.

3 See World Wide Fund for Nature, "Living Planet Report – 2018: Aiming Higher" (2018) and Intergovernmental Panel on Climate Change, "Global Warming of 1.5 °C: An IPCC Special Report on the Impacts of Global Warming of 1.5 °C Above Pre-Industrial Levels and Related Global Greenhouse Gas Emission Pathways" (2018) for just two examples.

4 World Commission on Environment and Development, "Our Common Future" (1987) Ch. 2.1. Available here: www.un-documents.net/ocf-02.htm (last accessed 11 Jun 2019).

of economic development, social justice and environmental protection.[5] To reach the goal of sustainability, and to ensure the protection and preservation of our natural resources, it is necessary to review our systems of regulation and consider how our laws should be reformed in light of the global challenges we are facing. Property law will not escape the critical eye of the law reformer in this process.

In this chapter, I consider the reform of property rights regarding water, otherwise known as private water rights, in the context of sustainability. Reflecting the global trend, there are mounting, urgent, multi-dimensional challenges facing water which threaten this vital resource. In the World Wide Fund for Nature's Living Planet Report 2018 it was stated: "Freshwater habitats, such as lakes, rivers and wetlands, are the source of life for all humans yet they are also the most threatened, strongly affected by a range of factors including habitat modification, fragmentation and destruction; invasive species; overfishing; pollution; disease and climate change."[6] Water has also been noted as being at the core of sustainable development.[7] I will explore the interactions between three different policy spheres, which relate to the reform of private water rights – each representing a pillar of sustainable development – in the particular context of small-scale hydro-schemes in Scotland. I argue that this micro-analysis has macro-implications, and that this case study shows that we must move beyond multiple boundaries in reforming our property laws in order to contribute to the transition to sustainability.

5.2 CURRENT LAW OF PRIVATE WATER RIGHTS

Before discussing three policy spheres, which impact on reform of private water rights, it is necessary to outline the current law in Scotland. Until recently, the law of private water rights was, like much of Scots law, obscure and under-researched. In the book *Private Water Rights*,[8] I undertook a comprehensive review of this area of law from a historical perspective and set out the principles and rules of the modern law. A central tenet of the law of private water rights in Scotland is that running water is among the *res communes*.[9] This means running water is categorised as incapable of private ownership due to its inherent nature and characteristics. As a result, in principle, running water is open to the use of all and the only right that anyone has to water is to appropriate portions of this

5 See generally J. Blewitt, *Understanding Sustainable Development* (3rd edn, 2017).
6 World Wide Fund for Nature, "Living Planet Report – 2018: Aiming Higher" (2018) p. 7.
7 United Nations World Water Assessment Programme, "The United Nations World Water Development Report 2015: Water for a Sustainable World" (2015), Foreword by M. Jarraud, Chair of UN-Water and Secretary-General of WMO p. vi.
8 J. Robbie, *Private Water Rights* (2015).
9 *Ibid.*, paras. 2-78-2-90.

resource, this being a public right.[10] Those with water running through their lands, however, have the best opportunity to exercise this public right.[11]

The fact that running water is among the *res communes* does not mean that there is complete freedom for landowners to abstract all the water in a river. If a river runs between several different plots of land, the landowners cannot materially interfere with flow of the river unless for primary purposes – these being drinking, washing, cooking and other requirements of a self-sufficient piece of land.[12] Each landowner along a river has a right to prevent any material interference with the natural flow of water for non-primary purposes and this results in a corresponding obligation on everyone, but particularly other landowners, not to interfere with this right. This network of reciprocal rights and obligations is a highly restrictive system of rules that arises by operation of law and is an aspect of the ownership of the land through which water runs. These private law rights are unaffected by any public law licences such as a Controlled Activities Regulations licence, discussed further below, obtained by the landowner.[13] The doctrine providing this regulation is called common interest.[14] These private rights are the "private water rights" I refer to in this chapter. This phrase is unsatisfactory as these rights are not rights *to* the water but merely *regarding* water.[15] Common interest rights are real rights held by one landowner in another's land rather than a right to appropriate the water, which as noted above is a public right. However, the phrase "private water rights" most immediately conveys the subject of discussion. These common interest rights crucially only arise when the ownership of a piece of land containing a river is split between several owners. If there is a river, which is wholly contained in one tract of land, the landowner is generally not restricted by common interest rights of others.[16]

The law of private water rights became settled in the 18th and 19th centuries in Scotland.[17] A significant contributing factor to the evolution of the restrictive rules of common interest was the effect of industry on water use and availability during the Industrial Rev-

10 *Ibid.*, para. 2-80.

11 It is difficult to place the conception of water in Scotland within the framework of private, public, common and open-access property. Although being outwith private ownership in its natural state, there are limitations on its appropriation. This reflects Tony Arnold's comment that "[d]istinctions among private property, public property, common property, and nonproperty are merely for conceptual convenience and do not reflect the actual reality that most – perhaps all – property regimes are mixed regimes." C.A. Arnold, "Sustainable Webs of Interests: Property in an Interconnected Environment" in D. Grinlinton and P. Taylor (eds), *Property Rights and Sustainability: The Evolution of Property Rights to Meet Ecological Challenges* (2011) p. 171.

12 J. Robbie, *Private Water Rights* (2015) para. 7-36.

13 *Ibid.*, para. 7-71.

14 *Ibid.*, Ch. 7.

15 *Ibid.*, para. 1-08.

16 *Ibid.*, para. 7-19.

17 *Ibid.*, Ch. 6.

olution. Although water-powered mills had a long history in Scotland,[18] with the beginning of the Industrial Revolution, water became an increasingly contested resource with industries such as brewing and distilling beginning to consume significant quantities of water.[19] There was also a demand for a centralised water supply due to increasing urbanisation, as water in the existing public wells in towns and cities was often insufficient or polluted.[20] In Chadwick's *Report on the Sanitary Condition of the Labouring Population of Great Britain* of 1842, lack of clean water was identified as a chief cause of the various cholera, typhus and tuberculosis epidemics across Britain.[21] There is evidence in the reported cases of this time that the use of water for primary purposes and industrial purposes often clashed such as when water was used for cooling steam engines and this then resulted in water shortages, or where use of water for a distillery, brewery or dye-works resulted in the pollution of rivers used for drinking, cooking and washing.[22] Judges acknowledged these conflicting uses of water and gave judgments against industry with comments such as "since there are evils, we should admit those only which are necessary: dwelling houses cannot be avoided, but manufactures may."[23] It is within this context that the natural flow principle outlined above was developed and became established.

The natural flow principle was finally settled in the case of *Morris v Bicket*[24] of 1864, with other rules being contained in a patchwork of older case law. The strict requirements of the law mean that the consent of all affected landowners along the river needs to be obtained to use water for any purposes which are commercial, agricultural or industrial. Unlike the law of England, there is no reasonableness requirement when considering what a landowner is entitled to do with the water running through her land.[25] However, the level of restriction is largely arbitrary and depends on the number of plots of land in separate ownership through which a river runs. The sources of the law of private water rights mean it is inaccessible to many and the particular historical origin of the rules suggest that the law should now be reviewed in light of modern concerns. Indeed, in 2014, the Land Reform Review Group, when considering this area of law in light of the recent reforms to the general regulatory framework governing water resources in Scotland,[26] identified common

18 *Ibid.*, para. 5-05.
19 *Ibid.*, para. 6-02.
20 *Ibid*,. para. 6-04.
21 E. Chadwick, *Report on the Sanitary Condition of the Labouring Population of Great Britain* (1842; reprinted M.W. Flinn (ed.), 1965, p. 4.
22 J. Robbie, *Private Water Rights* (2015) para. 6-51.
23 *Russell v Haig* (1791) Bell's Octavo Cases 338 at p. 347 (Lord Swinton).
24 *Morris v Bicket* (1864) 2 M 1082 (aff'd (1866) 4 M (HL) 44).
25 J. Robbie, *Private Water Rights* (2015) paras 7-14-7-17.
26 Including the Water Industry (Scotland) Act 2002, Water Environment and Water Services (Scotland) Act 2003, Water Services (Scotland) Act 2005, Flood Risk Management (Scotland) Act 2009 and Water Resources (Scotland) Act 2013.

interest as a doctrine requiring reform in order to "reflect the public interest in these resources as now defined".[27]

5.3 Tensions in Private Water Rights Reform

Although there are clear justifications for a review of the law of private water rights in Scotland, it is less obvious exactly how the law should be reformed. When considering reform of areas or institutions of property law, it is commonplace to focus on creating a doctrinally coherent and consistent system of rules, which fits with the principles of property law or private law in general. Stability and certainty are the goals. When examining water rights, however, it is evident that the factors to be considered in a reform process must be broader than those typically accommodated by doctrinal analysis. There are multiple functions which water plays in Scotland such as in providing a wholesome domestic supply to the general public, in growing food and within agriculture, in significant commercial purposes such as the whisky industry and supporting fish farms, for sporting and recreational activities as well as to sustain a diverse flora and fauna.[28] There are also a number of significant policy objectives, which could inform the reform of private water rights including protecting human health and wellbeing, maintaining biodiversity, tackling climate change and supporting the Scottish economy. In the following paragraphs, I will focus on and discuss three policy spheres that are influencing the operation of small-scale hydro-schemes to generate electricity. This analysis serves as a case study, which leads to greater claims regarding how to conduct research and implement property law reform to contribute to the transition to sustainability. The fact that there are conflicting policy objectives that require to be considered is more immediately obvious in relation to water rights reform than in other areas of property law. However, there are many barriers in doctrinal property law analysis, which will be outlined below, which result in the multifarious policy objectives that should influence property rules remaining unseen and unexplored.

5.3.1 *Economic Development: Scotland as a Hydro-Nation*

The Scottish Government is currently committed to making Scotland a "Hydro-Nation".[29] A Hydro-Nation is one where "water resources are developed so as to bring maximum

---

27 Land Reform Review Group, "The Land of Scotland and the Common Good" (2014) para 30.13. Available here: www.gov.scot/Resource/0045/00451087.pdf (last accessed 11 Jun 2019).

28 See the discussion in Scottish Government, "Building a Hydro Nation – A Consultation" (Dec 2010).

29 See Scottish Government, "Scotland the Hydro-Nation: Annual Report 2018" (Sep 2018).

benefit to the Scottish economy".[30] The Scottish Government states this is being done to fulfil the duty on the Scottish Ministers in the Water Resources (Scotland) Act 2013 to "take such reasonable steps as they consider appropriate for the purpose of ensuring the development of the value of Scotland's water resources".[31] Renewable energy is part of this agenda and, in 2011, the Scottish Government set the target of the amount of electricity generated through renewable sources (as a percentage of gross consumption) to increase to 100% by 2020.[32] Of course, Scotland's ambitious target must be viewed in light of the target set by the European Union (EU) under the Renewable Energy Directive of 2009 for 20% of the EU's total energy needs to be generated by renewable sources by 2020.[33] Within this framework, the UK has the target of 15% of all energy and 30% of electricity to be generated by renewables by 2020.[34] In 2017, hydro-power accounted for 11.4% of primary renewables production in the EU member states.[35] Future development of hydro-power will be important to reaching the EU's energy targets. However, as the sites for medium to large scale hydro-schemes have mostly been developed, the focus has now turned to small-scale hydro-schemes.[36]

In the Scottish Government's "2020 Routemap for Renewable Energy in Scotland", it was noted that in addition to reduction in carbon emissions and providing future energy security, by 2020 the renewables industry could provide up to 40,000 jobs and £30bn investment to the Scottish economy.[37] Small-scale hydro-power is a component in this industry. Although definitions of small-scale hydro differ, a generally accepted definition in Europe is that a small-scale hydro-scheme is one, which has an output of up to 10

30 See the statement on the Scottish Government website. Available here: https://beta.gov.scot/policies/water/hydro-nation/ (last accessed 11 Jun 2019).

31 Water Resources (Scotland) Act 2013 s1(1)(a). However, in this section, value expressly includes monetary or non-monetary value, s1(3)(a).

32 Scottish Government, "2020 Routemap for Renewable Energy in Scotland" (2011) p. 4.

33 Directive 2009/28/EC of the European Parliament and of the Council of 23 April 2009 on the promotion of the use of energy from renewable sources (OJ 2009 L 140). In Dec 2018, a revised renewable energy directive (2018/2011/EU) entered into force which establishes a new renewable energy target for the EU of 32% by 2030.

34 Department of Energy and Climate Change, "National Renewable Energy Action Plan for the UK" (Jul 2010). The extent to which energy policy will change following Brexit is, as is much concerning Brexit, a matter of considerable uncertainty. See A Reid, "Brexit: Energy Policy" SPICe Briefing (Nov 2016).

35 See EU's Eurostat website: Renewable Energy Statistics. Available here: https://ec.europa.eu/eurostat/statistics-explained/index.php/Renewable_energy_statistics#Renewable_energy_produced_in_the_EU_increased_by_two_thirds_in_2007-2017 (last accessed 11 Jun 2019).

36 D. Anderson, H. Moggridge, P. Warren and J. Shucksmith, "The impacts of 'run-of-river' hydropower on the physical and ecological condition of rivers" (2015) 29 Water and Environment Journal 268 at p. 268. There are also environmental objections to large-scale hydro-schemes mentioned below.

37 Scottish Government, "2020 Routemap for Renewable Energy in Scotland" (2011) p. 4. The Scottish Government's "Scottish Energy Strategy: The Future of Energy in Scotland" (Dec 2017) p. 76 states that in 2015, the renewable and low carbon technologies sector supported an estimated 58,000 jobs and generated a turnover of £10.5bn.

megawatts (MW), this being enough to power up to 10,000 homes.[38] A report commissioned by the Scottish Government in 2009 suggested that, at the time, up to a further 1200 MW of economically viable, small-scale hydro-power was potentially available in Scotland.[39] This report, however, needs to be reviewed in light of the negative changes since 2015 to Feed-in Tariffs and the subsequent closure of this subsidy by the UK Government, which has affected the viability of such schemes.[40] Despite these reforms, new schemes continue to be commissioned and constructed including, for example, a recently completed 2 MW scheme in Kinlochewe,[41] a scheme on the Allt Choille Rais which generates energy for Nevis Range[42] and the 4 MW Glasa scheme in Easter Ross which recently received planning permission.[43]

There has been significant progression towards the Scottish Government's renewable energy target. In 2016, Scotland generated 54% of its electricity needs from renewable sources, which is four times greater than the level in 2000.[44] The percentage is ever increasing.[45] Although this increase is largely attributable to onshore wind, small-scale hydro has also contributed to this figure.[46] In 2017, the Scottish Government set the new target of 50% of the energy for Scotland's heat, transport and electricity to be generated from renewable sources by 2030 in the "Scottish Energy Strategy: The Future of Energy in Scotland".[47] This again should be viewed against the background of an update to the EU's targets of at least 27% of the EU's total energy to be produced by renewable sources by 2030.[48] In introducing the new target, the Scottish Government noted that hydropower

38 T. Abbasi and S.A. Abbasi, "Small hydro and the environmental implications of its extensive utilization" (2011) 15 Renewable and Sustainable Energy Reviews 2134 at p. 2136. See also the guide provided by engineering firm Renewables First: www.renewablesfirst.co.uk/hydropower/hydropower-learning-centre/what-is-the-difference-between-micro-mini-and-small-hydro/ (last accessed 11 Jun 2019).

39 N. Wallace and J. Wallace, "The Employment Potential of Scotland's Hydro Resource" (2009). Available here: www.gov.scot/Resource/Doc/299322/0093327.pdf (last accessed 11 Jun 2019).

40 See Pöyry, "Analysis of Costs of Small-Scale Hydro and Implied Feed-in Tariffs" (2015). Available here: www.scottishrenewables.com/publications/analysis-costs-hydro-and-implied-fits-poyry-report/ (last accessed 11 Jun 2019); Department for Business, Energy & Industrial Strategy, "The Feed-In Tariffs Scheme: Government Response" (Dec 2018).

41 "Corks pop for Scottish hydro" (7 Sept 2017) http://renews.biz/108398/corks-pop-for-scottish-hydro/ (last accessed 11 Jun 2019).

42 "New hydro scheme powers Scottish mountain resort" (23 Oct 2017) www.nevisrange.co.uk/hydro-completion-ceremony/ (last accessed 11 Jun 2019).

43 "Highland blessing for Innogy hydro" (7 Nov 2018) https://renews.biz/49931/highland-blessing-for-innogy-hydro/ (last accessed 11 Jun 2019).

44 Scottish Government "Scottish Energy Strategy: The Future of Energy in Scotland" (Dec 2017) p. 21.

45 Scottish Government, "Energy Statistics for Scotland: Q4 Figures" (March 2019). Available here: www2.gov.scot/Resource/0054/00547118.pdf (last accessed 11 Jun 2019).

46 Scottish Government "Scottish Energy Strategy: The Future of Energy in Scotland" (Dec 2017) p. 21.

47 *Ibid.*, at p. 7.

48 European Commission, "2030 Energy Strategy" (2014). Available here: https://ec.europa.eu/energy/en/topics/energy-strategy-and-energy-union/2030-energy-strategy (last accessed 11 Jun 2019).

"has a long and illustrious history in Scotland which can continue, with small-scale hydro playing an important role in our economy and our energy mix as we make the transition into a low carbon future."[49] The Scottish Government also confirmed that it remains committed to helping the hydro industry overcome the challenges it has faced in recent years.[50]

Encouraging the construction and operation of more small-scale hydro-schemes creates the possibility of disputes and the private water rights system in Scotland does little to support many hydro-schemes along the course of one river due to its restrictive rules. As a hydro-scheme will inevitably interfere with the natural flow of the river, a landowner who wishes to set up a hydro-scheme will have to obtain the consent of the other affected landowners along the river.[51] Such consent may not be forthcoming particularly where the operation of existing hydro-schemes may be affected. Indeed, the early development of the rules of common interest in the 17th and 18th centuries in Scotland was in response to disputes in the courts between various mill owners along rivers.[52] Therefore, to support the renewable energy industry and the economic benefits it brings, greater flexibility in the law of private water rights would be required to allow more opportunities for the harnessing of this particular source of energy.

5.3.2 *Social Justice: Land for the Many and not the Few*

How does supporting small-scale hydro-power fit with the other objectives that the Scottish Government is pursuing? The land reform agenda in Scotland has recently been a much discussed topic.[53] Central to this agenda is the strengthening of the rights of communities to compulsorily acquire land. In 2013, the Scottish Government stated its aim for one million acres of land to be in community ownership by 2020.[54] In December 2017, there were approximately 547, 691 acres in community ownership.[55] Reforms being implemented to fulfil this aim include Part 4 of the Community Empowerment (Scotland) Act 2015 giving communities the right to buy abandoned, neglected or detrimental land and Part 5 of the Land Reform (Scotland) Act 2016 which gives communities the right to buy land

49 Scottish Government, "Scottish Energy Strategy: The Future of Energy in Scotland" (Dec 2017) at p. 50.
50 *Ibid.*
51 J. Robbie, *Private Water Rights* (2015) para. 7-71.
52 *Ibid.*, Ch. 5.
53 See, for example, A. Wightman, "Scottish land reform is on the agenda. And the rest of the UK should take note" (25 Jun 2015) Available here: www.theguardian.com/commentisfree/2015/jun/25/scottish-land-reform-bill (last accessed 11 Jun 2019). See generally Land Reform Review Group, "The Land of Scotland and the Common Good" (2014).
54 See generally Scottish Government, "One Million Acres by 2020" (2015).
55 See Scottish Government, "Estimate of Community Owned Land in Scotland 2017 – Revised Tables – Summary Note" (Dec 2018) p. 1.

to further sustainable development. The Scottish Land Fund[56] and Empowering Communities Fund[57] both provide access to funding for communities seeking to purchase land.

A driving force behind these reforms is the idea that Scotland's land is in the hands of too few people due to the claim that 432 private landowners own 50% of the private land in rural Scotland,[58] and the changes are also fuelled by a desire for greater community empowerment. However, to connect this policy with the renewable energy targets, large landowners, working with developers, are often in the best position to have renewable energy projects on their land. There are many reasons for this: owners of large estates can make decisions about the use of their land without needing to negotiate a consensus like communities; landowners and developers may already have an established relationship; developers often have access to finance; landowners and developers often have a relationship with experienced legal and technical advisers; and, perhaps most importantly for present purposes, landowners may own a tract of land large enough that they will require few or no private law agreements with other owners, for example, along the river for the development of a hydro-scheme.[59] Therefore, large landowners can effectively by-pass the private water rights constraints. These multiple factors result unsurprisingly in the statistic that in June 2016, 41% of the current operational capacity of renewable energy installations was on farms and estates in Scotland. This is the greatest single share of renewable energy. By contrast, only 11% was community owned.[60]

Connecting the land reform agenda with the renewables agenda, it is possible that the successful implementation of land reform policy, which is often argued as an issue of social justice in allowing more people access to land ownership, could potentially impact on the development of small-scale hydro-power. The existing private water rights system in Scotland would contribute to this. As soon as the ownership of a large area of land is fragmented by communities exercising their rights to buy, each section of land carries with it a right to object to any interference with the natural flow of a river, making the successful

56 See here: www.gov.scot/policies/land-reform/scottish-land-fund/ (last accessed 11 Jun 2019).

57 See here: www.gov.scot/policies/community-empowerment/empowering-communities-fund/ (last accessed 11 Jun 2019).

58 Land Reform Review Group, "The Land of Scotland and the Common Good" (2014) para. 24.1. The claim that the concentration of land ownership is a barrier to sustainable development in Scotland must be viewed in light of the report by S. Thomson et al, "The impact of diversity of ownership scale on social, economic and environmental outcomes: exploration and case studies" (Mar 2016). This report concluded (at p. 1) that "it is too simplistic to conclude that scale of land ownership is a significant factor in the sustainable development of communities". Available here: www.gov.scot/publications/impact-diversity-ownership-scale-social-economic-environmental-outcomes/ (last accessed 11 Jun 2019).

59 Many of these challenges are identified a report commissioned by the Scottish Government by D Roberts and A McKee, "Exploring Barriers to Community Land-Based Activities" (2015). Available here: www.gov.scot/Resource/0048/00485806.pdf (last accessed 11 Jun 2019).

60 Scottish Government, "Energy in Scotland 2017" at p. 13. Other owners are local authorities and housing associations.

establishment of a new hydro-scheme more difficult. This would be an example of the tragedy of the anti-commons where numerous right-holders prevent the effective management of a single asset.[61] Further, communities, understandably, often wish to acquire areas of land containing natural resources such as rivers in order to, among other things, operate their own renewable energy schemes. Indeed, this is being encouraged by the Scottish Government, which has an aim to have 1 gigawatt (GW) of community and locally-owned renewable energy by 2020 and 2 GW by 2030.[62] Support to communities is provided by the Community Renewable Energy Scheme,[63] which has resulted in successful projects like the 400 kilowatt Garmony hydro-scheme on the Isle of Mull.[64]

Consideration of the interaction between the renewable energy and land reform agendas in the context of small-scale hydro-schemes raises the possibility that reform of private water rights should also be considered as part of the land reform agenda, as suggested by the Land Reform Review Group.[65] As with renewable energy policy, the land reform policy aims would be consistent with creating more flexibility in the private water rights system in order to give a larger range of groups the opportunity to benefit from hydro-power. This would allow two economic and social justice goals relevant to private water rights to be pursued simultaneously.

5.3.3 *Environmental Protection: Are Hydro-schemes Really Green?*

There are, however, not only the social justice and economic aspects of private water rights reform to consider but also environmental protection. As noted above, hydro-power is often promoted as a "green" source of energy and important in the transition to renewable energy production. Whilst it is true that hydro-schemes produce carbon-free electricity, hydro-schemes can have considerably damaging environmental consequences.[66] It is now well-established that large-scale hydro-power projects have a number of adverse environmental, as well as social, effects resulting from the fundamental disruption to the river and its ecosystem, which needs to take place to implement them. Effects include degradation in water quality, increased siltation, increased numbers of disease carrying insects (such

61 M. A. Heller, "The Tragedy of the Anticommons: Property in the Transitions from Marx to Markets" (1998) 111 Harv Law Review 621.

62 Scottish Government, "Scottish Energy Strategy: The Future of Energy in Scotland" (Dec 2017) p. 43.

63 See here: www.localenergy.scot/funding/ (last accessed 11 Jun 2019).

64 See here: www.localenergy.scot/projects-and-case-studies/case-studies/community-owned/garmony-hydro/ (last accessed 11 Jun 2019).

65 See fn 27 above.

66 For an overview of the development of environmental controls of hydro-schemes in Scotland see C.T. Reid, A. Pillai and A.R. Black, "The Emergence of Environmental Concerns: Hydroelectric Schemes in Scotland" (2005) 17(3) Journal of Environmental Law 361.

as mosquitoes) and damage to fish populations.[67] It is often assumed that small-scale hydro-schemes are more environmentally friendly when compared with large-scale schemes.[68] This assumption was until relatively recently untested. Recent studies have, however, shown that even small-scale hydro-schemes can have significant negative consequences on the river ecosystem.[69] Indeed, there may also be cumulative effects where many small-scale hydro-schemes are positioned along one river.[70]

The Scottish Government is aware of the potentially negative environmental effects of hydro-schemes and in 2010 issued a policy statement regarding the balancing of benefits of renewables generation and protection of the water environment which stated that "in order to optimise the potential for hydropower generation emphasis will be placed on supporting hydropower developments which can make a significant contribution to Scotland's renewables targets whilst minimising any adverse impacts on the water environment."[71] There are a number of regulatory controls in place to establish and minimise the potential environmental impacts of a proposed hydro-scheme. When setting up a hydro-scheme in Scotland, the promoter of the scheme will need to obtain planning permission from the local authority.[72] As part of that, an environmental impact assessment (EIA) may need to be prepared if the project is likely to have significant effects on the environment by virtue of factors such as its natural, size or location.[73] An EIA report must consider any significant effects of the project on, among other things, biodiversity and in particular

67 T. Abbasi and S.A. Abbasi, "Small hydro and the environmental implications of its extensive utilization" (2011) 15 Renewable and Sustainable Energy Reviews 2134 at p. 2135.

68 *Ibid.*, at p. 2136.

69 See for example, T Abbasi and S A Abbasi, "Small hydro and the environmental implications of its extensive utilization" (2011) 15 Renewable and Sustainable Energy Reviews 2134; T.H. Bakken et al, "Development of small versus large hydropower in Norway – comparison of environmental impacts" (2012) Energy Procedia 185; D. Anderson, H. Moggridge, P. Warren and J. Shucksmith, "The impacts of 'run-of-river' hydropower on the physical and ecological condition of rivers" (2015) 29 Water and Environment Journal 268; R. Brackley, "Interactions between migrating salmonids and low-head hydropower schemes" (2016) Unpublished PhD Thesis, University of Glasgow. A recent article also indirectly links declining salmon populations to the rise of watermills in rivers across Europe through use of historical data, see H J R Lenders et al, "Historical rise of waterpower initiated the collapse of salmon stocks" (2016) Scientific Reports 6: 29269.

70 D Fraser, I Palmer and I Stewart-Russon, "Cumulative effects of hydropower schemes on fish migration and populations" (2015) Environment Agency Report.

71 Scottish Government, "Balancing the Benefits of Renewables Generation and Protection of the Water Environment" (Jan 2010). Available here: www.gov.scot/publications/balancing-the-benefits-of-renewables-with-protecting-the-water-environment/ (last accessed 11 Jun 2019).

72 Under the Town and Country Planning (Scotland) Act 1997. Over 50 MW, consent is granted by the Scottish Ministers under section 36 of Electricity Act 1989.

73 As required under the Town and Country Planning (Environmental Impact Assessment) (Scotland) Regulations 2017/102.

species and habitats protected under the EU Habitats Directive and Birds Directive.[74] Separately, the promoter of the scheme will also need a public law licence for interference with the water environment such as the abstraction and impoundment of water required as part of the hydro-scheme and also for temporary works undertaken through construction. This is a Controlled Activities Regulations (CAR) licence, which is granted by the Scottish Environmental Protection Agency (SEPA).[75] These regulatory requirements were enacted to fulfil Scotland's obligations under the EU Water Framework Directive and the Environmental Impact Assessment Directive.[76]

When deciding whether to grant the CAR licence, SEPA considers what the effect of any proposed scheme will have on plant and animal life. It is possible to predict a hydro-scheme will have negative environmental consequences but SEPA can nevertheless grant a licence if it considers the social and economic impacts of a scheme outweigh the environmental impact.[77] If a scheme will cause harm, SEPA has the power to impose conditions on the licence, which is granted in order to mitigate the negative effects of the scheme.[78] However, with the volume of licences that SEPA grants, it is difficult to ensure compliance with all licence conditions. SEPA has a compliance assessment scheme in order to target the highest risk and most poorly performing sites but of course this does not ensure complete compliance or prevent unlicensed activities taking place.[79] As a result, there can be environmental disasters such as when the operations for the Inverinian 1.5 MW hydro-scheme on the River Lyon killed fresh water pearl mussels in a large and actively breeding colony in 2010 due to silt from the hydro-scheme construction clogging up the river.[80] The freshwater pearl mussel is a priority species in Scotland and the UK,[81] a protected

74 Town and Country Planning (Environmental Impact Assessment) (Scotland) Regulations 2017/102 reg 4(3)(b); Council Directive 1992/43/EEC on the conservation of natural habitats and of wild fauna and flora; Directive 2009/147/EC of the European Parliament and of the Council on the conservation of wild birds.

75 Regulated by the Water Environment (Controlled Activities) (Scotland) Regulations 2011.

76 Directive 2000/60/EC of the European Parliament and of the Council establishing a framework for the Community action in the field of water policy (OJ 2000 L 327); Directive 2011/92/EU of the European Parliament and of the Council on the assessment of the effects of certain public and private projects on the environment (OJ 2012 L 26) as amended by Directive 2014/52/EU of the European Parliament and of the Council amending Directive 2011/92/EU on the assessment of the effects of certain public and private projects on the environment.

77 Scottish Environmental Protection Agency, "Guidance for Developers of Run-of-River Hydropower Schemes" (2015) p. 4. Available here: www.sepa.org.uk/media/383805/guidance-_for_developers_of_run_of_river_hydropower_schemes.pdf (last accessed 11 Jun 2019).

78 Water Environment (Controlled Activities) (Scotland) Regulations 2011 reg. 8(1).

79 SEPA, "Compliance Assessment Scheme Guidance Manual" (Jul 2018).

80 See "Firm directors admit killing endangered pearl mussels" (15 February 2013). Available here: www.heraldscotland.com/news/13092332.Firm_directors_admit_killing_endangered_pearl_mussels/ (lasted accessed 11 Jun 2019).

81 Scottish Government, "Priority Species of Mollusc in the UK Biodiversity Action Plan and the Species Action Framework for Scotland" (2008). Available here: www2.gov.scot/Resource/Doc/915/0062262.pdf (last accessed 11 Jun 2019).

species under the EU Habitats Directive and classified as a globally endangered species by the International Union for Conservation of Nature.[82] Scotland contains several of the largest remaining populations.[83] This event resulted in prosecutions of the hydro-power company and directors of the company's sub-contractors involved in the operations.[84]

How should evidence of the potentially negative environmental effects of small-scale hydro-scheme influence the reform of private water rights? There are great limitations to the extent that private law can act as a check on processes that may be environmentally harmful. However, historically private law has been used in attempts to prevent environmental harm and, in the modern law, private law actions can be an important additional option where other regulatory mechanisms fail.[85] As mentioned above protecting water from the abuses of industry is part of the history of Scotland, as this is why the restrictive regime of private water rights in Scotland became settled in the 19th century.[86] Therefore, to consider environmental protection policies in addition to a social justice and economic perspective of reform may suggest that there should still be some, quite significant, limitations on use of water by landowners through the private water rights system in order to minimise damage to the natural aquatic environment.

5.4 MOVING BEYOND BOUNDARIES

What does this micro-analysis of small-scale hydro-schemes in Scotland reveal about reforming property law in the light of sustainability? The three factors that have been discussed in the preceding paragraphs are only a handful of the multifarious influences on the development of hydro-power as a renewable energy source in Scotland. Further, these three factors are only a tiny selection of many varied and diverse issues which could impact generally on water use and availability, and which could therefore feed into the law reform process when considering private water rights. Here I am not providing an ideal system of private water rights for Scotland. Instead I am offering a brief insight into the difficulty and complexity of reforming this area of law. Clearly, the transition to sustainability will not be a straightforward or easy journey. However, there is a theme which is demonstrated

82 See here: www.iucnredlist.org/species/12799/128686456 (last accessed 11 Jun 2019).

83 Scottish Government, "Wildlife Crime Priority Areas: 2017 Annual Report" (Dec 2018). See also A Reid, "Freshwater Pearl Mussel: Frequently Asked Questions" SPICe Briefing (Aug 2013).

84 See *Nisbet v Shawater Ltd* (2013) GWD 8-171 and *Nisbet v Smith* (2013) GWD 12-249.

85 See discussion in D. McGillivray and J. Wightman, "Private rights, public interest and the environment" in T. Hayward and J. O'Neill (eds), *Justice, Property and the Environment* (1997); J. Lowry and R. Edmunds (eds), *Environmental Protection and the Common Law* (2000); B. Pozzo (ed), *Property and Environment: Old and New Remedies to Protect Natural Resources in the European Context* (2007); B Pontin, *Nuisance and Environmental Protection* (2013); G. Winter (ed), *Property and Environmental Protection in Europe* (2016).

86 See J. Robbie, *Private Water Rights* (2015) Ch. 6.

in the foregoing analysis, which is that to tackle the global challenges facing our natural resources and to evolve towards a more sustainable way of life, we must move beyond boundaries in our law reform processes in relation to property law, and therefore in our research. These boundaries are multiple and many are historically entrenched.

The first boundary is that between public and private law. In order to obtain a full overview of the regulation of water, it is necessary to consider provisions throughout the legal spectrum with a selection of examples given above relating to renewable energy, land reform and biodiversity. Yet, the influence of this legal spectrum is not limited to water. In particular, there are burgeoning regulations that focus on environmental protection and these regulations interact in complex and uncharted ways with our existing property rules. Property law researchers therefore need to give attention to the effect and impact of these regulations, both on our existing conception of property, and how our rules and principles should be reformed in light of these regulations.

It could be argued, in response to this assertion, that property law is concerned with the acquisition of wealth, and therefore primarily aimed at ensuring certainty and stability.[87] This area of law could be viewed as not being a vehicle for conceptions like social justice or environmental protection. Yet, social justice has been shown to have had a role in the historical development of private water rights in Scotland[88] as well as other jurisdictions.[89] Furthermore, the rules of property law clearly have *implications* for social justice and environmental protection. The cost of ignoring the social justice implications of property law has been notably demonstrated by the scholarship of Andre van der Walt in relation to South Africa.[90] Van der Walt states that supposedly apolitical doctrinal logic of property law in South Africa with its focus on certainty and stability often frustrated morally justified and legally authorised large-scale reforms.[91] In relation to environmental protection, there is growing scholarship, which is beginning to consider the environmental implications of property law and how we need to reconceive our doctrines in pursuit of sustainability.[92] However, much of this scholarship is from the Common Law world where the distinction between public and private law is less rigid than in European legal systems. Put simply by

87 S. van Erp, "From 'Classical' to Modern European Property Law?" in A. Sakkoulas and E. Bruylant (eds), *Essays in honour of Konstantinos D. Kerameus* (2009).

88 See discussion above.

89 See, for example, D. Schorr, *The Colorado Doctrine: Water Rights, Corporations, and Distributive Justice on the American Frontier* (2012) in relation to the prior appropriation doctrine of the western states of America.

90 See, for example, A.J. van der Walt, *Property in the Margins* (2009) Chs. 1 and 2.

91 *Ibid.*, p. 18-19.

92 Such as T.W. Frazier, "Protecting Ecological Integrity within the Balancing Function of Property Law" in (1998) 28 Environmental Law 53; P. Carrurthers, S. Mascher and N. Skead (eds), *Property and Sustainability: Selected Essays* (2011); D. Grinlinton and P. Taylor (eds), *Property Rights and Sustainability: The Evolution of Property Rights to Meet Ecological Challenges* (2011); R.A. Barnes, "The Capacity of Property Rights to Accommodate Social-Ecological Resilience" (2013) 18(1) Ecology and Society 6; U. Mattei and A. Quarta, *The Turning Point in Private Law* (2018) Ch. 1.

American scholar Eric Freyfogle, "[m]any times, how property is employed also affects the surrounding community – socially, economically and ecologically – so the community and its interests must be taken into account."[93]

The importance of social and environmental factors in the regulation of land has been explicitly recognised in Scotland by the Land Rights and Responsibilities Statement, which is a guidance document produced by the Scottish Ministers that seeks to inform the policy and practice regarding land. The Statement declares: "The overall framework of land rights, responsibilities and public policies should promote, fulfil and respect relevant human rights in relation to land, contribute to public interest and wellbeing, and balance public and private interests. The framework should support sustainable economic development, protect and enhance the environment, help achieve social justice and build a fairer society…The holders of land rights should exercise these rights in ways that take account of their responsibilities to meet high standards of land ownership, management and use. Acting as the stewards of Scotland's land resource for future generations they contribute to sustainable growth and a modern, successful country."[94] To fulfil a vision like this, which is inspired by sustainability, property law researchers are required to broaden their horizons beyond the factors that have traditionally been considered in analysis and in reform.

Conversely, public law is not sufficient in and of itself to regulate natural resources. As noted by Taylor and Grinlinton in the introduction to this chapter, property rules are a crucial component in the system of regulation. A hydro-scheme can still be prevented in Scotland if private law consents are not obtained despite all public law requirements being met. Indeed, in relation to water, when reviewing the plethora of governance tools which have emerged in recent years regarding this resource,[95] it is clear that one concept has gained international acceptance: integrated water resource management (IWRM).[96] The Global Water Partnership defines IWRM as "based on the equitable and efficient management and sustainable use of water and recognises that water is an integral part of the ecosystem, a natural resource, and a social and economic good, whose quantity and quality determine the nature of its utilisation."[97] The foundational principles of IWRM were established in the Dublin Statement on Water and Sustainable Development that was

93 E. Freyfogle, *The Land We Share: Private Property and the Common Good* (2003) p. 28.

94 Scottish Government, "Land Rights and Responsibilities Statement" (28 Sept 2017). Available here: https://beta.gov.scot/publications/scottish-land-rights-responsibilities-statement/pages/3/ (last accessed 11 Jun 2019).

95 OECD, "OECD Inventory: Existing Tools, Practices and Guidelines to Foster Governance in the Water Sector" (2014). Available here: www.oecd.org/cfe/regional-policy/Inventory.pdf (last accessed 11 Jun 2019).

96 See, for example, S Hendry, *Frameworks for Water Law Reform* (2014) Ch 2.

97 Global Water Partnership, "The need for an integrated approach" (2017). Available here: www.gwp.org/en/About/why/the-need-for-an-integrated-approach/ (last accessed 11 Jun 2019).

adopted by the International Conference on Water and the Environment in 1992.[98] Shortly after this conference, in the same year, Agenda 21, the action plan of the United Nations for sustainable development, adopted at the Rio Conference on Environment and Development, then went on to further elaborate on the concept and its objectives.[99] A key aspect of this concept is integration of land and water-related regulation. The crucial connection between the regulation of water and land, and the role of property rights within the matrix of regulation, is therefore beginning to be explored by various scholars[100] and international agencies such as the United Nations' Food and Agriculture Organization[101] (FAO) and the Global Water Partnership.[102] The appreciation of the role of property rights in relation to matters of sustainability, however, is not limited to water as shown by the recent development by the FAO of the Voluntary Guidelines on the Responsible Governance of Tenure of Land, Fisheries and Forests in the Context of National Food Security.[103] This wide-ranging document considers the regulation of property rights from the perspective of progressive realisation of the right to adequate food. The Guidelines recognise that natural resources and their uses are interconnected and thus adopts an integrated and sustainable approach to their administration.[104]

The second boundary is that of individual ownership. All land is connected to all other land. This has important consequences when considering the impacts of the use of one plot of land and therefore regulation of this use. This is easily demonstrated with respect to water as the law has historically been confronted with conflicts that relate to the use of a plot of land, which has consequences outwith that plot due to the flow of water. As explained above, this issue lies at the heart of the doctrine of common interest in Scotland. Yet, again this issue is not unique to water and the problem of how to rationalise the effects

---

98 United Nations, "The Dublin Statement on Water and Sustainable Development" (1992). Available here: www.wmo.int/pages/prog/hwrp/documents/english/icwedece.html (last accessed 11 Jun 2019).

99 United Nations, "Agenda 21" (1992) A/COND.151/26 Ch. 18. Available here: https://sustainabledevelopment.un.org/outcomedocuments/agenda21 (last accessed 11 Jun 2019).

100 See, for example, R. Meizen-Dick and L. Nkonya, "Understanding legal pluralism in water and land rights: lessons from Africa and Asia" in B. van Koppen, M. Giordano and J. Butterworth (eds), *Community-based Water Law and Water Resource Management Reform* (2007); L. Cotula, "The property rights challenges of improving access to water for agriculture: Lessons from the Sahel" (2008) 9(1) Journal of Human Development 5; L. Alden Wily, F. Dubertret, P. Veit, K. Reytar and N.K. Tagliarino, "Water Rights on Community Lands: LandMarks Findings from 100 Countries" (2017) 6(4) Land 77.

101 S Hodgson, "Land and Water: the Rights Interface" (2004) FAO Legislative Study 84.

102 Global Water Partnership, "Coordinating land and water governance – An essential part of achieving food security" (2014). Available here: www.gwp.org/globalassets/global/toolbox/publications/perspective-papers/07_perspectives_paper_land_water_governance.pdf (last accessed 11 Jun 2019).

103 Food and Agriculture Organization of the United Nations, "Voluntary Guidelines on the Responsible Governance of Tenure of Land, Fisheries and Forests in the Context of National Food Security" (2012).

104 *Ibid.*, p. 5.

of land use outwith individual plots has been discussed over centuries.[105] Nevertheless, as there is greater recognition of the interconnection and interdependence of ecosystems,[106] these developments in understanding should also be reflected in our legal conceptions. Ecosystems do not have boundaries that match property boundaries. Again Freyfogle notes that the "division of land into private shares merely divides the rights and responsibilities of ownership of a landscape: the landscape as a natural system remains at integrated as ever. Actions on one parcel do not stop at property boundaries."[107]

The third boundary is that of the national legal system. Property law is often regarded as the quintessential example of national law.[108] Land is a fixed resource within national borders and territories. However, the preceding paragraphs also emphasise the international aspect of property law reform by referencing targets and requirements, which are set at EU level. The EU's targets must, of course, also be seen in the context of broader international developments.[109] National legal systems are nested within an ever more complex set of international and transnational obligations. Some of these obligations are intended to contribute to tackling the global scale and nature of problems such as human rights abuses and increasing environmental degradation. Law reform choices within one system can have consequences far beyond national boundaries, which suggests the vital need to consider wide-ranging international factors and developments when reforming property law.

The final boundary is disciplinary. Reference was made above to research on the ecological impacts of small-scale hydro-schemes. The challenges facing our natural resources are not purely legal and therefore the solutions will not be produced solely by lawyers. A collective response is required to tackle these challenges and researchers, including property law researchers, need to engage with other disciplines, in order to understand the scope and scale of the problems facing us and also to collaborate on the crafting responses. Examples of such an interdisciplinary approach to the challenge of sustainability from Scotland is the volume *Lairds, Land and Sustainability: Scottish Perspectives on Upland Management*[110] which culminates in a practical sustainability tool for owners and managers of upland estates as well as the report commissioned by the Scottish Government on diversity of ownership in Scotland and its impact on social, economic and environmental

105 See, for example, J Gordley, "Immissionsschutz, Nuisance and Troubles de Voisinage in Comparative and Historical Perspective" 1998 Zeitschrift für Europäisches Privatrecht 13.

106 F Capra and U Mattei, *The Ecology of Law: Toward a Legal System in Tune with Nature and Community* (2015) p. 3-4.

107 E. Freyfogle, "Private Rights in a Connected Land" in C A Arnold (ed), *Wet Growth: Should Water Law Control Land Use?* (2005) p. 331.

108 See description in S. van Erp, "Comparative Property Law" in M. Reimann and R. Zimmermann, *The Oxford Handbook of Comparative Law* (2006) p. 1044.

109 Such as the United Nations Framework Convention on Climate Change (1992) 1771 UNTS 107 and the Convention on Biological Diversity (1992) 1760 UNTS 79.

110 J. Glass et al (ed), *Lairds, Land and Sustainability: Scottish Perspectives on Upland Management* (2013).

outcomes.[111] As Australian scholar Nicole Graham notes: "The Earth and jurisprudence are both systems. The Earth is a system of physical and interlinked relationships. Jurisprudence is a system of abstract laws. Jurisprudence is a human creation. As such, jurisprudence is a system that depends for its existence on the systems of Earth because the former is the creation of a species whose existence is of the latter. It is therefore important, indeed necessary, to situate the system of laws within the physical context of the Earth's systems, because although the law currently situates itself above or separate to the physical realm, in reality the converse is true."[112]

5.5 Conclusion

Barnes states that how to "best to manage dwindling, endangered, or finite resources in light of societies' expanding and changing demands is one of the most important and difficult tasks facing us today."[113] As property law rules are those which most directly regulate use of these resources, these rules cannot be untouched by the transformation of our laws, policies and lives that will be required in order to contend with this task. This chapter has provided a micro-analysis of an issue in Scottish property law, which I argue has macro-implications. Considering the reform of private water rights in this way throws into relief the limitations of the current doctrinal methodology of property law research and reform. Although these limitations are perhaps more apparent in relation to water due to the necessity of water for all forms of life, I argue that these limitations have significance beyond the narrow issue of private water rights. In order to reform property law to contribute to the transition to sustainability, there are multiple boundaries that need to be surpassed, which involves significant changes to our conception of property and the methodology of legal research and reform. Andre van der Walt noted the requirement to challenge the existing logic and assumptions of law in order to achieve social justice within property law.[114] In light of the ecological crisis of the Earth, I argue property lawyers need to continue this process of challenge and broaden their focus even further. As noted by Fritjof Capra and Ugo Mattei in their book *Ecology of Law*: "This, then, is the profound lesson we need to learn from nature: sustainability is not an individual property but a property of an entire web of relationships, and it always involves a whole community. A

---

111 S. Thomson et al, "The impact of diversity of ownership scale on social, economic and environmental outcomes: exploration and case studies" (Mar 2016).

112 N. Graham, "Owning the Earth" in P. Burton (ed), *Exploring Wild Law: The Philosophy of Earth Jurisprudence* (2011) p259.

113 R.A. Barnes, "The Capacity of Property Rights to Accommodate Social-Ecological Resilience" (2013) 18(1) Ecology and Society 6 at p. 6.

114 A. van der Walt, *Property in the Margins* (2009) p. 247.

sustainable human community interacts with other communities – human and nonhuman – in ways that enable each to live and develop according to their nature. Sustainability does not mean that things do not change. It is a dynamic process of coevolution rather than a static state."[115] Moving beyond boundaries in property law research and reform may help to ensure that property law, reflecting the global movement, is also working towards preserving the Earth's resources for future generations.

115 F. Capra and U. Mattei, *The Ecology of Law: Toward a Legal System in Tune with Nature and Community* (2015) p. 177.

6 Environmental Liability as a Tool to Promote Sustainability

Michael Faure and Shen Yayun

6.1 Introduction

It has especially been Harvard Professor Michael Porter who in many publications has pointed at the relationship between environmental regulation, innovation and economic growth.[1] He showed, both at the firm level as well as at the country level, that stringent environmental regulation should not restrict companies' profits, but that the efforts to comply with environmental regulation will force firms towards innovation which in turn will also lead to a generally higher profitability of those environmentally innovative firms. This has been known as the Porter Hypothesis[2] and at the state level, for example the success of California, combining stringent environmental regulation with economic growth, has underscored the importance of this story. Increasingly, the Porter Hypothesis is also enjoying empirical support.

As a starting point environmental law generally can therefore be considered as an important tool to promote sustainability. However, an interesting question is which instruments within environmental law are those that have the most important contribution to sustainability. The question more particularly arises what the contribution of instruments of private law, more particularly environmental liability can be. This is an interesting question as most instruments aiming at promoting sustainability are surely not of a private law character, but rather public regulation or, increasingly market-based instruments (such as taxation and emission trading). Given the primary role of other legal instruments in promoting sustainability a first question that arises is what the supplementary role of private law and more particularly environmental liability could be in promoting sustainability. This also raises the more general question as to the precise functions of environmental liability in promoting sustainability and the conditions under which liability rules may serve sustainable development. That leads inter alia to the question whether a negligence or a strict liability rule should be preferred, but also to more technical questions with

1 Porter 1991 and Porter & Vanderlinde 1995.
2 Ambec et al. 2013.

respect to the ideal shape of liability rules, such as the desirability of financial limits on liability and guarantees against insolvency.

In addition to a positive (rather descriptive) analysis of the role that environmental liability could play in promoting sustainability one could equally focus on the more normative question, being whether there are ways to improve the available remedies in environmental liability in order to strengthen the effectiveness of liability rules in promoting sustainability. In that respect one could for example examine the importance of collective action and standing by NGOs, more particularly in cases where harm is caused to environmental goods that are not privately owned.

The goal of this contribution is especially to show how private law rules can also play an important contribution in promoting sustainability. This may not be obvious given the primacy of regulatory instruments in this domain. We will try to show that private law can still have an important role to play, even though it is often a supplementary one, in promoting sustainability. The most important tool, to which we will pay most attention in this contribution, is environmental liability, even though there may be other rules that can play a role as well.

After this introduction we will briefly explain how according to Michael Porter environmental law can promote economic growth. This type of literature in a way constitutes the basis for sustainable development as it shows that, under specific conditions, economic development and environmental protection can go hand in hand (2). Next, we briefly sketch the goal of environmental law as an instrument to internalize externalities[3] (3); next, it will be explained that a variety of different instruments could in theory be used to reach the internalisation of externalities (4). However, in practice government ordered safety regulation will be the most important tool (5), even though there always is an important supplementary role of private law in the form of environmental liability (6). For environmental liability to promote sustainability it is important to take particular design features into account (7). There may be particular difficulties in applying liability rules to environmental harm, more particularly given the wide-spread nature of environmental harm that there are equally remedies for that problem as well (8). Finally, we equally discuss how private action increasingly may play a role in addition to government regulation via self-regulation, private regulation and CSR (9). Section 10 concludes.

---

3 As will be explained in section 3, this concept refers to the fact that polluters should take into account (internalize) the external effects, i.e. the effects on others than the polluter himself in their decision-making process.

6.2 Environmental Law and Economic Growth

There are two streams of literature that have addressed the relationship between environmental protection and economic growth, precisely the core of sustainable development. The first stream of literature, known as the Environmental Kuznets Curve (EKC) has focused on the relationship between economic development (more particularly rising income levels) and environmental quality. The other stream of literature, mostly developed by Michael Porter (and therefore known as the Porter hypothesis) holds that stringent environmental regulation forces firms to invest in innovation, leading not only to better environmental quality, but also to other gains (more particularly higher productivity) and therefore to more profits. We will briefly review both streams of literature.[4]

6.2.1 *Environmental Kuznets Curve*

The idea of the Environmental Kuznets Curve is named after the Nobel Prize winner Simon Kuznets who wrote on the relationship between income inequality and income levels in a country.[5] Since the 1980s scholars have also applied this concept to environmental pollution, establishing an empirical relationship between measures of environmental quality and national income.[6] This literature showed an inverted u-shaped relationship, meaning that in a first phase of economic development (at low income levels) increasing economic development led to increasing environmental degradation. However, there is a certain turning point (the top of the inverted u-curve) where income levels have increased to such a point that a demand for higher environmental quality emerges and where hence increased economic welfare leads to increased environmental improvements. This work has especially become known through the World Bank, which referred to it in its World Development Report 1992. The normative lesson that was drawn from this literature was obviously that developing countries would have an interest in fighting poverty and increasing income levels, since this would also lead to higher levels of environmental quality. This vision has been strongly voiced by Beckerman, who was involved in drafting the 1992 World Development Report of the World Bank.[7] He for example holds 'it is fairly clear that the best way to improve the environment of the vast mass of the world's population is to enable them to maintain economic growth' and 'the strong correlation between incomes and the

4 Of course within the scope of this chapter we cannot address that literature in an in-depth manner. For more details see *inter alia Faure* 2011.

5 Kuznets 1955.

6 See especially Grossman and Krueger 1993, and see Grossman and Krueger 1995.

7 Beckerman 1992.

extent to which environmental protection measures are adopted demonstrates that, in the longer run, the surest way to improve your environment is to become rich'.[8]

The Environmental Kuznets Curve (EKC) is at first blush surprising since the dominant view may be that more economic development (industrialisation) will automatically lead to more environmental pollution. The EKC shows that in the beginning of industrialisation and economic development that may indeed be the case, but that there is a point where environmental pollution peaks and subsequently increasing income levels lead to decreased pollution and higher levels of environmental quality. There is, as we will show below, empirical evidence (although debated) to support the EKC, but the difficulty is of course to identify the precise causation behind the relationship. Simply stating that increasing income levels in the end leads to less pollution is obviously too simple. Strand presents five reasons why, theoretically the EKC may work, in other words why higher income levels in a country could lead to lower pollution levels.[9]

1. When incomes grow there may be a tendency for a larger share of total demand to consist of services rather than manufactured goods. This could explain why environmental and resource burdens decrease as income grows.
2. General technological process leads to greater efficiency in the use of energy and materials. This idea is also strongly related to the work of Michael Porter, holding that environmental improvement does not necessarily come at the expense of competitiveness. Porter showed that, to the contrary increased environmental performance would also lead to an increased competitiveness of nations and industries.[10] This has been known as the 'Porter hypothesis', showing that not only countries, but also companies may benefit from investments in environmental protection since it could increase their competitiveness.
3. The increase of income can also lead to changing preferences of the population: once the basic needs are satisfied the population may value a clean environment especially since it wants to enjoy free time and recreate in a clean environment. In the words of Arrow *et al.* 'People spend proportionally more on environmental quality as their income raises'.[11]
4. With increasing economic development an educated population may pressure for democratic reform and democratic societies tend to be more environmentally friendly.
5. Given different levels of income between countries increasing income may lead to an environmentally burdening production to move to low income countries. This envi-

8 Beckerman 1992, 491.
9 Strand 2002, 6-8.
10 Porter and Van der Linde 1995.
11 Arrow *et al.* 1995, 92.

ronmental dumping to pollution havens[12] may reduce pollution levels in the rich countries, which are able to relocate polluting activities to lower income countries.

It has more particularly been the contribution of Dan Esty and Michael Porter who examined empirically to what extent not only income levels, as suggested by the Environmental Kuznets Curve literature, but also a nation's regulatory regime influences environmental quality. The result of this powerful research, based on an examination of regulatory intensity and environmental quality in a great number of developed and developing countries, is that economic development and environmental protection go hand in hand with the improvement of a country's institutions and more particularly the environmental regulatory regime.[13] They find that not only the rigour and structure of environmental regulations have a particular impact on environmental performance, but also the enforcement. The empirical evidence hence suggests that a country can benefit environmentally not only from economic growth, but equally from developing the rule of law and strengthening its governance structures.[14] Interestingly, they also found evidence that countries that adopted a stringent environmental regime relative to their income were able to speed up economic growth rather than retarding it.[15]

6.2.2 *The Porter Hypothesis*

In contrast to the traditional economics paradigm that environmental regulation imposes additional costs on firms and thus may damage firms' competitiveness in the market,[16] Porter basically argues in many publications that firms that move beyond environmental compliance will automatically not only do more investments in environmental protection, but become more innovative in general. The innovations needed to reach higher environmental standards would, according to Michael Porter, also provide other benefits to the firm. In particular, Porter and Van der Linde believe that regulation can exert substantial influence on firms' environmental innovation in at least six aspects.[17] Consequently, this further innovation would provide strategic gains to the firm because of which those firms that strive for higher standards of environmental protection in the end would also be more profitable.[18] Porter has defended this "Porter hypothesis" not only with respect to individual

12 On which more in section 3 below.
13 See Esty and Porter 2005.
14 Esty and Porter 2005, 424.
15 Esty and Porter 2005, 425.
16 Jaffe et al. 1995, 133.
17 Porter and Van der Linde summerized these six aspects in Porter & Van der Linde 1995, 99-100.
18 This has *inter alia* been defended in Porter & Van der Linde 1995, 97-118. For a summary see Faure and Johnston 2009, 205-274.

corporations, but also with respect to states. He holds that increased environmental performance will lead to increased competitiveness, of both nations and industries.[19]

An overview of literature shows that the empirical evidence of the Porter hypothesis, although being mixed, to a large extent supports it. Ambec *et al.* distinguish between a "weak" and a "strong" version of the Porter hypothesis. The weak version only indicates that properly designed environmental regulation may spur innovation.[20] The strong version implies a relationship between environmental regulation and the business performance of a firm.[21] The authors conclude that the evidence for the weak version of the Porter hypothesis (that stricter environmental regulation leads to more innovation) is fairly clear and well-established. Empirical evidence concerning the strong version of the Porter hypothesis (that stricter regulation enhances business performance) is mixed: some studies find that environmental regulation has a direct negative effect on business performance,[22] but newer studies also provide clearer support for that hypothesis.[23]

This interesting economic literature has somewhat set the scene for the remainder of this contribution. Both the EKC literature as well as the Porter hypothesis show that sustainable development can be a reality in the sense that it is possible to let economic growth and environmental quality go hand in hand. However, an important conclusion from the literature is that this combination (and thus sustainable development) can only be reached if there is a solid institutional framework, in other words environmental law. That brings us to the question of what goals environmental law should precisely achieve (3) and through which instruments (4).

6.3 The Goal of Environmental Law and Policy

Environmental pollution is described in environmental law and economics as being created by the existence of 'externalities;' of data missing from or ignored by the decision maker, as might happen when the market does not require the decision maker to pay those costs. These side effects are external to the industrial activity itself since the company committing the pollution is in principle not affected by the negative side effects it causes by its actions.

19 See Porter 1991.

20 Ambec *et al.* 2013, 9. In line with the Porter Hypothesis, a study also shows that market-based instruments, such as subsidies or taxation, can score equally or even better than the mandates when the regulator uses them immediately after firms have adopted the technology. By contrast, if regulators make the first move ahead of the firms' investment, the use of command and control instruments (e.g. permitting) is more likely to achieve best allocation. Requate and Unold 2003, at 142.

21 Id.

22 Id.

23 Id., 16.

Environmental law and economics makes the argument that this form of pollution could be prevented by ensuring the decision makers to internalize the external costs, by ensuring that they bear the costs of the injuries and damages they impose on those third parties.

Precisely because pollution is an externality, the starting point of the economic analysis of environmental pollution is that a decision maker, such as the pharmaceutical company of our example, will not take into account the externality when it makes decisions on the production level and the investments in measures to avoid pollution, such as the instalment of a water treatment plant. Environmental pollution is considered by many scholars to be the classic example of an externality.[24] When environmental externalities exist, when actors are unable to discern the costs of environmental damages, then the harm is likely to continue; the market cannot function properly when data, especially cost data, is missing. By re-connecting that data to the actor, by making them aware of the costs they imposed on third parties, the decisions of the actor(s) will become responsive to those acts that create those environmental injuries and their damages.

This analysis indicates an economic goal of environmental law: environmental rules should (i) force the potential polluter to include in her decisions the damages caused by the pollution emitted by her activity choices by (ii) enabling the internalisation of related externalities back into her decision process.[25]

The need for environmental rules to connect potential polluters to the consequences of their acts is clear from the economic analysis of environmental law. Thus the scholar and policy maker of environmental law turn their focus to developing legal policies to solve the problem of externalities.

6.4 INSTRUMENT CHOICE

Having identified that the goal of environmental law is to internalise externalities, the next question is obviously through which types of instruments those externalities can be internalised? The literature distinguishes a wide variety of instruments. The most important one for the purposes of this chapter is the use of instruments of private law, more particularly civil liability. Civil liability has been stressed as one of the more robust tools in correcting the problems of internalising environmental externalities.[26] The essence of a rule of civil liability is that it forces, when particular conditions are met, polluters to compensate victims; and by holding polluters liable, the liability rule also leads to deterrence. The lia-

24 See generally Van den Bergh 1988, at 234.
25 See Faure 1996, at 85-109.
26 Shavell 2011.

bility rules do not, however, prescribe a particular behaviour like a specific emission standard or the use of a particular technology. Under civil liability systems the polluter remains permitted to pollute, as long as he is able to pay the price, i.e., to pay the adjudicated damages to the victim.[27]

The alternative, which is de facto most often used as tool of environmental policy, is regulation by the government. Economists often qualify this as "command and control" rules. They consist of an administrative system based on licenses, permitting and standard-setting by administrative agencies. We will discuss the choice between command and control (also referred to as safety) regulation and private liability rules in more detail in the next section.

In the interest of pollution reduction and innovations for sustainability, command and control is not the only way for public agencies to influence behaviour. A different approach, in fact already advocated as early as the 1920s by Pigou, is the use of financial instruments to internalise externalities. These economic instruments are often referred to as 'incentive-based', 'market-based', or 'economic' instruments.

The basic idea of those incentive mechanisms is to correct an externality by returning an appropriate fee or cost to the potential polluter. This is based on the economic premise that a particular actor, in this case a polluter, bases his decision on cost-benefit analyses. Increased costs (resulting from a threat of having to pay a tax), being held liable or incurring a sanction would lead to costs that would be higher than the benefits to the polluter and could therefore correct his behaviour. In that case, public regulation would not need to provide specific behavioural guidance, nor would bureaucrats need to audit the polluter's behaviour to those requirements. Instead, the restored information, the re-internalised externality, would provide sufficient information to guide the actor's behaviour.

The most commonly implemented are those Pigouvian taxes discussed earlier, but there is in fact a range of options, including positive payments such as subsidies for desired behaviours. For example, the polluter could be taxed according to the amount of pollution emitted; giving the polluter better incentives, tax-reducing incentives, for pollution reduction and more particularly for innovative investments in pollution reduction tools.[28] Apart from the Pigouvian tax, green public procurement (GPP) is increasingly used to jump-start the uptake of green technologies.[29] In the case of GPP, governments use their purchasing power to buy services or products with fewer environmental impacts. As a

27 In that sense a liability rule can be considered as a price instrument, just like taxes or subsidies. See Wiener 1999, at 706-709.

28 Wiener 1999, at 714-726; Stewart 2007, at 151-152.

29 See United Nations Environment Programme (UNEP) 2013 'Sustainable Public Procurement: a Global Review', UNEP Final Report, December 2013, at. 16-24. Full text available at: www.unep.org/resourceefficiency/Portals/24147/SPP_Full_Report_Dec2013_v2%20NEW%20(2).pdf.

result, the GPP per se can directly boost the quantity demanded in the short run.[30] In the long run, GPP may also indirectly increase the demand of private parties, in a way of making professionals and customers better aware of environmental performance.[31]

The traditional 'carrots and sticks' aside, some persuasive instruments making use of private information and voluntary compliance are also around for environmental governance.[32] The idea of 'responsive regulation' on the one hand hints that regulators may go for persuasion in the first place, as persuasion can be effective and cheap, particularly when it comes to changing individual behaviour.[33] On the other hand, regulators can put mandates in the background,[34] as mandates may fail to crowd in the intrinsic motivations of individuals.[35] In theory as in practice, informational tools have been around as behavioural interventions to motivate environmental compliance. A case in point is the Opower program that provided the end-users of buildings with real-time information and peer-comparison feedback about energy use. Some empirical evidence has shown that the Opower program did result in more efficient energy use.[36]

Although there is a large variety of instruments available, Gunningham and Grabosky established in the seminal text, *Smart Regulation* (1998), that in fact all legal instruments have particular advantages, but also their own particular weaknesses; but they can be combined in bespoke arrangements.[37]

An important question in the 'choice of instrument' literature is therefore which type of policy instrument is indicated under which particular circumstances. The insight that no instrument alone can lead to optimal results also indicates that in most cases a combination of different instruments may be necessary to optimally internalise externalities. That leads to a growing literature on the search for smart mixes between different legal and policy instruments. The crucial question in that respect is how an optimal combination of a variety of legal and policy instruments can be designed to optimally internalise the externality caused by environmental pollution.

There are different mixes between various instruments but are theoretically possible. This chapter will provide the example of a mix between regulation and liability. It will be shown that as a result of (administrative) costs, imperfect information and the judgment

30 See e.g. Commission of the European Communities, 'Buying Green: A Handbook on Green Public Procurement', 2016, at. 4. Full text available at: http://ec.europa.eu/environment/gpp/pdf/Buying-Green-Handbook-3rd-Edition.pdf.
31 See e.g. Simcoe, Timothy, and Toffel 2014, at 413.
32 Oates and Baumol 1996, at 108-109.
33 Ayres and Braithwaite 1992, at 19-26.
34 Id.
35 See Frey 1997, at 56-57 and 64; Boussalis, Feldman and Smith 2018, at 281-283.
36 Ayres, Raseman and Shih 2012, at 1016.
37 This choice of instruments is discussed in a detailed manner by Wiener 1999 and may also lead to hybrid regulatory approaches. See Stewart 2007, at 154.

proof problem neither regulation, nor liability is as such able to perfectly internalize environmental externalities. Hence a mix of regulation and liability is needed, and the supplementary role of liability is justified. The regulation-liability mix is meant to cancel out the weaknesses around each other, as with the Supplementary Environmental Projects (SEPs) for sustainable site development, which will be presented in Section 6.

6.5 Criteria for Regulation

Law and economics have paid a great deal of attention to the question of whether safety in society can best be reached through liability rules or through regulation. An important contribution to this debate comes from Steven Shavell,[38] who examined the choice between liability rules and regulation. Both liability rules and regulation can be used to reach the same goal – the optimal prevention of environmental harm. However, the way in which both instruments reach this goal is totally different. If tort law is used, the risk creator remains free to choose the way in which environmental damage can be prevented. Tort law assumes that the preventive function of liability rules will give incentives to the potential risk creator to introduce optimal preventive mechanisms. This is the case either because it is the optimal way for him to prevent the damage (under strict liability) or because it is a way to avoid having to pay compensation to the victim (under a negligence rule). Under regulation, the government will ex ante impose the use of a particular standard. Non-compliance with this standard will also be enforced and can lead to the imposition of administrative or criminal sanctions. Regulation is therefore considered to be an ex ante system aiming for prevention, whereas liability rules mainly intervene ex post after the damage has occurred. The criteria advanced by Steven Shavell that influence the choice between safety regulation and liability are:

- Information asymmetries;
- Insolvency;
- The underdeterrence of tort law.

Information deficiencies have often been advanced as a cause of market failure and as the justification for government intervention through regulation.[39] For the proper operation of a liability system, information on the existing legal rules, the accident risk, efficient measures to prevent accidents, etc. is a precondition for efficient deterrence. According to Shavell, the parties in an accident setting generally have much better information on

38 Shavell 1984a, 1984b, 1987.

39 See the basic article by Stigler 1961; Schwarz and Wilde 1979; Mackaay 1982.

the accident risk than that possessed by the regulatory body.[40] The parties themselves have, in principle, the best information on the costs and benefits of the activity that they undertake and of the optimal way to prevent accidents. This "assumption of information", however, will be reversed if it becomes clear that some risks are not readily appreciated by the parties in an accident setting. This may be more of a problem if costs are external, as they cannot always be easily assessed by the parties involved.

If the potential damages can be so high that they will exceed the wealth of the individual injurer, liability rules will not provide optimal incentives. The reason is that the costs of care are directly related to the magnitude of the expected damages. If the expected damages are much greater than the individual wealth of the injurer, the injurer will only consider the accident as having a magnitude equal to his wealth. He will, therefore, only take the care necessary to avoid the total accident risk.[41] This is a simple application of the principle that the deterrent effect of tort liability works only if the injurer has sufficient assets to pay for the damages he causes. If an injurer is protected against such liability, a problem of underdeterrence arises.[42] Regulation can overcome the problem of underdeterrence caused by insolvency (if insurance were to come into the picture, it could overcome the problems of underdeterrence, provided that the moral hazard problem, caused by insurance, can be solved). In that case, the efficient care will be determined ex ante by regulation and will be affected by enforcement instruments, which induce the potential injurer to comply with the regulatory standard, irrespective of his wealth. Therefore, a problem might still arise if the regulation were also enforced by means of monetary sanctions. Again, if these were to exceed the injurer's wealth, the insolvency problem would remain. Hence, if a safety regulation is introduced because of a potential insolvency problem, the regulation itself should be enforced by non-monetary sanctions.[43]

Some activities can cause considerable damage, but even so a law suit to recover these damages may never be brought. If this were the case, there would be no deterrent effect of liability rules. Therefore, the absence of a liability suit would again be an argument to enforce the duty of efficient care by means of regulation, rather than through liability rules.[44] There can be a number of reasons why a law suit is not brought, even though considerable damage has been caused. Sometimes an injurer can escape liability because the harm is thinly spread among a number of victims. As a consequence, the damage incurred by every individual victim is so small that he has no incentive to bring a suit. In particular, this problem will arise if the damage is not caused to an individual but to common property,

40 Shavell 1984a.

41 Id.

42 Shavell 1986. It was mentioned above that insolvency causes a problem under a strict liability rule, but less so under negligence.

43 Shavell 1985.

44 Shavell 1984a.

such as the surface waters in which each member of the population has a minor interest. In addition, a long time might have elapsed before the damage becomes apparent; in this case, much of the necessary evidence may be either lost or not obtained. Another problem is that if the damage only manifests itself years after the activity, the injurer might have gone out of business. A related problem is that it is often hard to prove that a causal link exists between an activity and a type of damage.[45] The burden of proof of a causal relationship becomes more difficult with the increasing passage of time since the damaging incident took place. Often a victim will not recognise that the harm had been caused by a tort, but might think that his particular ailment, for example cancer, had a "natural cause", associated with general ill health. For all these reasons, a liability suit might not be brought and hence safety regulation is necessary to ensure that the potential polluter takes efficient care.[46]

6.6 Supplementary Role of Environmental Liability

According to Shavell's criteria there is a strong argument to control environmental risk through ex ante regulation (or taxation). However, in individual cases there can still be damage to the environment. Then again, liability under tort may come into the picture when victims claim compensation. But also irrespective from the question of compensation, there may be particular weaknesses in command and control regulation, which justify a combination of liability rules and regulation. The criticism found in the literature with respect to the command and control approach can be summarised as follows:

First, traditional command and control systems indeed focus on a permit or licensing system. Within this system, traditionally, permits set emission standards, but these often disregard the effect of the aggregate level of emissions on the environmental quality of the receiving environmental medium. This was a criticism that was formulated, particularly in the 1970s, in situations where the approach was heavily focusing on emission systems. Whereas environmental policy had indeed been focusing on the control of emissions, the total effect of the emissions on environmental quality was disregarded. As a result, the effect was that, notwithstanding severe emission controls, total environmental quality was seriously reduced. It is indeed striking that within the USA emission trading could develop within the context of the Clean Air Act, which had set target standards referred to as National Ambient Air Quality Standards (NAAQS).[47] Hence, the focus should of course be on target standards or environmental quality standards. However, this criticism on the use of emission standards is not necessarily a criticism on the use of command and control

45 Landes and Posner 1984; Kunreuther and Freeman 2001.

46 For alternatives to liability, see Bocken 1987, 1988.

47 Hahn and Hester 1989.

as such. Indeed, even within a system that would largely focus on target standards, one could still have either command and control or economic instruments. However, there are several other criticisms that can be formulated.[48]

A second criticism on command and control is that it requires high information and enforcement costs. Indeed, each industry must be scrutinised in detail to determine the appropriate level of emission control. Hence, on the one hand, the government needs to set optimal standards. It must be remembered that the traditional regulatory approach only works optimally if there is also optimal enforcement. In many cases polluters will balance the possibility of being fined (when they breach a regulation) against a marginal profit that can be realised with additional pollution. However, enforcement costs will be too high. If, on the other hand, the level of control is too low, the damage costs for society as a result of the environmental pollution will be too high.[49] Absent information about the desirable level of intervention, regulation may fail to fully internalise the externalities. For instance, the information problem may lead to the inaccuracy of the variables of a tax based on expected outcomes.[50] A possible result of such inaccuracy would be that, the amount collected is less than the loss of actual harm, and the expected harm will be excessive when the untaxed variables also contribute to the harm.[51] Of course one could argue that the authorities may reduce enforcement (and information) costs by relying on information provided by industry. However, the private interest theory of regulation will teach that it is still likely that the industry will distort the information in favour of its own interests.

As far as administrative costs are concerned, liability may generally score better than regulation. A study has shown that the negligence rule may cost less than regulation in terms of enforcement.[52] The study further pointed out that, if compliance with regulation is certain, the cost of enforcement will occur anyway under regulation; whereas under the negligence rule, the enforcement cost will occur with the possibility that harm occurs.[53] In this case, the enforcement cost of regulation will be greater than that of the negligence rule. If compliance with regulation is not certain and compliance with regulation can eliminate accidents, the enforcement cost of regulation will be positive, and that of the negligence rule will be none since there will be no accident.[54] All else being equal in the second case, if compliance with regulation cannot eliminate accidents, the negligence rule can reduce the number of instances in which behaviour is examined; regulation, however,

48 For a summary of these criticisms see also Faure and Ubachs 2003.
49 Tietenberg 2000.
50 Shavell 2011, at 255.
51 Id.
52 Shavell 2013, at 275.
53 Id., at 276-277.
54 Id., at 277-278.

may not reduce the instances in which behaviour is examined.[55] In either case, the negligence rule will be cheaper than regulation in terms of enforcement. Another study likewise shows that, in dealing with harmful externalities, liability, either the negligence rule or strict liability, is in theory superior to the corrective taxes in terms of administrative costs.[56]

Third, it has often been argued that the command and control approach has in many cases failed to generate sufficient incentives for polluters to reduce their pollution levels. The problem is that a command and control type regulation only requires a polluter to follow the regulatory standard, as this is, for instance, incorporated in a permit. However, as soon as the polluting firm complies with the regulatory standard there is no additional incentive to invest in, for example, research and development towards innovative environmental technologies.

A fourth criticism is that the command and control approach has the disadvantage that it cannot equalise the marginal pollution costs of pollution control among the different polluters that produce the same pollution. This has to do with the fact that a command and control approach is often too general. Indeed, with regulation the standard set by the regulatory agency will often be similar for each polluter and will therefore not take into account the fact that, for example, an efficient pollution reducer could reduce pollution at much lower costs. This constitutes a major shortcoming of a command and control system. This failure to equalise the marginal pollution costs will excessively increase the costs of pollution control. This, of course, has to do with the difficulty that administrative agencies will in many cases not be able to determine what the efficient emission for each individual polluter is. Indeed, the efficient pollution will of course vary from case to case. Ideally, authorities should be able to identify the polluters and should also determine the efficient pollution for that specific polluter. For certain factories the efficient pollution level will probably be higher than the imposed standard; for other factories it may be lower. If the authorities are not able to acquire the correct information about the actual pollution of certain polluters, they might demand that all polluters reduce their emissions by a same percentage. This will inevitably lead to inefficiency and thus to welfare losses because the possibilities for pollution abatement will of course be different for each polluter.[57] The essential problem with the command and control approach is indeed that those polluters that have the capacity to abate the pollution above the regulatory standard do not have any financial incentive to do so under a command and control system.

---

55 Id.

56 Shavell 2011, at 251-253. Apart from the administrative costs, Shavell's study also looks into other factors, such as how liability and the corrective tax differ in their impacts on the level of activity and the level of care. The study in the end points out that liability should on the whole be superior to the corrective tax in dealing with most harmful externalities, except for general pollution; and puts forward a joint use of liability and the corrective tax. For an in-depth discussion see Shavell 2011, at 249-266.

57 This point has also been made by Rosen 1999.

Fifth, under a command and control approach the polluters will only pay the prevention costs required to comply with the regulatory standard. However, polluters will not necessarily be required to pay for the costs of residual damages associated with the pollution that they have produced in conformity with the standard.

Last but not least, regulation can sometimes be less flexible, given the rule of law and environmental uncertainty. On the one hand, regulations made by the government are taken as law that should be general, certain and neutral; and regulatory power should take shape and be used through a due process. On the other hand, regulation may do well in environmental governance when causation is clear, outcomes are foreseeable, and abatement technologies are available.[58] Yet in the face of environmental uncertainty, regulators might not dash off regulatory rules, in deference to the precautionary principle. One of the reasons could be that reckless regulation may do more harm than good when the outcomes are neither foreseeable nor reversible.[59] On that account, the government should consider the extent to which regulation should address risks that may not be real but "have significant economic consequences where the markets may react to perceptions rather than actual risks".[60]

These criticisms show that there are considerable disadvantages with the traditional command and control approach, which can be summarised by the fact that the regulatory standard is often too general and not flexible and differentiated enough.

These weaknesses of command and control regulation are on the one hand used to justify the introduction of flexible and market-based instruments (like taxes or emissions trading). However, in the context of this contribution it is important that these weaknesses of regulation are also used as an argument to supplement regulation with liability rules. An exposure to liability can therefore provide additional incentives to polluters to promote sustainable development.

A case to show the supplementary role of liability could be the Supplemental Environmental Project (SEP), in which regulation uses liability in pursuit of sustainable site development. The SEP policy was made by the federal environmental regulator in the US, viz the US Environmental Protection Agency (USEPA). The SEPs are pro-environment projects undertaken by defendants as part of the settlements for violations.[61] In its latest policy, the USEPA made brownfield redevelopment part of the SEP, and laid out more detailed requirements for a project to be an SEP. The idea of the SEP is that the detection

58 Faure 2014, at 694.

59 For instance, there has been a study showing that, when the public has a very inaccurate perception of the risks posed by hazardous waste sites, the housing prices will be adversely affected. See Viscusi 2007, at 599.

60 Id.

61 More about the SEP policy see USEPA, 'U.S. Environmental Protection Agency Supplemental Environmental Projects Policy 2015 Update', March 10, 2015, at 1. Full text available at: www.epa.gov/sites/production/files/2015-04/documents/sepupdatedpolicy15.pdf.

of harm can be done by private parties through litigation, e.g., citizen suits. When a defendant seeks a SEP, the settlement of the suit will be handed over to the USEPA, who will then decide and oversee what the defendant should do to compensate the harm through a proposed SEP. In this way, regulation and liability may improve each other: on the one side, the regulator can make use of private information to detect environmental harm; on the other side, the SEP may ease the judgment proof concern around liability, in the sense that the SEP allows the defendant to pay the price over a long term, instead of paying a lump sum at once or even going insolvent.[62] Yet the liability-regulation mix through the SEP may have some limits. For, instance, a study has shown that the SEP tends to deter parties already subject to the SEP and bring them back to compliance, but it may not give general deterrence as damages do; it is also likely that the SEP can deter large firms more than it does to small companies.[63] However, it goes beyond this chapter to go into the details of the SEP project.

6.7 The Optimal Design of Environmental Liability

In the previous section we just indicated that environmental liability rules can play an important role to back up command and control regulation. Private law therefore can play a role in promoting sustainable development. However, the literature has also indicated that for liability rules to play this important supplementary role, particular design features have to be respected.

6.7.1 *Strict Liability Versus Negligence*

A basic question, often addressed in the literature,[64] is whether the operator – the tortfeasor in a liability context – should be exposed to a strict liability or a negligence rule. A distinction is usually made between the case where only one party, the injurer, can influence the accident risk – this is referred to as a unilateral accident situation – and the situation where both the injurer and the victim can influence the accident risk; the latter is referred to as a bilateral accident situation.[65] The goal of tort law should be to provide parties that can influence the accident risk with incentives in order to reduce the total sum of accident costs. Those costs consist, on the one hand, of the cost of prevention and, on the other

62 Id., at 17-25.

63 See Glicksman and Earnhart 2007.

64 The seminal article is by Shavell 1980. See generally Schäfer and Müller-Langer 2009, 3-45 (providing a recent overview of the economic literature with respect to the choice between strict liability and negligence).

65 Id.

hand, of the costs of the accident (the damage). Efficient care levels can be found where the marginal costs of care equal the marginal benefits in reduction of the expected loss.[66]

In a unilateral accident case, where only the injurer can influence the accident risk, both negligence and strict liability will provide incentives to follow an efficient care level. On the condition that the due care required in the legal system is equal to the efficient care, the injurer will take the efficient care level. The simple explanation is that the injurer will be found liable under the negligence rule if he spends less than the due care level required in the legal system. Hence, for the injurer following the due care level is a mechanism to reduce his expected costs. The negligence rule can therefore in principle give a tortfeasor an incentive to spend on care to reach the optimal standard. However, in order for the negligence rule to work optimally, the legal system must set the due care level equal to the efficient care level.

Additionally, a strict liability rule will lead to optimal incentives for care taking for the polluter, since taking efficient care will minimise the expected accident costs which the potential polluter has to bear under a strict liability system.[67] Therefore, the literature generally accepts that both a negligence rule and a strict liability rule will provide a potential polluter with incentives to take the efficient care level. However, this is only valid in a unilateral accident setting, whereby only the injurer can influence the accident risk.

In a bilateral accident situation the potential victim also needs to be provided with incentives for mitigation. In that case a contributory negligence defence should be added to the strict liability rule. Under a negligence regime, victims will always have an incentive to take efficient care as well since they will – in principle – not be compensated by the injurer, who will take efficient care to avoid liability under a negligence rule.

In the joint care or bilateral case, strict liability with contributory negligence and a negligence rule – with or without contributory negligence – will incite parties to adopt efficient levels of care. However, the accident risk cannot be completely minimised by increasing the levels of care. Accident losses also depend on the extent to which parties participate in the activity that might cause the damage (e.g., the miles driven). Therefore, reducing the activity level will also reduce the accident risk.[68] The activity level can be interpreted as any control variable not taken into account in setting the optimal level of care. Under a negligence rule, an injurer has no incentive to adopt an optimal level of activity. This cannot be remedied, because judges cannot easily calculate the optimal activity level into the due care standard.[69] A strict liability rule has the advantage that the injurer will automatically adopt an optimal activity level. This is also a means to minimise

66 See Landes and Posner 1984, 417.

67 Polinsky 1983, 44-47; Shavell 1987, 8.

68 Diamond 1974, 109-111; Polinsky 1983, 44; Shavell 1980.

69 It is difficult to determine both the optimal and the actual activity level. See, e.g., Polinsky 1983, 47; Shavell 1980, 2.

his costs. If the victim's activity has no influence on the accident risk, strict liability might have a slight advantage, because it might also lead to an optimal activity level of the injurer. Nevertheless, in a joint care case this advantage is cancelled out by the fact that the victim will not adopt an optimal activity level. This is due to the impossibility of calculating the activity level into the due care standard when considering contributory negligence.[70]

What is the importance of the activity level for the choice between negligence and strict liability? In a unilateral accident model, wherein only the behaviour of the injurer influences the accident risk, strict liability seems to be the preferred rule since it is the only liability rule which will lead both to efficient care and to an optimal activity level. In a bilateral case the answer is more balanced.

Since activity level changes are not calculated into the due care standard, strict liability with a defence of contributory negligence will encourage activity level changes on the part of the injurer. On the other hand, a negligence rule will encourage activity level changes of the victim. Therefore, several authors suggest that in bilateral cases strict liability will be a superior device if giving injurers an incentive to change their activity level is more important than giving victims a similar incentive.[71] This implies that if the injurer's activity is very dangerous and creates a high accident risk, even if optimal care is taken, it will be more desirable to control the injurer's activity than it is to control the victim's.

Even though a clear-cut test is thus difficult to provide, Landes and Posner describe several factors that may lead to a preference for a strict liability rule. These elements are: (1) high expected accident costs; (2) the impossibility that more care by the injurer would reduce the accident risk; (3) the impracticability of constraining the victim's activity in favour of the injurer's; and (4) the desirability of reducing the risk by an activity level change of the injurer.[72]

Since tortfeasors such as petrochemical plant operators are undoubtedly much more influential than victims with respect to technological accident risks that could lead to man-made disasters, there are strong arguments in favour of applying a strict liability rule to such ultra-hazardous activities. The strong appeal of the strict liability rule (of course combined with a comparative negligence defence to account for the victim's influence on the risk as well)[73] is that it advantageously shifts all social costs of the accident to the operator. Thus, the operator will appropriately weigh costs and benefits concerning optimal

70 Landes and Posner 1981, 875; Shavell 1987, 23-24.

71 Landes and Posner 1981, 877; Shavell 1987, 7, 19.

72 Landes and Posner 1981, at 907; for a more recent overview of the literature see Schäfer and Müller-Langer 2009, at 36.

73 The literature makes a distinction between a contributory negligence defense (where the plaintiff would be completely barred from compensation if he would be at fault) and a comparative negligence defense (where the victim's claim on compensation would only be reduced to the proportion in which he contributed to the loss as well). Both defenses are generally considered sufficient to provide incentives for appropriate victim care. For an overview of the literature see Artigot i Golobardes and Gómez Pomar 2009, at 46.

preventive measures and activity levels.[74] For this reason, it is no surprise that the literature generally advocates strict liability both for environmental harm[75] and for technological disasters.[76]

6.7.2 Solvency Guarantees

Unfortunately, strict liability may only be efficient if the insolvency problem can be cured. Insolvency should be seen here as a situation where the amount of the damage is higher than the tortfeasor's wealth. This scenario is very likely with environmental harm. The literature has even indicated that, if an insolvency problem persists, strict liability may more easily lead to underdeterrence than negligence.[77] This is because strict liability leads to underdeterrence as soon as the total amount of the damage is lower than the injurer's wealth. Under a negligence regime, the tortfeasor still has an incentive to spend on care as long as the costs of due care required in the legal system are less than his wealth. Spending on due care will in that case still be attractive for the injurer since it implies that he will not be held liable.[78]

When strict liability is introduced, it should hence be accompanied with some guarantee against insolvency. This is, moreover, a more general point made in economic literature: liability rules only work efficiently (in the terms of both deterrence and compensation) if the solvency of the tortfeasor can be guaranteed. Otherwise, a so-called "judgment proof" problem will arise whereby liability rules may generally fail to lead to a deterrent effect.[79] There is, therefore, a strong economic argument in favour of imposing a duty to purchase financial coverage (e.g., compulsory liability insurance) for environmental pollution simply because the magnitude of the damage caused by the incident can greatly outweigh the assets of an individual tortfeasor.[80]

6.7.3 No Limits

In sum, although strict liability can, in principle, be efficient for environmental harm, due to a potential insolvency problem it should be accompanied with solvency guarantees since it could otherwise lead to underdeterrence. Precisely for that reason there should likewise

74 Shavell 1980.
75 For a summary of the literature see Faure 2009, at 252-253 (summarizing the literature defending a strict liability rule for environmental pollution).
76 See Faure 2007, at 342-343; Bruggeman 2010, at 38-39.
77 Faure and Grimeaud 2003, at 35-36; Landes and Posner 1984, at 418.
78 Faure and Grimeaud 2003.
79 Shavell 1986.
80 See also Kunreuther and Freeman 2001.

be no limit on the liability of the potential tortfeasor. A so called "financial cap", which limits the tortfeasor's liability to a particular amount, will have the same effect as insolvency, i.e., it will lead to underdeterrence and thus negatively affect incentives for prevention.

An obvious disadvantage of a system involving financial caps is the serious impairment of the victim's right to full compensation. However, if the cap is indeed set at a much lower amount than the expected damage, this would not only violate the victim's right to compensation, but would also prevent the full internalisation of the externality mentioned above. From an economic point of view, a limitation on compensation therefore poses a serious problem, since the risky activity will not be internalised.

Indeed, if one believes that exposure to liability has a deterrent effect, limiting the amount of compensation owed to victims poses yet another problem. There is a direct linear relationship between the magnitude of the accident risk and the amount spent on care by the potential wrongdoer. Therefore, if the liability is limited to a certain amount, the potential injurer will assess the accident's magnitude in proportion to that limited amount. Hence, he will only spend on care to avoid causing an accident with a magnitude equal to his limited amount of liability, and he will not spend the care necessary to reduce the total accident costs. Obviously, the amount of care spent by the potential injurer will be lower, causing a problem of underdeterrence. The amount of optimal care reflected in the optimal standard — that is to say the care necessary to efficiently reduce the total accident costs, — will exceed the amount the potential injurer will spend to avoid an accident equal to the statutory limited amount.[81] Thus, as a result of the cap too little care is taken.[82]

Moreover, another effect of imposing a financial limit on liability (in addition to victim undercompensation and operator underdeterrence) is that it would constitute an indirect subsidisation of the industry that enjoys a particular limit on liability.[83]

6.7.4 *Attribution*

Another point that remains important in the design of efficient liability rules is that liability should be attributed in such a way that all parties that contributed to the risk should be held liable to the extent that their actions actually affected the accident risk. When several tortfeasors (the case of so called multiple tortfeasors) have acted together, a joint and several

81 See Faure 1995, at 27-28.

82 The reason for the underdeterrence is obviously the same as for the underdeterrence that results from the insolvency of the injurer. Underdeterrence arises because the injurer is not exposed to full liability, either as a result of his insolvency or as a result of a cap.

83 See also Radetzki and Radetzki 2000, at 180 (arguing that the top layer of compensation provided by the governments in fact constitutes a subsidy to nuclear power generation).

liability rule may provide incentives to the joint tortfeasors for mutual monitoring.[84] In any case, liability of other actors who contributed equally to the loss should not be excluded by, for example, exclusively channelling the liability to one selected tortfeasor, e.g. the licensee of a particular plant. Doing so would negatively affect the incentives of others who could have equally contributed to the loss.[85]

However, inefficiencies may arise in case of insolvency of one of the actors, since recourse may become impossible.[86] Joint and several liability is debated since an injurer could, in principle, also be held liable for a part of the damage not caused by his activity, thus potentially increasing his liability exposure.[87]

The application of joint and several liability is a general rule in all cases where more than one tortfeasor is involved. Many legal systems adopt a joint and several liability rule where more than one party (e.g. an operator and a subcontractor) has contributed to the accident risk.[88] Joint and several liability has, however, been criticised from an insurance perspective, based on the argument that it increases the necessity to purchase insurance coverage for all parties involved.[89]

6.7.5 *Summary*

To summarise, liability rules can be used to provide incentives for preventing environmental harm, but particular conditions must be met:
- a strict liability rather than a negligence rule should apply;
- solvency guarantees should exist;
- no statutory limit (a so-called cap) should be imposed on the operator's liability; and
- liability should be attributed to all actors who can influence the risk.[90]

Under these conditions liability rules can have the desirable effect of incorporating the social costs of environmental risks into the prices of the activity concerned and to provide incentives for operators to reduce environmental risk. The liability rules only provide incentives to take optimal care,[91] which can thus reduce the chilling effects that could follow

84 See Tietenberg 1989, at 305 (discussing this incentive mechanism).
85 Faure and Hartlief 2003, at 127-128.
86 See Kornhauser and Revesz 1989, at 831 (providing an analysis of joint and several liability under full solvency); Kornhauser and Revesz 1990, at 617 (analysing liability in case of insolvency).
87 For this reason, joint and several liability in case of environmental harm is opposed by Bergkamp 2000, at 153-156.
88 See Rogers 2004, at 276-279.
89 See Faure and Hartlief 2003, at 127.
90 For a more detailed discussion of those conditions see Faure and Grimeaud 2003, at 18-50.
91 Recall, this is the care where the marginal costs of accident prevention equal the marginal benefits reduction of the expected damage.

from what the literature considers "crushing" liability. For example, the latter could occur when operators would also be held liable for harm that was not caused by their own activity.[92] However, the mere fact that the application of a liability rule will lead to increased prices of particular products or services (resulting from higher investments in preventive efforts) is from a social welfare perspective desirable. Efficient operators – those taking optimal care to reduce environmental risks – will be able to produce at lower prices than inefficient ones, who would not take optimal preventive measures and would thus be confronted with higher liability risks and higher insurance premiums. That is precisely the desirable result of the application of liability rules: efficient operators will be rewarded with lower liability risks and, therefore, lower prices.

6.8 Standing and Access to Justice

There is one particular problem that rises in the context of applying environmental liability to promote sustainable development. The problem is that private law remedies to be used by individual victims in classic tort or nuisance cases may not work in environmental cases.

Shavell offers many reasons why private enforcement of environmental standards may not work: the damage may be too widespread, resulting in low damage amounts to individual victims even if the totality of the damages is very high.[93] These circumstances produce, in the words of Schäfer, a "rational apathy" on the part of the individual victims.[94] Therefore, none of them are motivated to take on the expense of litigation. Moreover, a private law suit may never be brought due to problems of causation or latency, which is characterised by long time lapse between the emission and the actual occurrence of the harm.[95] These problems are especially prevalent in environmental cases. Moreover, collective litigation does not always follow either, since the transaction costs for the group to get organised can in some cases be high.[96] This may be an argument in favour of allowing a lower threshold for *locus standi* in case of environmental harm and even allowing the development of so-called environmental Public Interest Litigation (PIL).[97]

---

92 *Inter alia* as a result of a shift in the burden of proving causation. Faure and Hartlief 2003, at 126-127. On the dangers of such a crushing liability more particularly, see Trebilcock 1987, at 958-960 (arguing that the attempt to pursue deterrence objectives and compensation objectives — traditionally in social insurance — through this tort system leads to a destabilization of the tort system and to a lacking availability and affordability of liability insurance).

93 Shavell 1984, at 372-374.

94 Schäfer 2000.

95 See Kaplow 1986 and Faure and Fenn 1999.

96 Schäfer 2000.

97 See on environmental Public Interest Litigation in India Faure and Raja 2010.

Before addressing the rationale for (in some particular cases) widening access to justice (via environmental Public Interest Litigation) first we need to address the economic justification for the traditional legal standing requirement. The basic rationale is that parties should only be able to sue when they have a direct interest at stake for damages they have personally suffered.[98] Traditionally, *locus standi* is an admissibility condition that acts as a gatekeeper for the filing of cases.[99] A central issue of the standing doctrine is that a plaintiff should indicate an injury and, moreover, which substantive rights were violated.

The traditional economic argument against expanding standing contents that it would lead to many inefficient procedures, resulting in an inefficient use of the court system and potentially to overdeterrence. A distinction should in that respect, however, be made between *locus standi* in private law and in public law. A strict *locus standi* in private law may make sense from an economic perspective in order not to overburden courts and not to create overdeterrence of operators. However, the argument may be different in public law, such as in judicial review cases and in common law public nuisance cases.[100] There are various approaches to understanding why the standing requirement may not always work in the interest of justice (and hence why enlarged standing and access to justice should be considered).

There is equally a literature justifying collective redress since in environmental cases damage may often have a wide-spread nature as a result of which the private incentive to bring litigation may be too limited.[101]

That is precisely an economic justification, not only for a widened access to justice, but also for either collective redress mechanisms (in case of widespread losses) or environmental Public Interest Litigation. In that sense environmental PIL (e.g. granting standing to environmental NGOs can, from an economic perspective, be considered as an essential instrument to deal with cases of environmental harm where the losses to individual victims would be relatively low as a result of which private incentives to litigate (e.g. suing for injunctive relief) may be limited.

The first approach to standing and access to justice hence follows from a pure rational choice (economic) perspective: apart from the problem of "rational disinterest", discussed earlier, the verdict in a case with a large number of stakeholders takes on the nature of a public good, which would not be provided for, or risk, at best, undersupplied by a rational victim.[102] In that case, *locus standi* can become an impediment to the redress process. A similar failure could occur where the affected population has no judicial access.

98 Divan and Rosencranz 2001, at 137.
99 Van Aaken 2005.
100 Stein 1979.
101 See on collective redress inter alia Keske, Renda and Van den Bergh 2010.
102 Van Aaken 2005, at 50.

A second approach can be presented from a justice standpoint. Since, judicial review, broadly defined, is the power of a court to review the actions of public sector bodies in terms of their legality or constitutionality, it becomes imperative to have a mechanism that accomplishes this.[103] A broadened access to justice (and more particularly environmental PIL) can be seen as one way of bringing the courts the claims of unlawful exercise of power or violation of rights by a government entity.

Summarising, it is important to broaden access to justice (either via more generous standing requirements or by allowing collective redress) as those are also tools to internalise environmental externalities and therefore instruments to promote sustainable development.

6.9 CSR, Private and Self-Regulation

There is one other way in which private actors can play an important role in promoting sustainable development, which we should briefly touch upon, even though it is not directly related to private law. It refers to the increasingly popular phenomenon of corporate social responsibility (CSR). It has especially been John Elkington who has posited the so-called triple bottom-line of people, profit and planet (PPP), which should each get equal attention and be balanced within corporate policy.[104]

CSR is typically defined as going beyond compliance on a voluntary basis.[105] In that sense CSR could be considered as a form of self-regulation whereby stakeholders, more particularly corporations, would spontaneously take engagements to go beyond compliance with government imposed environmental standards. In some cases other parties may stimulate corporations to engage in this CSR. Of course many environmental NGOs, in a consultation with corporations, will try to convince corporations to move to CSR. In other cases it is more particularly partners in the supply chain that impose high(er) environmental standards upon their business partners. The latter is sometimes referred to as supply chain control or private environmental governance.[106] The latter can equally be important in the context of developing countries: often large retail chains downstream in the supply chain (often situated in Europe and in the US) may impose private environmental (for example food safety) standards on providers upstream in the supply chain, sometimes located in the South. Via this supply chain control private parties (buyers) will impose high standards

103 See broadly the contributions in Seerden 2007 and in Seerden, Heldeweg and Deketelaere 2002.
104 Elkington 1998.
105 Kitzmueller and Shimshack 2012, at 53.
106 Van den Bergh 2013, at 129-199.

upon suppliers in order to be able to correspond to demands of consumer markets in Europe.[107]

Again, the contracting via the supply chain control can to a large extent fit into the private contracting and thus be considered as an application of the Coase theorem.[108] Self-regulation more generally has in some cases been advanced in law and economics literature as an effective tool to regulate externalities at lower costs than via government regulation. Arguments presented in law and economics literature in favour of self-regulation relate *inter alia* to the higher expertise of the stakeholders involved (thus leading to lower information costs), lower organisational and administrative costs and to the fact that business actors may have a larger willingness to apply norms and standards that they would have created themselves.[109] Self-regulation could in that sense lead to a "crowding in" of norms.[110] The main advantage of self-regulation from that perspective would be that it could lead to a higher intrinsic motivation of the stakeholders to comply, given that they were involved in the creation of the norms and standards. Those could hence all be valuable arguments in favour of CSR, even as a cost effective alternative for governmental (command and control) regulation.

However, the law and economics literature on self-regulation has equally indicated that there are many problems with self-regulation as well. One problem is that there may be free-riding of particular members. Hence, some may join the body that would be responsible for self-regulation, thus benefiting from reputational gains, but have no incentives to comply with the agreed standards. Second, compliance with self-regulation is also based on voluntarism. Enforcement may hence be weak, which can be particularly risky since some emissions can cause substantial environmental harm. Indeed, there are a few typical features of environmental pollution, which make it not necessarily a good candidate for self-regulation (only). In this respect we more particularly refer to the latency problems inherent in environmental pollution.[111] This indicates that environmental damage often has a so-called long-tail character. Moreover, environmental damage may be widespread and problems of causal uncertainty may occur. Environmental pollution can also have a transboundary character. Finally, environmental issues often involve the public interest, but self-regulation may not always work in the public interest. Self-regulation is no stranger to rent-seeking and lobbying.[112] Self-regulators may by these means become

107 For example, the flower industry of Colombia, as one of the major exporters of cut flowers to Europe, had created the Florverde program to encourage members to adopt a set of environmental friendly standards to satisfy the high standards of the European Union. See Lyon and Maxwell 2008, at 244.

108 See Coase 1960.

109 See for example Cheffins 1997, Chapter 8; Arora et al. (1995), at 305.

110 See Frey 1997, at 56-57 and 64; Frey 1999, at 395-408; Boussalis, Feldman and Smith 2018, at 281-283.

111 Indicating a potential long time laps between the moment of the emission and the moment that the damage may occur.

112 Ogus 2000, at 591-592.

powerful if the lobbying succeeds. In that case, self-regulators are able to water down private standards on sustainability and create entry barriers against more efficient standards.[113] It could also be the case that self-regulation, particularly that via voluntary environmental agreements, will be used by industries as a shield from regulations. A relief from regulation or a lower rate of inspections can sometimes be the reasons for industry's participation, as has been the case with the USEPA's Project XL[114] and the 33/50 program.[115] A voluntary environmental agreement is likely to exclude other possibly more effective regulations to come, if the government promises not to induce new mandates in return for voluntary compliance by the industry. All those typical features of environmental pollution may make it substantially more difficult to generally control, especially emissions, via self-regulation. That implies that in general government intervention, either via command and control or market-based instruments, may still be the primary tool needed to control environmental externalities. There are, however, some successful stories with respect to private environmental governance as well as with environmental branding. For example, consumers do reward traders that engage in CSR with an "environmental premium" or cases where buyers are able (via supply chain control) to enforce private safety standards upon suppliers. The empirical evidence of the marketing literature also supports this claim that an increasing number of consumers express their willingness to pay a premium for environmentally friendly and socially responsible products.[116] According to a consumer survey of The Body Shop, their natural and fair trade products are becoming a purchasing trend among consumers. Also, it is assumed that 83% of their regular customers tend to choose products or services from retailers that take social and environmental issues seriously, and meanwhile 64% of them are willing to pay a premium for an ethical product.[117] Moreover, private supply chain standards are becoming a popular business strategy for more and more companies (buyers) who would like to impose private environmental standards on their suppliers. For example, in order to achieve the target of a safe and

113 Id. A real-world case could be the Leadership in Energy and Environmental Design (LEED) created by the US Green Building Council (USGBC). The USGBC and its LEED system, were established to pursue building sustainability and reduce the environmental impacts of buildings. When the USGBC was still young, they fought against some trade associations from watering down the LEED standards. Over a long term, the LEED has become one of the most-commonly used GB rating systems around the world, and accordingly, the USGBC gained control over GB certification as well as the licensing of GB professionals. However, the LEED has in some cases been accused of manipulating and availing easy points for building stakeholders in GB certification. See USA Today, 'In U.S Building Industry: Is it Too Easy to be Green?', published on October 24, 2012, full text available at: www.usatoday.com/story/news/nation/2012/10/24/green-building-leed-certification/1650517/, last visited August 2017.

114 See the USEPA 2016, 'Project XL-New England Universities Laboratories', available at: https://archive.epa.gov/projectxl/web/html/index-66.html; Innes and Sam 2008, at 292-293.

115 See Innes and Sam 2008.

116 See Kitzmueller and Shimshack 2012, at 52.

117 The data is from *The Body Shop International Values Report 2011*. An English version of this report can be found at: www.thebodyshop.com/content/pdf/global-values_report.pdf.

responsible supply chain, Wal-Mart imposes high standards on their suppliers regarding their social and environmental conditions.[118] In respect of the environment, besides the mandatory compliance with domestic environmental law, local law and regulation, and international treaties and protocol, Wal-Mart requires its global suppliers also comply with its specific standards on waste management, air emissions management, water management, energy consumption and greenhouse gas management, land use and biodiversity, environmental management system, hazardous substances management and pollution prevention, noise pollution and nuisance.[119] Again, as the pioneer of ethical business in beauty industry, the Body Shop is always proud of their natural and ethical products. As a result, in order to manage the sourcing process of natural ingredients, the Body Shop requires the new suppliers to comply with their ethical, social and quality criteria, besides the compliance with legal and financial checks.[120] At some point self-regulation may also make the first move in pursuing better environmental performance. A case in point could be the US Green Building Council (USGBC), to whom green building owed its survival in early times. The idea of green building (GB) is to reduce the environmental impacts of buildings. The USGBC as a professional association created one of the most commonly-used GB standards around the world, namely the Leadership in Energy and Environmental Design (LEED). With the LEED system, the USGBC not only increases the stock of GB knowledge, but also helps to showcase the benefits of GB and speed up the GB movement by the competition and comparison the LEED causes on the real estate market.[121] Over time, the US governments began to make their buildings LEED-certified, and the LEED has been incorporated into some state and local regulations for sustainable buildings.

However, as was indicated in the cases above, in many of those cases it relates to examples where traders already comply with basic mandatory environmental regulation and the CSR (in all of its different forms and shapes) again mainly is an instrument to go beyond compliance with mandatory standards, not a substitute for those standards.

It goes beyond the scope of this chapter to analyse the strengths and weaknesses of CSR and other forms of private regulation.[122]

---

118 Wal-Mart publishes and regularly updates *Standards for Suppliers*, which are utilized to evaluate employment practices and environmental compliance in facilities producing merchandises for sale by Wal-Mart. The latest version was adopted in April, 2014 and can be found at: http://corporate.walmart.com/global-responsibility/ethical-sourcing/standards-for-suppliers

119 See Wal-Mart' *Standards for Suppliers*. Mengxing, please provide precise website or source where this can be found.

120 See The Body Shop International Values Report 2011. An English version of this report can be accessed at: www.thebody.com/content/pdf/global-values_report.pdf.

121 See Building Design + Construction, A report on the Green Building Movement, BD+C White Paper on Sustainability, 23 November, 2003, at 8. Full text available at: https://archive.epa.gov/greenbuilding/web/pdf/bdcwhitepaperr2.pdf.

122 For a further analysis see *inter alia* Lu and Faure 2016 and Scheltema 2014.

6.10 Concluding Remarks

The goal of environmental law is undoubtedly to promote sustainability. Also environmental liability and, more generally, private law arrangements in the area of environmental law undoubtedly aim at promoting sustainable development as well. We used an economic approach to show how environmental law generally, but more particularly environmental liability and other rules of private law contribute to sustainable development. We started by pointing at the importance of the so-called Environmental Kuznets Curve literature, which has indicated a positive relationship between economic growth and environmental quality, but only on the condition that adequate legal rules and regulations are put in place (in other words institutions) to promote sustainable development. The work of Michael Porter has, moreover, indicated that stringent environmental law should not necessarily retard economic growth (or firm profits), but can to the contrary promote innovation and economic growth (at the country level) or profits (at the firm level). We indicated that a variety of instruments and institutions could be employed to promote sustainable development. Even though instruments of public law (like regulation or taxation) may play a primary role in that respect, there is still an important role to play for environmental liability, more particularly as an instrument to back up the weaknesses inherent in regulation. However, we equally indicated that for environmental liability to play this supplementary role it is important that in the specific design of environmental liability rules, particular conditions are met. For example a strict liability rule would be preferred to a negligence rule, but it should be accompanied with solvency guarantees. Liability should in principle also be unlimited and should be attributed to all actors who can influence the risk.

An important feature of environmental harm is that it often is widespread. As a result an individual victim to bring a liability suit may not be available. In that case the market failure caused by the negative environmental externality will not be externalised. It is for that reason important to enlarge the possibilities of standing in case of environmental harm in order for the polluter still to be exposed to liability. This could for example take the form of allowing many suits to be brought together in a collective action or to allow for example a non-governmental organisation to bring public interest litigation on behalf of the environment. Those developments are of crucial importance to expose polluters to the environmental externalities they have caused.

In the final section of this chapter we pointed at the important role to be played by private actors in various ways. In some cases the industry takes initiative to regulate via so-called self-regulation. Even though this may be beneficial given the information advantage with industry, there is always a danger that the (self-)regulation will be strongly in the interest of the parties who draft it. Private regulation (for example eco-labelling or certification systems) increasingly plays a role in environmental law and can be an important complement in addition to government regulation. The same is true for actions taken by corporations under the heading of corporate social responsibility. Even though CSR will and can never replace public regulation, actions taken by corporations under the heading of CSR can play an important role to supplement public regulation as CSR allows corporations to go beyond public regulation and enjoy a reputational (price) premium as a result.

Summarising, a variety of interventions by private law and private parties do and can play an important role in the promotion of sustainable development. Even though the primary instrument in this respect will often still be of a public nature, it is important to stress that public regulation often has important limits. For that reason rules of private law will play a crucial role in supplementing an effective environmental legal framework, promoting sustainable development.

List of References

Ambec, S., Cohen, M., Elgie, S. & Lanoie, P., 'The Porter Hypothesis at 20: Can Environmental Regulation Enhance Innovation and Comparativeness', *Review of Environmental Economics and Policy*, 2013, Vol. 7(1), p. 2-22.

Arora *et al.*, 'Towards a Theoretical Model of Voluntary Overcompliance', *Journal of Economic Behavior & Orgainization*, 1995, Vol. 28, p. 289-309.

Arrow, K. *et al.*, 'Economic Growth, Carrying Capacity and the Environment', *Ecological Economics*, 1995, p. 91-95 (reprint from *Science*, Vol. 268, p. 520-521).

Artigot i Golobardes, M. & Gómez Pomar, F., 'Contributory and Comparative Negligence in the Law and Economics Literature', in M. Faure (ed.), *Tort Law and Economics*, Cheltenham, Edward Elgar, 2009, p. 46-79.

Ayres, I. & Braithwaite, J., *Responsive Regulation: Transcending the Deregulation Debate*, Oxford University Press, 1992.

Ayres, I., Raseman, S., & Shih, A., 'Evidence from Two Large Field Experiments that Peer Comparison Feedback Can Reduce Residential Energy Usage', *Journal of Law, Economics & Organization*, 2013, Vol. 29, p. 992-1022.

Beckerman, W., 'Economic Growth and the Environment: Whose Growth? Whose Environment?', *World Development*, 1992, p. 481-496.

Bergkamp, L., 'The Proper Scope of Joint and Several Liability', *Tijdschrift voor Milieuaansprakelijk-heid*, 2000, Vol. 14, p. 153-156.

Bocken, H., 'Alternatives to Liability and Liability Insurance for the Compensation of Pollution Damages', *Tijdschrift voor Milieuaansprakelijkheid*, 1987, p. 83-87 and *Tijdschrift voor Milieuaansprakelijkheid*, 1988, p. 3-10.

Bruggeman, V., *Compensating Catastrophe Victims: A Comparative Law and Economics Approach*, Alphen aan den Rijn, Kluwer Law International, 2010.

Boussalis, C., Feldman, Y. & Smith, H. E., 'Experimental analysis of the effect of standards on compliance and performance', *Regulation & Governance*, 2018, Vol. 12, p. 277-298.

Cheffins, B.R., *Company Law: Theory, Structure and Operation*, Oxford, Clarendon Press, 1997.

Coase, R.A., 'The Problem of Social Cost', *Journal of Law and Economics*, 1960, p. 1-44.

Diamond, P.A., 'Single Activity Accidents', *Journal of Legal Studies*, 1974, Vol. 3, p. 107-111.

Divan, S. & Rosencranz, A., *Environmental Law and Policy in India: Cases, Materials and Statutes*, 2nd edition, New Delhi India, Oxford University Press, 2001.

Elkington, J., *Cannibals with Forks: The Trippe Bottom-line of Sustainability*, New Society, Gabriola Island, 1998.

Esty, D.C. & Porter, M.E., 'National Environmental Performance: An Empirical Analysis of Policy Results and Determinants', *Environment and Development Economics*, 2005, p. 391-434.

Faure, M.G., 'Economic Models of Compensation for Damage Caused by Nuclear Accidents: Some Lessons for the Revision of the Paris and Vienna Conventions', *European Journal of Law and Economics*, 1995, p. 21-43.

Faure, M.G., 'Economic Aspects of Environmental Liability: An Introduction', *European Review of Private Law*, 1996, Vol. 4(2), p. 85-110.

Faure, M.G., 'Financial Compensation for Victims of Catastrophes: A Law and Economics Perspective', *Law & Policy*, 2007, Vol. 29(3), p. 339-367.

Faure, M.G., 'Environmental Liability', in M. Faure (ed.), *Tort Law and Economics*, Vol. 1, Cheltenham, Edward Elgar, 2009, p. 247-286.

Faure, M., 'Does Environmental Law Matter?', in M. Faure & J. Smits (eds.), *Does Law Matter? On Law and Economic Growth*, Antwerp, Intersentia, 2011, p. 385-416.

Faure, M. & Fenn, P., 'Retro-active Liability and the Insurability of Long-tail Risks', *International Review of Law and Economics*, 1999, Vol. 19, p. 487-498.

Faure, M. & Grimeaud, D., 'Financial Assurance Issues of Environmental Liability', in M. Faure (ed.), *Deterrence, Insurability and Compensation in Environmental Liability: Future Developments in the European Union*, Vienna, Springer, 2003, p. 7-255.

Faure, M. & Hartlief, T., *Insurance and Expanding Systemic Risks*, Paris, OECD, 2003.

Faure, M. & Johnston, J.S., 'The Law and Economics of Environmental Federalism: Europe and the United States Compared', *Virginia Environmental Law Journal*, 2009, p. 205-274.

Faure, M. & Raja, A.V., 'Effectiveness of Environmental Public Interest Litigation in India: Determining the Key Variables', *Fordham Environmental Law Review*, 2010, Vol. 21(2), p. 239-294.

Faure, M. & Ubachs, S., 'Comparative Benefits and Optimal Use of Environmental Taxes', in J. Milne, K. Deketelaere, L. Kreiser & H. Ashiabor (eds.), *Critical Issues in Environmental Taxation. Vol. I: International and Comparative Perspectives*, Richmond, Richmond Law and Tax, 2003, p. 29-49.

Faure, M., 'The Complementary Roles of Liability, Regulation, and Insurance in Safety management: Theory and Practice', *Journal of Risk Research*, 2014, Vol. 6, p. 689-707.

Frey, B.S., *Not Just for the Money. An Economic Theory of Personal Motivation*, Cheltenham, Edward Elgar, 1997.

Frey, B.S., 'Morality and Rationality in Environmental Policy', *Journal of Consumer Policy*, 1999, Vol. 22, p. 395-408.

Grossman, G.M. & Krueger, A.B., 'Environmental Impacts of a North-American Free Trade Agreement', in P.M. Garber (ed.), *The US, Mexico Free Trade Agreement*, Cambridge: MIT Press, 1993, p. 13-56.

Grossman, G.M. & Krueger, A.B., 'Economic Growth and the Environment', *Quarterly Journal of Economics*, 1995, p. 353-377.

Glicksman, R.L. & Earnhart D., 'The Comparative Effectiveness of Government Interventions on Environmental Performance in the Chemical Industry', *Stanford Environmental Law Review*, 2007, Vol. 26, p. 317-368.

Hahn, R.W. & Hester. G.L., 'Where Did All The Markets Go? An Analysis of EPA's Emissions Trading Programme', *Yale Journal on Regulation*, 1989, Vol. 6, p. 109-153.

Innes, R. & Sam, A. G., 'Voluntary Pollution Reductions and the Enforcement of Environmental Law: An Empirical Study of the 33/50 Program', *The Journal of Law and Economics*, 2008, Vol. 51, p. 271-296.

Jaffe, A.B. *et al.*, 'Environmental Regulation and the Competitiveness of US Manufacturing: What Does the Evidence Tell Us?', *Journal of Economic literature*, 1995, Vol. 33(1), p. 132-163.

Kaplow, L., 'An Economic Analysis of Legal Transitions', *Harvard Law Review*, 1986, Vol. 99, p. 509-617.

Keske, S., Renda, A. & Van den Bergh, R., 'Financing and Group Litigation', in M. Tuil & L. Visscher (eds.), *New Trends in Financing Civil Litigation in Europe. A Legal, Empirical and Economic Analysis,* Cheltenham, UK and Northampton, MA, USA, Edward Elgar, 2010, p. 33-56.

Kitzmueller, M. & Shimshack, J., 'Economic Perspectives on Corporate Social Responsibility', *Journal of Economic Literature,* 2012, Vol. 50(1), p. 51-84.

Kornhauser, L.A. & Revesz, R., 'Sharing Damages Among Multiple Tortfeasors', *Yale Law Journal*, 1989, Vol. 98(5), p. 831-884.

Kornhauser, L.A. & Revesz, R., 'Apportioning Damages among Potentially Insolvent Actors', *Journal of Legal Studies,* 1990, Vol. 19, p. 617-651.

Kunreuther, H. & Freeman, P., 'Insurability, Environmental Risks and the Law', in A. Heyes (ed.), *The Law and Economics of the Environment*, Cheltenham UK, Edward Elgar Publishing, 2001, p. 304-305.

Kuznets, S., 'Economic Growth and Income Inequality', *American Economic Review*, 1955, p. 1-28.

Landes, W. & Posner, R., 'The Positive Economic Theory of Tort Law', *Georgia Law Review*, 1981, Vol. 15, p. 851-924.

Landes, W. & Posner, R., 'Tort Law as a Regulatory Regime for Catastrophic Personal Injuries', *Journal of Legal Studies*, 1984, Vol. 13, p. 417-434.

Lu, M. & Faure, M., 'The Regulation of Corporate Environmental Responsibility', in N. Philipsen *et al.* (eds.), *Market Integration: The EU Experience and Implications for Regulatory Reform in China*, China EU Law Series, Berlin/Heidelberg, Springer, 2016, p. 239-265.

Lyon, T.P. & Maxwell, J.W., 'Corporate Social Responsibility and the Environment: A Theoretical Perspective', *Revi. Environ. Econ. Policy*, 2008, Vol. 2(2), p. 240-260.

Mackaay, E., *Economics of Information and the Law*, Boston, Kluwer Nijhoff Publishing, 1982.

Oates, W.E. & Baumol, W.J., 'The Instruments for Environmental Policy', in W.E. Oates (ed.), *The Economics of Environmental Regulation*, Cheltenham, Edward Elgar, 1996, p. 101-103.

Ogus, A., 'Self-regulation', in B. Bouckaert & G. De Geest (eds.), *Encyclopedia of Law and Economics*, Cheltenham, Edward Elgar, 2000, Vol. IX, p. 587-597.

Polinsky, A.M., *Introduction to Law and Economics*, Boston, Little, Brown & Co., 1983.

Porter, M., 'America's Green Strategy', *Scientific American*, 1991, Vol. 264(4), p. 168-170.

Porter, M.E. & Van der Linde, C., 'Towards a New Conception of the Environment – Competitiveness, Relationship', *The Journal of Economic Perspectives*, 1995, Vol. 9(4), p. 97-118.

Radetzki, M. & Radetzki, M., 'Private Arrangements to Cover Large-Scale Liabilities Caused by Nuclear and Other Industrial Catastrophes', *Geneva Papers on Risk & Insurance*, 2000, Vol. 25, p. 180-195.

Rogers, W.V.H., 'Comparative Report on Multiple Tortfeasors', in W.V.H. Rogers (ed.), *Unification of Tort Law: Multiple Tortfeasors*, Vienna, Springer, 2004, p. 271-279.

Rosen, H.S., *Public Finance*, Chicago, Irwin, 1999.

Requate, T. & Unold, W., 'Environmental Policy Incentives to Adopt Advanced Abatement Technology: Will the Time Ranking Please Stand Up?', *European Economic Review*, 2003, Vol. 47, p. 125-146.

Schäfer, H.B., 'The Bundling of Similar Interest in Litigation. The Incentives for Class Action and Legal Actions taken by Associations', *European Journal of Law and Economics*, 2000, Vol. 3, p. 183-213.

Schäfer, H.-B. & Müller-Langer, F., 'Strict Liability Versus Negligence', in M. Faure (ed.), *Tort Law and Economics*, Cheltenham, Edward Elgar, 2009, p. 3-45.

Scheltema, M., 'An Assessment of the Effectiveness of International Private Regulation in the Corporate Social Arena: A Legal Perspective', *Maastricht Journal of European and Comparative Law*, 2014, p. 383-405.

Schwartz, A. & Wilde, L., 'Intervening in Markets on the Basis of Imperfect Information: A Legal and Economic Analysis', *University of Pennsylvania Law Review*, 1979, p. 630-682.

Seerden, R.J.G.H. (ed.), *Administrative Law of the European Union, its Member States and the United States. A Comparative Analysis*, Ius Commune Europaeum 68, Antwerp, Intersentia, 2007, p. 155-219.

Seerden, R.J.G.H., Heldeweg, M.A. & Deketelaere, K. (eds.), *Public Environmental Law in the European Union and the United States. A Comparative Analysis*, The Hague/London/Boston, Kluwer Law International, 2002.

Shavell, S., 'Strict Liability versus Negligence', *Journal of Legal Studies*, 1980, Vol. 9(1), p. 1-25.

Shavell, S., 'Liability for Harm versus Regulation of Safety', *Journal of Legal Studies*, 1984a, p. 357-374.

Shavell, S., 'A Model of the Optimal Use of Liability and Safety Regulation', *Rand Journal of Economics*, 1984b, p. 271-280.

Shavell, S., 'Criminal Law and the Optimal Use of Non-Monetary Sanctions as a Deterrent', *Columbia Law Review*, 1985, p. 1232-1262.

Shavell, S., 'The Judgement Proof Problem', *International Review of Law and Economics*, 1986, Vol. 6, p. 43-58.

Shavell, S., *Economic Analysis of Accident Law*, Cambridge MA, Harvard University Press, 1987.

Shavell, S., 'The Corrective Tax versus Liability as Solutions to the Problem of Harmful Externalities', *The Journal of Law and Economics*, 2011, Vol. 54, p. 249-266.

Shavell, S., 'A Fundamental Enforcement Cost Advantage of the Negligence Rule over Regulation', *Journal of Legal Studies*, 2013, Vol. 42, p. 275-302.

Stein, L.A. (ed.), *Locus Standi*, Sydney, Law Book Co, 1979.

Stewart, R.B., 'Instrument Choice', in D. Bodanksy, J. Brunnée & E. Hey (eds.), *The Oxford Handbook of International Environmental Law*, Oxford, Oxford University Press, 2007, p. 147-181.

Stigler, G., 'The Economics of Information', *Journal of Political Economics*, 1961, p. 213-225.

Strand, J., *Environmental Kuznets Curves: Empirical Relationships between Environmental Quality and Economic Development*, March 2002, Memorandum No. 04/2002, Department of Economics, University of Oslo, www.oekonomi.uio.no/memo.

Simcoe, T. & Toffel, M.W, 'Government Green Procurement Spillovers: Evidence from Municipal Building Policies in California', Journal of Environmental Economics and Management, 2014, Vol. 68, p. 411-434.

Tietenberg, T., 'Indivisible Toxic Torts: The Economics of Joint and Several Liability', *Land Eco*nomics, 1989, Vol. 65(4), p. 305-319.

Tietenberg, T., *Environmental and National Resource Economics*, Reading, Addison-Wesley, 2000.

Trebilcock, M.J., 'The Social Insurance-Deterrence Dilemma of a Modern North-American Tort Law: A Canadian Perspective on the Liability Insurance Crisis', *San Diego Law Review*, 1987, Vol. 24, p. 929-960.

Van Aaken, A., 'Making International Human Rights Protection more Effective: a Rational Choice Approach to the Effectiveness of Use Standi Provisions', Max-Planck Institute for Research on Collective Goods, Preprint No. 2005-16, 2005.

Van den Bergh, R., 'Le droit civil face à l'analyse économique du droit', *Revue Internationale de Droit Économique*, 1988, p. 229-254.

Van den Bergh, M., 'Private Environmental Governance', *Cornell Law Review*, 2013, Vol. 99, p. 129-199.

Viscusi, W.K., 'Regulation of Health, Safety, and Environmental Risks', in A.M. Polinsky & S. Shavell (eds.), *Handbook of Law and Economics*, Amsterdam, Elsevier, 2007, Vol. 1, p. 591-645.

Wiener, J., 'Global Environmental Regulation: Instrument Choice in Legal Context', *The Yale Law Journal*, 1999, Vol. 108, p. 677-800.

7 Tort Law and Greenhouse Gas Emission Reductions

Gijs van Dijck[*]

7.1 Introduction

A 2017 UN report mentions cases filed in 24 countries (25 if one counts the European Union), with "654 cases filed in the U.S. and over 230 cases filed in all other countries combined" and "governments (...) almost always the defendants", while observing five trends: "holding governments to their legislative and policy commitments; linking the impacts of resource extraction to climate change and resilience; establishing that particular emissions are the proximate cause of particular adverse climate change impacts; establishing liability for failures (or efforts) to adapt to climate change; and applying the public trust doctrine to climate change".[1] One of the legal grounds is liability or negligence for failure to adapt and implement climate change regulation.[2]

Research conducted at the intersection of tort law and environmental law has argued that tort law is not designed to protect environmental interests. Dewees concluded that tort law has a limited role in the reduction of pollution emissions in the US and Canada since 1970, arguing that tort doctrines' focus on the protection of private property (rather than on public lands and ecosystems) makes it unlikely to obtain a successful tort claim.[3] The same applies to establishing that pollution harmed one's property or health, given the lack of scientific evidence that convincingly shows effects of pollution on individuals' current or future well-being.[4] Latham et al., in turn, have argued that (and why) tort law is not equipped to address environmental harm and should not be reshaped to do so.[5]

---

* The author thanks Marjan Peeters for her comments on a draft version.

1 United Nations, 'The Status of Climate Change Litigation', 10-14, available at http://wedocs.unep.org/bitstream/handle/20.500.11822/20767/climate-change-litigation.pdf?sequence=1&isAllowed=y (last accessed 11 July 2019).

2 United Nations, 'The Status of Climate Change Litigation', 14ff, available at http://wedocs.unep.org/bitstream/handle/20.500.11822/20767/climate-change-litigation.pdf?sequence=1&isAllowed=y (last accessed 11 July 2019).

3 Donald N. Dewees, 'The Role of Tort Law in Controlling Environmental Pollution' 18 Canadian Public Policy / Analyse de Politiques 425.

4 *Ibid.*

5 Mark Latham, Victor E. Schwartz and Christopher E. Appel, 'The Intersection of Tort and Environmental Law: Where the Twains Should Meet and Depart' 80 Fordham L Rev 737.

In this contribution, the claim that tort law is not designed to deal with environmental matters is further explored. Since tort law encompasses a variety of concepts and elements, which can differ depending on the applicable jurisdiction, this contribution focuses on the requirements of a loss and causality, and compares two types of claims in this respect: an injunction (to stop the wrong or injustice) and a damages claim. It will be concluded that the loss and causality requirement may not be an impediment for a successful tort claim.

The Urgenda case will be used to illustrate the differences between the two types of claims. In Urgenda, a Dutch court of first instance decided to hold the State of the Netherlands liable for not meeting emission targets. Since the Urgenda case was decided under Dutch law, this contribution illustrates the two types of claims with Dutch law.

This contribution is structured as follows. After an explanation of the Urgenda case and the reactions to it (*Section 2*), a damages claim (*Section 3*) will be compared to an injunction (*Section 4*). The contribution concludes that tort law is more suitable for deciding environmental matters than some have suggested (*Section 5*).

7.2 The Urgenda Case[6]

The Urgenda Foundation, aimed at contributing to a more sustainable environment[7] and acting on its own behalf as well as on behalf of 886 individuals who authorised Urgenda to initiate legal proceedings, essentially claimed that the state of the Netherlands (hereafter: the State) had a legal obligation towards Urgenda to limit greenhouse gas emissions. Among other things,[8] Urgenda claimed that the joint volume of the annual greenhouse gas emissions in the Netherlands was unlawful, that the State was liable for these gas emissions, and that the State had acted unlawfully by having failed to sufficiently reduce the annual greenhouse gas emissions in the Netherlands.[9] Additionally, it requested the court to order the State to reduce greenhouse gas emissions.

Urgenda argued that the State violated several provisions, including Article 21 of the Dutch Constitution (the obligation to keep the country habitable and to protect and

6 For a more elaborate description, see District Court the Hague 26 June 2015, ECLI:NL:RBDHA:2015:7196; Marjan Peeters, 'Case Note – Urgenda Foundation and 886 Individuals v. The State of the Netherlands: The Dilemma of More Ambitious Greenhouse Gas Reduction Action by EU Member States' 25 RECIEL 123; Marc A. Loth, 'Climate Change Liability After All: A Dutch Landmark Case' 21 Tilburg Law Review: Journal on International and Comparative Law 5, 7-30. For the appeal case, see Court of Appeal The Hague 9 October 2018, ECLI:NL:GHDHA:2018:2591.

7 Article 2 of the by-laws ("purposes and principle"), cited from Court of Appeal the Hague 27-6-2017, ECLI:NL:GHDHA:2017:1761.

8 Additional claims can be found in the decision, see District Court the Hague 26 June 2015, ECLI:NL:RBDHA:2015:7196.

9 District Court the Hague 26 June 2015, ECLI:NL:RBDHA:2015:7196.

improve the environment) in conjunction with a variety of treaties and international obligations, Article 2 ECHR (right to life), Article 8 ECHR (right to private and family life), and Article 6:162 Dutch Civil Code (tort, duty of care) in conjunction with Article 5:37 Dutch Civil Code (owner needs to prevent or reduce nuisance to others).

The court, in its 2015 decision, rejected that Article 5:37 Dutch Civil Code was violated. It also rejected the notion of a violation of the Dutch constitution, but it did state that the provisions could be relevant in the context of assessing liability based on national provisions:

> "Urgenda may not derive a legal obligation of the State towards it from these legal rules. However, this fact also does not stand in the way of the fact that stipulations in an EU treaty or directive can have an impact through the open standards of national law described above" (4.44).

A similar reasoning can be found with respect to the obligations laid down in Articles 2 and 8 ECHR:

> "Therefore, Urgenda itself cannot directly rely on Articles 2 and 8 ECHR. (...) However, both articles and their interpretation given by the ECtHR, particularly with respect to environmental right issues, can serve as a source of interpretation when detailing and implementing open private-law standards in the manner described above (...)" (4.45-4.46).

The court constructed the violation of a duty of care by finding that the only effective option to protect the environment is to reduce emissions, and that cost considerations with respect to mitigating the damage do not justify deviating from taking such measures. Because the court also found that the plaintiff suffered a loss and that the loss was causally related to the violation of the duty of care, it concluded that the State acted negligently. As a result, it ordered the State to

> "(...) limit the joint volume of Dutch annual greenhouse gas emissions, or have them limited, so that this volume will have reduced by at least 25% at the end of 2020 compared to the level of the year 1990" (5.1).

Regarding the State's discretionary power, the court concluded that this power is not unlimited, particularly in situations where there is "a high risk of dangerous climate change with severe and life-threatening consequences for man and the environment", and that the measures taken by the State insufficiently protected its citizens against environmental damage. In a section devoted specifically to the State's discretionary power, the court held:

> "4.74 (…) If, and this is the case here, there is a high risk of dangerous climate change with severe and life-threatening consequences for man and the environment, the State has the obligation to protect its citizens from it by taking appropriate and effective measures".

The court justified its decision to not see the discretion of power as an obstacle for imposing liability by arguing that mitigation measures needed to be taken, since adaptation measures would only reduce consequences of climate change (i.e. reduce the loss rather than preventing or stopping it) for current and future Dutch residents, that the costs of the measures were not disproportionally high, and that the fact that reducing Dutch emissions according to the set target would only limitedly reduce global emissions was not a proper reason for not imposing a duty of care nor was the lack of scientific uncertainty regarding the effect of the measures. The Urgenda decision was upheld in appeal,[10] whereas the decision of the Supreme Court is expected in the course of 2019.

Particularly the discretionary power reasoning caused quite some controversy in the Dutch legal community. Some scholars criticised the Court's decision and reasoning. They claimed that the court should not have gone beyond what the administrative court would have determined, which is assessing whether the State sufficiently weighed the interests of all parties involved and whether it had taken adequate and sufficient measures to reduce the gas emissions.[11] Others argued that the court's judgment is borderline political,[12] and that it should simply have refrained from political questions involving environmental issues.[13] Moreover, it has been claimed that the decision might hamper EU negotiation power regarding the conclusion of climate treaties, as ordering the State of the Netherlands to reduce its greenhouse gas emissions for that same year with at least 25 per cent whereas 20 per cent (by the year 2020) is the norm[14] might signal a lack of unity that, consequently, frustrate the EU capacity to act united.[15] It has been argued that a preliminary reference procedure would therefore have been preferred.[16]

The decision also received support. Considering that the court was confronted with rules and principles governed by public law on the one hand, and a tort claim on the other hand, the decision was seen as an attempt to reconcile the two domains.[17] The question

10 Court of Appeal The Hague 9 October 2018, ECLI:NL:GHDHA:2018:2591.

11 R. Schutgens, 'Urgenda en de trias: Enkele staatsrechtelijke kanttekeningen bij het geruchtmakend klimaatvonnis van de Haagse rechter' NJB 2270.

12 S.M.N. Fikkers, 'Urgenda, de zorgplicht en toekomstige generaties' NJB 2289.

13 L. Bergkamp, 'Het Haagse klimaatvonnis: Rechterlijke onbevoegdheid en de negatie van het causaliteitsvereiste' NJB 2278.

14 Peeters, 124.

15 *Ibid.*, 126-127.

16 *Ibid.*, 125.

17 Rob van Gestel and Marc Loth, 'Urgenda: roekeloze rechtspraak of rechtsvinding 3.0?' NJB 2598.

whether the court made a political question was also challenged, since the decision still left discretion to the State how to achieve the emission targets.[18] According to the proponents of the decision, the court essentially held that the State should comply with the targets that states had agreed on to meet.[19] They considered the decisions as an attempt to find an institutional balance between public law, private law, and the various legislative bodies active in those domains at the domestic and European level.[20] Since the separation of powers theory does not provide directions or instructions on how to achieve such a balance, criticism on the decision from a separation of powers perspective is not straightforward.[21]

7.3 Damages Claim

One type of redress is to claim damages. Another possibility is to seek a declaratory judgment containing that certain behaviour (or the lack thereof) is tortious. Urgenda opted for a declaratory judgment at the court of first instance. It requested the court to rule that:

> (3.1) "*principally*: the State acts unlawfully if it fails to reduce or have reduced the annual greenhouse gas emissions in the Netherlands by 40%, in any case at least 25%, compared to 1990, by the end of 2020;
> *alternatively*: the State acts unlawfully if it fails to reduce or have reduced the annual greenhouse gas emissions in the Netherlands by at least 40% compared to 1990, by the end of 2030".

Under Dutch law, a declaratory judgment for negligence does not require an order involving damages by any party. Consequently, the amount of damages does not need to be established for obtaining a declaratory judgment. However, proving negligence does require the loss criterion to be met.

A loss is commonly determined by comparing the situation the victim is in with the situation it would have been in had the injustice not taken place (*Differenzhypothese* or *difference theory*).[22] For example, article 10:101 of the Principles of European Tort Law (PETL) states that:

---

18 *Ibid.*, 2603.

19 *Ibid.*, 2603.

20 *Ibid.*, 2599, 2601.

21 *Ibid.*, 2601.

22 B. Winiger and others, Digest of European Tort Law: Essential Cases on Damage, vol 2 (Bénédict Winiger and Hakan Andersson eds, De Gruyter 2011) 18 (Germany), 22 (Switzerland), 23 (Greece), 26 (Belgium), 30 (Italy), 33 (Spain), 35-36 (Portugal), 46 (Finland), 52 (Lithuania). For the Netherlands, see for example Supreme Court 11 January 2013, ECLI:NL:HR:2013:BX9830, *NJ* 2013, 48. The loss criterion is related to

> 'Damages are a money payment to compensate the victim, that is to say, to restore him, so far as money can, to the position he would have been in if the wrong complained of had not been committed'.

The comparison between the situation with and without the injustice follows from the theory of corrective justice. Corrective justice is generally understood as the repair of an injustice inflicted by one person on another person.[23] The concept essentially entails that the law needs to restore an injustice by means of rectification or by re-establishing the initial equality between the doer and sufferer of an injustice.[24] Corrective justice requires an injustice, a connection between the remedy and the injustice as well as a relation between the doer and the sufferer of the injustice.[25]

According to Weinrib, an injustice occurs when one person deprives another person of what lawfully belongs to them.[26]

As a result, the goal of corrective justice is to restore the original situation by correcting the gain and the corresponding loss. It aims to do so by correcting the injustice, and only the injustice. The notion that a remedy should repair the injustice explains why, for example, punitive damages are not reconcilable with the concept of corrective justice, as punitive damages can provide more to the plaintiff than what he or she is entitled to based on the injustice. Instead, the duties that a wrongdoer has should be the mirror image of the victim's rights.[27]

From this, three features of corrective justice can be derived. First, the application of corrective justice presupposes an injustice.[28] Second, the remedy and the wrong should be connected, that is, the remedy should address the injustice.[29] It does not suffice to merely take away the gain from one person if the loss of the sufferer remains, as the injustice then

---

the causality test, more specifically the 'but for' test. This entails that the loss, harm or injury would not have occurred if the injustice did or will not take place.

23 Aristotle, Nicomachean Ethics (translated by W. D. Ross) (350 B.C.), V, 2-5. Corrective justice is not undisputed with respect to whether it can sufficiently explain or justify what tort law is and why it differs from other fields, see for example John Goldberg and Benjamin C. Zipursky, 'Torts as Wrongs' 88 Texas Law Review 917 (arguing that it is wrongs, not losses, lie at the heart of tort law). Corrective justice is not used in this paper as a theoretical justification for a proportionality test in relation to a legal apology, not in the context of justifying why tort law differs from other fields.

24 Ernest J. Weinrib, Corrective Justice (Oxford University Press 2012), Chapter 1, section 3.

25 *Ibid.*, 16-17.

26 *Ibid.*, 16.

27 *Ibid.*, 17.

28 What constitutes an injustice (eg a wrong, a loss, a combination of the two, or neither one) is subject to debate. This topic is not further discussed, as it is not essential for the purpose of this study. For an overview, see for example Jules L. Coleman, Risks and Wrongs (Oxford University Press 1992), 306-326.

29 Weinrib, 16; Ernest J. Weinrib, 'Corrective Justice in a Nutshell' 52 The University of Toronto Law Journal 349, 350.

continues.[30] Third, the doer and sufferer should be connected in that they are both part of the same injustice.[31] They need to be the 'active and passive poles of the same injustice'.[32] Put differently, correcting an injustice should not involve correcting a loss by having this loss repaired by a person who was not involved in the specific injustice. Weinrib summarises the latter two features as the requirement 'correlatively structured', with the correlativity addressing two aspects: (1) the process of simultaneously removing the excess and the deficiency and (2) the injustice itself being correlatively structured (i.e. the doer and sufferer need to be part of the same injustice).[33]

In cases such as Urgenda, a strict application of the difference theory poses problems, as it would force the plaintiff to prove that the environmental wrong has resulted or will result in harm for the individual plaintiff. It would have required Urgenda to establish that one or more claimants suffered a loss or will suffer one, and that the loss was causally related to the injustice. According to the State, the loss requirement was not met because Urgenda's interests were not concretely at risk of being affected, and because it is not sufficient that the risk is abstract or that anyone in the world will be affected,[34] thereby essentially challenging the correlative structure between the doer and the sufferer.

It was 1951 when the Dutch Supreme Court defined the loss requirement for instances where plaintiffs sought a declaratory judgment.[35] In the 1951 case, a husband who separated from his spouse sought support from another person. That person subsequently wrote the husband's employer a letter, which, according to the husband, constituted a deliberate insult and / or injured the husband's honour or reputation. The husband then initiated legal proceedings, seeking a declaratory judgment confirming that the content of the letter was indeed unlawful, at least in part – the husband would possibly claim damages later. The court of first instance and the court of appeal both rejected the claim. The Dutch Supreme Court upheld the decision of the court of appeal, stating that plaintiffs may only split a declaratory judgment from a damages claim in case of special circumstances, and that such special circumstances could not be established in this instance.

Fast-forward to 2015, when the Dutch Supreme Court was presented a personal injury case. The plaintiff suffered injuries as a result of being hit by the wrongdoer's car and of subsequently being overrun by the car following a hostile confrontation between the plaintiff and the wrongdoer. Both the plaintiff and the wrongdoer were prosecuted and convicted, the plaintiff for threatening, the wrongdoer for battery. The plaintiff claimed a declaratory judgment entailing that the wrongdoer's insurer was liable for the victim's

30 Weinrib, Corrective Justice, 16-17.
31 *Ibid.*, 1.
32 *Ibid.*, 2; Weinrib, 'Corrective Justice in a Nutshell', 350.
33 Weinrib, Corrective Justice, 16-17.
34 District Court the Hague 26 June 2015, ECLI:NL:RBDHA:2015:7196, at 3.3.
35 Dutch Supreme Court 30 March 1951, *NJ* 1952/29.

losses. The court of first instance rejected the claim, whereas the court of appeal decided that the insurer was liable for 75 per cent of the losses suffered by the victim.

In cassation, following the 1951 case, the insurer argued that a declaratory judgment may only be claimed in case of special circumstances, that such circumstances were lacking, and that the declaratory judgment should consequently be dismissed. The Dutch Supreme Court rejected the insurer's argument, revoking the 1951 decision ("insofar he decided differently") in the 2015 decision. In 2015, the Court held that plaintiffs can rightfully seek declaratory judgments in liability cases for which damages may be claimed if a "possibility of a loss" can be established.[36]

The court in the Urgenda case, three months after the Dutch Supreme Court decision that introduced the 'possibility of a loss' criterion, applied the same criterion and found that the loss requirement was met:

> "4.89. (...) It is an established fact that climate change is occurring partly due to the Dutch greenhouse gas emissions. It is also an established fact that the negative consequences are currently being experienced in the Netherlands, such as heavy precipitation, and that adaptation measures are already being taken to make the Netherlands "climate-proof". Moreover, it is established that if the global emissions, partly caused by the Netherlands, do not decrease substantially, hazardous climate change will probably occur. In the opinion of the court, the possibility of damages for those whose interests Urgenda represents, including current and future generations of Dutch nationals, is so great and concrete that given its duty of care, the State must make an adequate contribution, greater than its current contribution, to prevent hazardous climate change".

Consequently, it alleviated the burden on Urgenda, as a loss becomes easier to establish on the side of the plaintiff (i.e. to conclude there will be a possible difference between the situation with and without meeting the emission reduction targets) if a possible difference is sufficient rather than that an actual difference has to be established.

Not only did the 'possibility of a loss' criterion alleviate the burden for establishing a loss, it also made proving 'but for' causality easier. The difference test prescribes that the situation with and without the injustice differs, whereas the 'but for' test entails that the situation with the injustice would not have occurred had the injustice not taken place. Regarding the 'but for' test, the court pointed out that emission reduction requires a global approach where the Dutch government plays an important role:

36 Dutch Supreme Court 27 March 2015, ECLI:NL:HR:2015:760. See also Dutch Supreme Court 19 March 2010, ECLI:NL:HR:2010:BK8146, where a declaratory judgment was made without reference to the 'damages' or 'loss' requirement.

> "4.79. It is an established fact that climate change is a global problem and therefore requires global accountability. It follows from the UNEP report that based on the reduction commitments made in Cancun, a gap between the desired CO2 emissions (in order to reach the climate objective) and the actual emissions (14-17 Gt CO2) will have arisen by 2030. This means that more reduction measures have to be taken on an international level. It compels all countries, including the Netherlands, to implement the reduction measures to the fullest extent as possible. The fact that the amount of the Dutch emissions is small compared to other countries does not affect the obligation to take precautionary measures in view of the State's obligation to exercise care. After all, it has been established that any anthropogenic greenhouse gas emission, no matter how minor, contributes to an increase of CO2 levels in the atmosphere and therefore to hazardous climate change. Emission reduction therefore concerns both a joint and individual responsibility of the signatories to the UN Climate Change Convention. In view of the fact that the Dutch emission reduction is determined by the State, it may not reject possible liability by stating that its contribution is minor, as also adjudicated mutatis mutandis in the Potash mines ruling of the Dutch Supreme Court (HR 23 September 1988, NJ 1989, 743)".

In the Urgenda case, the court assumed a link between failing to meet emission reduction targets and the living environment:

> "4.90. From the above considerations, particularly in 4.79, it follows that a sufficient causal link can be assumed to exist between the Dutch greenhouse gas emissions, global climate change and the effects (now and in the future) on the Dutch living climate [living environment, GD]. The fact that the current Dutch greenhouse gas emissions are limited on a global scale does not alter the fact that these emission[s] contribute to climate change. The court has taken into consideration in this respect as well that the Dutch greenhouse emissions have contributed to climate change and by their nature will also continue to contribute to climate change".

Taken together, the courts' reasoning regarding the presence of a loss and causality between the loss and not meeting the emission reduction targets is threefold:

1. The State has been failing to meet the emission reduction targets it politically agreed to;
2. Emission reductions reduce or prevent climate change, even if the impact is limited;

3. Climate change is likely to negatively affect the interests of Urgenda, that is, the interests of those it represents.

The 'possibility of a loss' criterion particularly plays an important role under 3. For the same reason as described above, it is easier to establish a causal relationship between not meeting emission reduction targets, climate change and a possible loss than with an actual loss.

The approach adopted by the court can be reconciled with corrective justice theory. The correlative structure is an issue in environmental cases like Urgenda, as the collective nature of the issue does not necessarily correspond with the individual protection offered by corrective justice theory. More specifically, questions may be raised regarding both the requirement that the doer and sufferer are connected and that the remedy should mirror the injustice. With respect to the latter, an injunction that orders the State to meet emission targets is unlikely to mirror the injustice if there is insufficient evidence for the loss or relationship. As explained above, requiring a possibility of a loss is much more likely to be established than an actual loss, as long as individual plaintiffs can potentially be affected by not meeting emission targets.

Regarding the relationship between doer and sufferer, it is not a given that they are necessarily related in environmental issues. Emissions do not affect individual plaintiffs in the same manner, if at all, because they may only or primarily affect future generations. The fact that the plaintiff may no longer be alive when the effects of global warming set in, or that it is uncertain that the environmental harm will affect the victim's standard of living, makes a tort claim difficult to reconcile with the connectivity requirement that corrective justice imposes (i.e. a relationship between the doer and sufferer of the injustice).

The 'possibility of a loss' criterion preserves the symmetry between the doer and sufferer in case of a successful claim, particularly in instances of collective redress with multiple claimants of which at least one is likely to suffer a possible loss. A tort law that allows anyone to sue anyone for any violation causes a tension with corrective justice, as the symmetry between doer and sufferer may diminish or disappear. The 'possibility of a loss' also prevents *actio popularis* like claims where the plaintiffs initiate legal proceedings without the possibility of suffering harm or the loss themselves.

7.4 Injunction

In the procedure at first instance, Urgenda did not only seek a declaratory judgment, but also an injunction:

(3.1) '*principally*: to reduce or have reduced the joint volume of annual greenhouse gas emissions in the Netherlands that it will have been reduced by 40% by the end of 2020, in any case by at least 25%, compared to 1990;
alternatively: reduce or have reduced the joint volume of annual greenhouse gas emissions in the Netherlands that it will have been reduced by at least 40% by 2030, compared to 1990'.

The decision of the court of first instance focused on whether or not meeting the emission targets had introduced a possibility of a loss for Urgenda and those whose interests Urgenda represented. The Court of Appeal noted that Urgenda sought an injunction, not damages, and that causality (and the loss requirement) is of less importance when an injunction is sought compared to when damages are claimed. Consequently, instead of examining whether the loss criterion was met, the Court of Appeal derived a different test from ECtHR case law on Article 2 and Article 8 ECHR.[37] It held that the relevant test for ordering an injunction is to determine whether there was a

'(...) realistic threat against which measures need to be taken (...)'.[38]

In appeal, the court rejected the State's argument on the lack of causality.

The test the court of appeal adopted follows the conditions developed for an injunction under Dutch law in general. Already in 1944, the Dutch Supreme Court detached the loss requirement from injunctions.[39] Under Dutch law, one can file a claim in order to prevent or stop tortious behaviour, for which it is sufficient to establish a realistic threat that a legal obligation is or will be violated.[40] The burden to establish a violation of a legal obligation is lighter than the burden to prove a loss or the possibility thereof.

Not having to prove or establish a loss implies an alleviation of proving causality as well. Nonetheless, issues that would have been causality issues in a damages claim (or declaratory judgment procedure) become issues of representation when an injunction is sought. When seeking an injunction, it will still need to be established that the plaintiff sufficiently represents the interest at stake, with the interests consisting of the consequences of Dutch government not meeting emission targets. The question then becomes whether

37 Referring to *Öneryildiz/Turkije* (ECHR 30 November 2004, no. 48939/99), *Budayeva/Russia* (ECHR 20 March 2008, no. 15339/02, 21166/02, 20058/02), 11673/02 and 15343/02), *Kolyadenko/Russia* (ECHR 28 February 2012, no. 17423/05, 20534/05, 20678/05, 23263/05, 24283/05 and 35673/05), and *Fadeyeva/Russia* (ECHR 9 June 2005, no. 55723/00).

38 Court of Appeal The Hague 9 October 2018, ECLI:NL:GHDHA:2018:2591, at 64.

39 Tim Bleeker, 'De knellende criteria van het rechterlijk bevel en verbod' in F.Q. van de Pol and others (eds), Vijftig Weeffouten in het BW – Een ode aan het Burgerlijk Wetboek, ter ere van zijn 25-jarig bestaan (Ars Aequi Libri 2017), at 187-188.

40 *Ibid.*, at 188-189.

the plaintiff has sufficient interest in seeking an injunction regarding meeting greenhouse gas emission targets by the State. The question was answered affirmatively in the Urgenda case, but it could also have been answered differently if the court had been less sympathetic towards the claim.

7.5 Final Remarks

The Urgenda case illustrates how existing tort law concepts can be preserved when deciding on matters that consist of environmental harm, greenhouse gas emission reduction in particular. An injunction, at least under Dutch law, alleviates the burden of proof for plaintiffs, as they are no longer required to prove a loss and 'but for' causality between the tortious behaviour and the loss.

However, a successful tort claim is also possible when having to prove a loss, and causality between the loss and the legal obligation that is or was violated, as a loss may be interpreted as an actual loss or as a possible loss, with the latter being easier to prove in environmental matters. Interpreting a loss as a possibility of a loss allows deciding within the individual protection paradigm, which prevents persons to file *actio popularis* like tort claims where they initiate legal proceedings without even the possibility of suffering harm or the loss themselves. This way, the possibility of a loss preserves the symmetry between the doer and sufferer. The symmetry can also be found in situations of an injunction, as in order for the plaintiff to have standing a relationship needs to be established between the plaintiff and the interests he represents on the one hand and the issue for which an injunction is sought on the other hand.

The approach adopted by the Dutch courts illustrates that tort law can be applied in a manner that allows for environmental claims to be successful, at least in cases such as Urgenda. Consequently, the concern that tort law is not designed to decide on environmental matters is less problematic than is sometimes suggested in legal scholarship. The concern that tort claims stand in the way of environmental matters might ultimately be more a matter of desirability than of possibility.

Nevertheless, an environmental-friendly approach chosen in cases such as the Urgenda case does not go without warning. The actions of one state may not be evaluated in isolation of the actions of other states. In the Urgenda case, the State of the Netherlands was ordered to do more than required by EU regulation and by The Paris Agreement (or Protocol) Paris Agreement that included a variety of national commitments toward the goal of averting average global warming in excess of 1.5°C and 2°C. By EU standards, the greenhouse gas emissions should be reduced by 20% by the year 2020,[41] whereas the court in

41 Peeters, 124. Here, it is also explained that 'part of these emissions may be covered by international credits'.

the Urgenda case ordered the State of the Netherlands to reduce its greenhouse gas emissions for that same year with at least 25% (compared to 1990).

The question arises whether compliance with gas emission targets of one member state can be looked at in isolation of other member states. Greenhouse gas emissions are regulated by a mix of EU regulatory instruments.[42] Under the existing regulation, a gas allowance market has emerged, which allows the auctioning and free distribution of allowances of greenhouse gas emissions.[43] The allowance market includes the auctioning, distribution and trade of emission rights between Member States and industries. As a result of this market mechanism, the total emission rights do not diminish if one Member State applies stricter rules on gas emissions, since a Member State that reaches its targets may trade the rights that are not used (consisting of the difference between the EU targets and the higher national targets) to other Member States, which can distribute the allowances among their industries.[44] Consequently, the total greenhouse gas emissions can only be reduced if allowances are not traded, cancelled or otherwise not used.[45] It may therefore not be realistic to expect emission reduction when only one Member State is ordered to reduce emissions, whereas imposing all EU Member States to increase gas emission reductions would go beyond the jurisdiction of a national court and to be considered a violation of international law.[46]

As a result, well-meant tort liability may stimulate one state to increase its emission reduction activities, but it may at the same time discourage other states from doing the same. This issue was brought up in appeal, but rejected by the court. It did not consider it a given that other countries would allow an increase of emissions if the Netherlands would do more than it is obliged to. Additionally, the court noted that the State did not find the same arguments decisive when deciding to reduce gas emissions per 2030 with a higher percentage than internationally agreed upon.[47]

The relationship between tort law and environmental matters remains complicated. Even when tort law is designed for dealing with environmental matters, the question remains whether tort law is an effective means to protect the environment or enhance sustainability. Tort law is merely one of the instruments for reaching sustainability goals, and certainly not the most effective one compared to for example political interventions. This, however, does not take away from the fact that it is still one of the instruments, and one that is worth exploring.

42 Peeters, 124.
43 Peeters, 124-125.
44 Peeters, 125.
45 Peeters, 125.
46 Peeters, 125 (arguing that ruling that 'the EU overall target is insufficient, this implies a negative assessment on the lawfulness of the core aim of EU climate law').
47 Court of Appeal The Hague 9 October 2018, ECLI:NL:GHDHA:2018:2591, at 56-57 and 59.

8 Company Law is Bananas

Kim Berg and Mark Kawakami[*]

8.1 Introduction

We are slowly waking up to the uncomfortable realisation that the costs associated with global industrialisation are increasingly overshadowing many of its perceived benefits. From global warming to the acidification of our oceans, our planet is noticeably deteriorating and we often wag our collective finger at corporate greed, which we blame as one of the main culprits of these plights.[1] The question that we aim to address in this contribution is therefore the following: If corporate malfeasance is indeed contributing to various environmental harms, what is the role of company law – or what should the role of company law be – in curbing these socially undesirable behaviours?

Before diving into the issue of what company law can do, it is worth making two observations at the onset: First, it is no hyperbole to suggest that corporations wield tremendous amounts of power,[2] which – in theory – can be used for the benefit of society. Second, even in the absence of any legislative or extrinsic incentives, there are various stakeholders that are voluntarily sacrificing material comforts and percentages of their profits in order to prevent further degradation of the environment.[3] For example, in the wake of these emerging global challenges, some companies are organising their businesses in a more socially conscious manner by putting environmental and social needs on par with their corporate objectives. Some companies are even implementing codes of conduct

* We are grateful to Mieke Olaerts and her invaluable comments and feedback while editing this contribution.

1 J. Cook, et al, 'Consensus on Consensus: A Synthesis of Consensus: Estimates on Human-Caused Global Warming', *Environmental Research Letters*, Vol. 11, No. 4, 13 April 2016.

2 S. Vitali, J.B. Glattfelder & S. Battiston, 'The Network of Global Corporate Control', *PLoS ONE*, Vol. 6, No. 10, 26 October 2011 (hypothesising that among the 37 million companies and investors worldwide, 147 firms – like Barclays, and the Walton Enterprises LLC, which is a holding company of Wal-Mart – control 40% of the wealth).

3 Companies like the LEGO Group have made public commitments to reduce their carbon footprints by pledging to be 100% reliable on renewable energy by 2030. LEGO has also partnered with the World Wildlife Fund and has shifted their manufacturing process to a more environmentally friendly process through the establishment of its own Sustainable Materials Center. *See*, K. Strauss, 'The 10 Companies with the Best CSR Reputations in 2017', *Forbes*, 13 September 2017. Retrieved from: www.forbes.com/sites/karsten-strauss/2017/09/13/the-10-companies-with-the-best-csr-reputations-in-2017/#656eab64546b (last accessed 6 June 2018). Other companies are also taking guidance from various soft law measures.

to ensure that their supply chains are more sustainable,[4] while others are increasing their transparency by fully disclosing to the general public the manner in which they operate.[5] Similarly, some socially responsible investors are carefully combing through these disclosures and choosing to divest from otherwise lucrative opportunities to forge a new, more holistic and responsible way of investing, the aim of which is to change corporate behaviour typically characterised by short-termism and profit maximisation.

8.1.1 *Issues that Company Law Aims to Address*

While there are those that heed the call to action by voluntarily choosing to be more socially responsible, the majority of corporate stakeholders still operate under the mantra of profit maximisation and forgo most other considerations. This reality can be evidenced by how some companies have brazenly taken the societal demand for increased sustainability merely as an opportunity to further increase their profit margins. For example, in a practice commonly referred to as *greenwashing*, companies are increasing their marketing and advertising efforts to dupe consumers (and investors) into mistakenly thinking that the company is taking active measures to be sustainable, without actually implementing any meaningful course of action.[6] Similarly, there are investors that – regardless of how much non-financial information a socially conscious company discloses – pay zero attention to factors other than the value of their shares.

So if we are to seriously consider whether company law can be utilised to reduce socially undesirable corporate behaviours for the sake of sustainability, we must determine whether company law can: 1) preserve the intrinsic motivations of stakeholders already attempting to be socially responsible on their own accord, while incentivising more and more stakeholders to follow suit; 2) shift the existing paradigm from one that prioritises profit maximisation to a more holistic and socially conscious framework; and 3) effectively differentiate socially responsible companies from those that are not (e.g. the greenwashers) and

4 *See e.g.*, Apple's Environmental Responsibility Report: Progress Report 2018 (Covering Fiscal Year 2017). Retrieved from: www.apple.com/environment/pdf/Apple_Environmental_Responsibility_Report_2018.pdf (last accessed 24 July 2018).

5 For example, companies are voluntarily adhering to guidelines and soft law measures such as Global Reporting Initiative's Sustainability Reporting Guidelines, UN Global Compact backed SDG Compass, UN Guiding Principles on Business and Human Rights, ISO 26000, OECD Guidelines for Multinational Enterprises, the ILO's Tripartite Declaration, and the Consultation Draft of the International Framework published by the International Integrated Reporting Council all of which stress the importance of integrated reporting and urge companies to be transparent and open in their reports about their ESG metrics.

6 B. Watson, 'The Troubling Evolution of Corporate Greenwashing', *The Guardian*, 20 August 2016. Retrieved from: www.theguardian.com/sustainable-business/2016/aug/20/greenwashing-environmentalism-lies-companies (reporting that companies like the American auto manufacturer Chevron advertised that they were environmentally conscious, when in fact they were only following mandatory regulations imposed on them by the government) (last accessed 6 June 2018).

possibly incentivising the latter to change. If company laws can be designed and implemented to address these issues, then we can conclude that company law does have a significant role to play in promoting sustainability and reversing the trend of companies causing environmental harm.

8.1.2 *Research Question & Structure*

While company law could potentially hold the key to incentivising and modifying the behaviours of various corporate stakeholders and nudging companies to being more socially responsible, the main question that this short contribution will address is whether company law is indeed a feasible or even desirable tool for driving such changes. In order to answer this question in a structured manner, this contribution will first lay out some of the prevailing assumption that courses through any discussion of company law, corporations, and their objectives (Section 2). Next, this contribution will present a brief overview of two relatively recent EU legislations that aim to modify corporate stakeholders to be more sustainable (Section 3), followed by an analysis of some of the challenges and shortcomings that they pose (Section 4). Lastly, we will offer some alternative approaches and considerations that could potentially better incentivise corporate stakeholders to be more pro-social (Section 5), before making our concluding remarks to answer the question posed above (Section 6).

8.2 Prevailing Assumptions in Company Law

Before addressing the impact of existing legislative measures and what untapped opportunities company law measures may hold in enabling corporate sustainability drives, this section will first lay out a few underlying issues such as: a) historical roots of company law; b) agency theory in modern company law; and c) a company's *raison d'être* and objectives.

8.2.1 *Historical Roots of Company Law*

The roots of modern company law can be traced back to the early nineteenth century when, due to industrialisation and rising economic prosperity, companies evolved into large organisations greater in size than the traditional private partnerships of the previous decades. This is significant because the law of *joint stock companies* once resembled the law of partnership in a sense that joint stock companies were also conceptualised as an aggregate of individuals joining together in an organisational form for the benefit of their business activity.[7] However, the economic natures of the joint stock company and the shares in joint stock companies evolved differently in that era. Due to the growing scale of investments into joint stock companies, shareholders were no longer required – nor really expected – to have direct interests in the assets of the company nor its day-to-day operation. Instead, their near singular task became the exercising of their right to dividends and to sell their shares on the market for their personal gain.[8] The shares being the sole property to the shareholders (rather than a shared property over the company's assets) lead to the development of the share market that we know today. Indeed, the share in itself became an asset, which the shareholders were permitted to transfer freely to a third party. As a result, shares of most companies today are held by a diverse group of shareholders and individual investors not having any or little interest in the daily activities of the company.[9] This created, if not further polarised, the division of ownership and management with the latter taking more control over the day-today operation of the company and the shareholders taking the metaphorical backseat.

8.2.2 *Agency Theory in Modern Company Law*

With the separation of ownership and management serving as one of its underlying assumptions, company law evolved as an instrument to protect and serve the principle of shareholder value, which is the idea that the shareholders ought to be protected from suboptimal functioning of the management and that the core aim of a company was to serve the financial interests of the shareholders. Accordingly, economists strongly influenced by the likes of Friedman, have long argued that the company's purpose is profit maximisation for the benefit of the shareholders and to maintain a strong position towards its competitors in the market.[10]

Berle and Means conceptualised this relationship between shareholders and management according to the agency theory,[11] which assumes that the aforementioned separation of ownership and control of the company, with the shareholders serving as the principal and

7 P. Ireland, 'Company Law and the Myth of Shareholder Ownership', *The Modern Law Review*, Vol. 62, No. 1, January 1999, p. 32-57, p. 56.

8 As ruled by the English court in Bligh *v.* Brent (1836). A similar approach in other jurisdictions follows from landmark cases in such as HR 18 januari 1901, W. 7553 in The Netherlands. The Supreme Court ruled that the Dutch joint stock company (*Naamloze Vennootschap*) is a legal entity possessing assets and liabilities on its own and separate from its shareholders.

9 L. Stout, *The Shareholder Value Myth: How Putting Shareholders First Harms Investors, Corporations, and the Public*, San Francisco, Berrett-Koehler Publishers, 2012, p. 15.

10 M. Friedman, 'The sole responsibility of the corporation is to increase its profits', *The New York Times Magazine*, 13 September 1970. Retrieved from: http://umich.edu/~thecore/doc/Friedman.pdf (last accessed 25 July 2018).

11 A. Berle & G. Means, *The Modern Corporation and Private Property*, New York, Macmillan, 1932.

the management as the agents. Jensen and Meckling further developed the notion of shareholders owning the company and the separation of ownership in their seminal work, *Theory of the Firm*, which undeniably influenced the conceptualisation of a modern company.[12] These assumptions originating from economics have often been paired with the aforementioned concept of shareholder primacy, and the belief that it is the primary duty of the corporate board to squeeze as much profit as possible for the sake of the shareholders. Anything less than that would be tantamount to a breach of their fiduciary duties, as exemplified by notorious cases such as *Dodge v. Ford Motor Company* in the US, where the court controversially ruled that the board must always keep at least one eye on the main prize, which is the company's valuation.[13]

What is striking about the aforementioned theories, however, is that they are abstract theories based on *economic* conceptualisation of the company rather than a *legal* understanding of the company. Inevitably, the assumption has lead legal scholars to challenge the underlying (economic) concepts of company law over the past decades. As markets expanded, new opportunities for investors were created and along with the benefits of a globalising world economy, the nature of corporate shareholding changed, which made the problem more evident. Modern stock markets offer fast and easy trades, facilitating those investors investing in companies merely for the sake of enjoying a share in the company's profit. In light of the legal context in which this development has taken place, a clear mismatch between the corporate legal framework and actual economic practice came to the surface. Indeed, when shareholding is considered merely as an investment opportunity, shareholders are less concerned with material issues on the (long term) functioning of the company. According to Stout, shareholders therefore do not necessarily own the company as such, but merely its shares, which puts them on equal footing with other debtors of the company such as bondholders, suppliers, or even employees.[14] Consequently, there is no legal ground to maintain the thought that shareholders need influential control over management following agency theory.[15]

---

12 C. Jensen & W. Meckling, 'Theory Of The Firm: Managerial Behavior, Agency Costs and Ownership Structure', *Journal of Financial Economics*, Vol. 3, No. 4, p. 305-360.

13 *Dodge v. Ford Motor Company*, 201 Mich. 459, 170 N.W. 668 (Mich. 1919) (holding that the board's primary duty is to protect the interest of the shareholders); *cf. Aronson v. Lewis*, 473 A.2d 805 (Del. 1984). The authoritative meaning of Dodge v. Ford Motor Company as a source for defining the corporate purpose by, amongst others, L. Stout, 'Why We Should Stop Teaching Dodge v. Ford', *Cornell Law Faculty Publications*, Paper 724 (2008). Retrieved from: http://scholarship.law.cornell.edu/facpub/724/) and T. Henderson, 'Everything Old Is New Again: Lessons from Dodge v. Ford Motor Company', *John M. Olin Program in Law and Economics Working Paper*, No. 37 (2007). Retrieved from: https://chicagounbound.uchicago.edu/law_and_economics/198/.

14 L. Stout, 'The shareholder Value Myth', *Cornell Law Faculty Publications*, Paper 771 (2013). Retrieved from: http://scholarship.law.cornell.edu/facpub/771 (last accessed 25 July 2018).

15 *Ibid.*

8.2.3 A Company's Raison d'Être & Objectives

In more recent times, however, shareholder primacy is slowly losing its initial meaning in defining the company's core objective. Management decisions have been given some flexibility and leeway to take into consideration more factors in determining the company's valuation. This breathing room is essentially what enabled the corporate social responsibility movement to grow into what it is today.[16] Based on the assumption that exhibiting sensitivity towards environmental, social, and government issues – often indicated as issues relating to 'ESG metrics' – can serve in the long-term interest of a company's profit maximisation scheme, management has been enabled to take into consideration the company's sustainability initiatives. While this is a positive step towards the path of sustainability, it is still a risk for the management to invest in various CSR initiatives, as there are no guarantees that investing in sustainability initiatives actually results in profits down the line for the company. In the event that the shareholders feel that particular sustainability initiatives will not result in profit maximisation, the shareholders still reserve the right to oust the management.[17]

In short, while the shareholder expectations and corporate cultures are increasingly becoming more tolerant of sustainability initiatives, shareholder wealth and profit maximisation still remain an integral part of corporate objectives. Similarly, company law, the purpose of which is primarily to regulate how stakeholders of the company interact with one another, has not significantly changed either. In other words, the basic function of company law has never been, nor is it now to transform corporate stakeholders into environmentally conscious activists.[18] Moreover, although the aggregate actions of corporations

16 For example, John Elkington's triple bottom line framework suggests that companies should not only care about profits, but also about people and the planet. *See also*, M.E.P. Seligman, *Flourish*, New York, Atria, 2011, p. 23 (noting that "[t]he new bottom line of the positive corporation in this view is profit... plus meaning... plus positive emotion... plus engagement... plus positive human relations").

17 For example, shareholders can persuade the management by using the tools of offered in company law such as forum rights. Another more radical example would be the removal of the board, if permitted by national law.

18 Given the shareholder primacy and the incentives placed on short term profit maximisation, some have argued that company law – at least as they are currently composed and enforced – almost have nothing to do with the welfare of the general public, including that of promoting and ensuring sustainability. *See e.g.* K. Greenfield, *The Failure of Corporate Law: Fundamental Flaws and Progressive Possibilities*, Chicago, University of Chicago Press, 2006, p. 1 ("Public corporations are not public in any sense of having responsibilities to society, or of being owned by the community, or of being subject to particular stringent public oversight. In fact, managers of most large, 'public' companies are *prohibited by law* from taking into account the interests of the public when making decisions, if in doing so those of the company's shareholders are harmed"). European Commission, "European Commission proposes to strengthen shareholder engagement and introduce a 'say on pay' for Europe's largest companies," (9 April 2014). Retrieved from: http://europa.eu/rapid/press-release_IP-14-396_en.htm?locale=en (last accessed 14 March 2016); *see also*, European Commission, 'Shareholders' Rights Directive Q&A Fact Sheet' MEMO/17/592, 14 March 2017. Retrieved from: http://europa.eu/rapid/press-release_MEMO-17-592_en.htm (last accessed 7 April 2017).

have significant impacts on the general public, the converse is not necessarily true in the sense that the voice of the public does not always seem to sway corporate actions, as many companies are more inclined to cater to their shareholders. In other words, shareholder value, which has been at the core of how company law developed historically, almost ensures that short term interests of the investors will be prioritised above that of the general public, that is unless there is a sudden uptick in the number of socially responsible and sustainability conscious investors.

8.3 Recent EU Legislations on Company Law

Having covered the history and the prevailing assumptions of company law, let us now take a closer look at two recent changes made at the EU legislative level that aim to shake up the role of stakeholders and corporate reporting: They are the recent amendments made to the Shareholder's Rights' Directive[19] and the Non-Financial Disclosure Directive,[20] which amended Directive 2013/34/EU (on the annual financial statements). While these two developments are, by no means, the only legislative endeavours related to company law that the EU is working on, these two measures in particular overlap with the sustainability and CSR circles.[21]

These changes suggest that – as far as the EU sees it – increasing corporate transparency and enhancing shareholder engagement are the necessary steps to transforming companies

19 Directive 2007/36/EC of the European Parliament and of the Council of 11 July 2007 on the exercise of certain rights of shareholders in listed companies, L 184/17 (listing the various rights of the shareholders, including but not limited to their right to put items on the agenda of the general meeting (Article 6), right to vote at the general meeting (Article 7), and their right to ask questions (Article 9)). On 9 December 2016, the EU's committee of permanent representatives (COREPER) approved the agreement between the Slovak presidency and the European Parliament representatives to "strengthen shareholder engagement in big European companies". *See*, European Council, 'Shareholders' rights in EU companies: Presidency strikes deal with Parliament', *Press Release*, 16 December 2016. Retrieved from: www.consilium.europa.eu/en/press/press-releases/2016/12/16-shareholders-rights-eu-companies/ (last accessed 7 April 2017) (noting that the aim of the agreement is to "encourage transparent and active engagement by shareholders of listed companies…").

20 Directive 2014/95/EU of the European Parliament and of the Council of 22 October 2014 amending Directive 2013/34/EU as regards disclosure of non-financial and diversity information by certain large undertakings and groups. *See also*, European Commission Press Release, 'Statement: Disclosure of non-financial information: Europe's largest companies to be more transparent on social and environmental issues', 29 September 2014. Retrieved from: http://europa.eu/rapid/press-release_STATEMENT-14-291_en.htm (last accessed 16 January 2016).

21 For example, Directive 2017/1132 has recently codified and merged various aspects of company law into a single Directive and Regulation No 2019/876 has updated and amended capital requirements and issues of remuneration for financial institutions. *See*, European Commission, 'What the EU is doing: Company Law and Corporate Governance'. Retrieved from: https://ec.europa.eu/info/business-economy-euro/doing-business-eu/company-law-and-corporate-governance_en (last accessed 17 June 2019).

into more sustainable and socially responsible entities. For example, the second paragraph of the preamble in the newly amended Shareholder's Rights Directive states:

> "The financial crisis has revealed that shareholders in many cases supported managers' excessive short-term risk taking. Moreover, there is clear evidence that the current level of 'monitoring' of investee companies and engagement by institutional investors and asset managers is often inadequate and focuses too much on short-term returns, which may lead to suboptimal corporate governance and performance."

Here, the Commission alleges that the combination of shareholder primacy and short-term profit maximisation mentality – what this contribution discussed in the previous section as the prevailing assumptions in company law – are culpable to creating a 'suboptimal' state of affairs, which mostly disregards the needs of the general public (e.g. sustainability initiatives). The ideal solution to this problem – at least at the EU level – appears to be the empowerment of the shareholders so that they can better monitor the way companies are run: If only the shareholders and institutional investors would generate a more holistic valuation for a company's worth – in other words, not just the valuation of the company in terms of share values, but in terms of the company's role in society and how it treats their employees – then companies might start behaving differently all together. This section will now present how the EU envisions to stimulate these changes through their company law based measures.

8.3.1 Shareholders' Rights Directive ('SRD II')

The European Commission's recent revision of the Shareholders' Rights Directive aims to make it "easier for shareholders to use their existing rights over companies and enhance those rights where necessary... [which] would ensure shareholders were more engaged; [and to] better hold the management of the company to account and act in the long-term interests of the company."[22] To provide more detail, the revision to the Shareholders' Rights Directive (henceforth referred to as "SRD II"), which Member States are starting to implement in 2019, attempts to enable corporate sustainability initiatives by: 1) "strengthening the transparency requirements for institutional investors and asset managers

22 European Commission, 'European Commission proposes to strengthen shareholder engagement and introduce a 'say on pay' for Europe's largest companies', 9 April 2014. Retrieved from: http://europa.eu/rapid/press-release_IP-14-396_en.htm?locale=en (last accessed 14 March 2016). *See also*, European Commission, 'Shareholders' Rights Directive Q&A Fact Sheet', MEMO/17/592, 14 March 2017. Retrieved from: http://europa.eu/rapid/press-release_MEMO-17-592_en.htm (last accessed 7 April 2017).

on their investment and engagement policies regarding the companies in which they invest [in]", 2) creating "a framework to make it easier to identify shareholder so [that] they can more easily exercise their rights like voting rights," and 3) introducing a "say on pay" scheme that would link management pay with their performance (i.e. "oblige companies to disclose, clear, comparable and comprehensive information on their remuneration policies").[23] In short, the SRDII gives the shareholders access to more corporate information and the tools to amplify their voices.

The empowerment of shareholders, however, is balanced with the EU's wishes for shareholders to take on more responsibility to oversee the companies in which they invest. This sentiment is noted in the SRD II under Preamble 14:

> "Greater involvement of shareholders in corporate governance is one of the levers that can help improve the financial and non-financial performance of companies, including as regards environmental, social and governance factors, in particular as referred to in the Principles for Responsible Investment, supported by the United Nations."

The SRD II can be labelled as an instrument that encapsulates the EU's current position, which is that *enlightened* shareholder engagement is a prerequisite for successful governance of companies.[24] Therefore, any increase in corporate sustainability drives would prove to be difficult in the absence of increased shareholder engagement.

However, as noted back in Section 2, the shareholder's primary task nowadays is not the day-to-day operation of the company, but to pay attention on the financial aspects and the general direction of the company. As a matter of fact, shareholders are not supposed to have direct influences on most corporate decisions as that task is primarily reserved for the board of directors.[25] Nevertheless, the proposal to increase shareholder engagement was set on the legislative agenda because the EU strongly believes that doing so will improve corporate accountability and prevent new corporate scandals that harm society at large. By combing through the legislation, the EU's intent becomes quite evident: place more

---

23 European Commission, 'European Commission proposes to strengthen shareholder engagement and introduce a 'say on pay' for Europe's largest companies', 9 April 2014. Retrieved from: http://europa.eu/rapid/press-release_IP-14-396_en.htm?locale=en (last accessed 14 March 2016) (suggesting that the proposal, if implemented would "improve the corporate governance of around 10,000 companies listed on Europe's stock exchanges"); *see also*, National Transposition of Directive 2017/828. Retrieved from: https://eur-lex.europa.eu/legal-content/EN/NIM/?uri=CELEX:32017L0828 (last accessed 29 April 2019).

24 Enlightened shareholders are those that seek profits whilst considering factors such as long-term sustainable growth and stakeholder interests. *See generally*, A. Keay, 'The Enlightened Shareholder Value Principle and Corporate Governance,' London: Routledge, 2013.

25 *See generally*, J. Fox & J.W. Lorsch, 'What Good Are Shareholders', *Harvard Business Review*, July-August 2012. Retrieved from: https://hbr.org/2012/07/what-good-are-shareholders (last accessed 18 June 2018).

tools at the disposal of the so-called enlightened shareholders so that they can keep a better eye on what the companies are doing and nudge them down a more righteous path as necessary.

In an ideal world, the EU would not only want to see the shareholders take up a more overseeing role of companies, but for investors to drastically change the way in which they invest in companies. As noted previously, if shareholders paid less attention on purely financial considerations and more on various other factors (e.g. ESG metrics noted above), then the management of the company would inevitably start operating more holistically (e.g. hold sustainability initiatives on par with the valuation of the company). This view is based on the assumption that most companies are currently forced into prioritising short-term profit maximisation because of their shareholders. After all, the performance of the management is assessed based on the financial results of the company, but moreover, for the management there is a constant threat of removal in cases where the shareholders are disappointed by their decisions. If only the shareholders' objectives could be more multifaceted rather than singular (or if only they could be more enlightened), the management could be liberated from the tyranny of short termism and be allowed to focus on other factors without suffering the repercussions, perhaps sustainability initiatives could be allowed more attention. So in these ways, company law measures that modify shareholder engagement, at least according to the EU, is the key to how company law can curtail harmful corporate behaviours.

One underlying concern that this contribution will note here with the EU's vision is the aforementioned reality that not all shareholders are enlightened nor do they all care about sustainability initiatives. The argument that this contribution will make in the next section is that while SRD II might potentially empower shareholders, it does not necessarily incentivise shareholders that do not care about sustainability initiatives to be more socially responsible. For the time being, however, let us table this concern and move on to the second recent legislation that the EU sees as a vital measure to enhance corporate sustainability initiatives.

8.3.2 *Directive on Disclosure of Non-Financial and Diversity Information ('NFRD')*

The EU Directive on Disclosure of Non-Financial and Diversity Information (henceforth referred to as the Non-Financial Reporting Directive or "NFRD"),[26] which went into effect

26 Directive 2014/95/EU of the European Parliament and of the Council of 22 October 2014 amending Directive 2013/34/EU as regards disclosure of non-financial and diversity information by certain large undertakings and groups. *See also*, European Commission Press Release, 'Statement: Disclosure of non-financial information: Europe's largest companies to be more transparent on social and environmental

on 1 January 2017, "require large companies with more than 500 employees to disclose relevant and material environmental and social information in their annual reports."[27] This means that the NFRD requires companies to release integrated reports with ESG metrics contained within.[28] With this Directive, the EU aims to "improve the kinds of information that companies need to provide on their socially responsible conduct."[29] As organisations tend to prioritise considerations that are actually measured (e.g. economic or financial indicators), by requiring the measuring of ESG metrics along with the financial indicators, the idea is that the NFRD forces directors to *care* about the companies social responsibilities.

Given that it is a European Directive, all Member States are expected to transpose this requirement into their national legislations,[30] meaning that the Member States will soon be requiring large companies located within their jurisdiction to release information related to their policy and status on pollution prevention, sustainable water use, social impact, and so on. In theory, requiring companies to conduct such internal assessment will inevitably require them to pay some attention on these important issues; and by releasing this information into the market, investors will be able to evaluate these companies, not only on their fiscal standing, but on various other factors. The EU's vision here is an

issues', 29 September 2014. Retrieved from: http://europa.eu/rapid/press-release_STATEMENT-14-291_en.htm (last accessed 16 January 2016).

27 Directive 2014/95/EU of the European Parliament and of the Council of 22 October 2014 amending Directive 2013/34/EU as regards disclosure of non-financial and diversity information by certain large undertakings and groups. Preamble 6 and Article 4 (stating that the Directive will compel "certain large undertakings [to] prepare a non-financial statement containing information relating to at least environmental matters, social and employee-related matters, respect for human rights anti-corruption and bribery matters"). *See also*, A. Rühmkorf, *Corporate Social Responsibility, Private Law and Global Supply Chains*, Cheltenham, Edward Elgar, 2015, p. 59 (adding that in accordance with Article 1(1)(a), "the Directive stipulates that the annual report of these companies must include a non-financial statement containing information relating to at least environmental, social and employee matters, respect for human rights, anti-corruption and bribery matters").

28 R.G. Eccles & D. Saltzman, 'Achieving Sustainability Through Integrated Reporting', *Stanford Social Innovation Review*, Vol. 9, No. 3, Summer 2011, p. 56-61 at p. 57 (stating that an integrated report is "a single document that presents and explains a company's financial and nonfinancial - environmental, social, and governance (ESG) - performance").

29 A. Rühmkorf, *Corporate Social Responsibility, Private Law and Global Supply Chains*, Cheltenham, Edward Elgar, 2015, p. 61.

30 Moreover, this Directive has the potential to significantly impact even foreign companies located outside of the EU as well, to the extent that if they are conducting businesses within the EU or are listed in an EU exchange, this Directive could potentially require them to disclose integrated reports as well. *See*, Directive 2014/95/EU of the European Parliament and of the Council of 22 October 2014 amending Directive 2013/34/EU as regards disclosure of non-financial and diversity information by certain large undertakings and groups. Article 1. The Directive will be applicable, not only to companies incorporated in the EU that fit these elements, but possibly to foreign companies that are listed in an EU exchange or are conducting significant business within the EU.

understandable one: more information and more transparency lead to better decision-making and higher accountability by the stakeholders.

In addition, while some companies might perceive these requirements to disclose additional information as an unnecessary and unwanted burden, there are alleged benefits that could possibly outweigh the burden. For example, Eccles and Saltzman note the following benefits: 1) there are internal benefits, where the work required to compile the ESG report could lead to better allocation of resources; 2) external market benefits where the ESG report would invite socially conscious investors; and 3) management and reduction of regulatory risk.[31] In short, conducting the necessary assessment and audits to publish ESG metrics enables corporate risk management that can benefit the companies.[32]

While it is an accomplishment in and of itself for the EU legislators to compel companies to collect and release more information to the public and potential investors, it is worth asking the critical question of who will actually be reading them. Similar to the concern that was raised in the previous subsection about whether or not the SRD II actually incentivises shareholders to engage and be more active *in a socially responsible manner*, the NFRD might increase the amount of information that the shareholders and investors can rely on to make their investment decisions, but it leaves some of us wondering whether the availability of ESG metrics alone will actually incentivise shareholders to move companies to be more pro-social. These lingering questions lead us to the next section on the problems with the current approach.

8.4 Problems with the Status Quo

As mentioned at the onset, the primary aim of this contribution is to discuss the role of company law – if any – in curtailing environmentally and socially harmful corporate behaviours. The previous section presented how the EU has recently implemented company law based measures in their attempts to make companies more accountable and socially responsible (i.e. activating shareholders and increasing the amount and type of corporate disclosures). While the European Commission's work could be lauded as steps in the right direction, as the previous section already hinted, some doubts linger as to whether these measures actually work towards achieving sustainability goals or whether they really change the nature of how companies operate. With these concerns in mind, this section will now analyse the problematic aspects of the Directives by asking: a) whether the existing measures are sufficient, or perhaps worse; b) whether they are counterproductive measures; and c)

31 R.G. Eccles & D. Saltzman, 'Achieving Sustainability Through Integrated Reporting', *Stanford Social Innovation Review*, Vol. 9, No. 3, Summer 2011, p. 56-61 at p. 59.

32 *Ibid.*, at p. 58.

whether these measures can compel – with any certainty – companies to behave in a more pro-social manner.

8.4.1 Insufficient Measures?

As noted earlier, enlightened shareholders or socially responsible investors could utilise the measures implemented by the EU to steward companies into becoming more socially responsible entities that bring positive impact. If the significant resources that corporations wield could be used for social good, we could have a better chance at fighting back against challenges such as global warming and other environmental degradation. However, it would be highly unrealistic to expect companies and stakeholders to do so without being properly incentivised and as previously noted, enlightened shareholders and socially conscious investors do not grow on trees as if they were bananas. Moreover, even if they did, there is evidence to suggest that what shareholders can do to steer a company is rather limited even with the help of SRD II in effect. To substantiate this claim, this subsection will look at the issue of i) shareholder proposal on ESG issues and ii) shareholders' use of their forum rights to address ESG issues.

8.4.4.1 Shareholder Proposals on ESG Issues

Let us offer some empirical findings that suggest shareholders do not necessarily use the rights afforded to them, and even if they did, they do not have much impact on the direction of the companies. For example, Grewal, Serafeim and Yoon[33] investigated the relationship between shareholder proposals on ESG issues and the companies' subsequent ESG performance and market valuation.[34] In their study, 2,665 ESG shareholder proposals were analysed, which were classified as either financially material or immaterial.[35] Their research found that 42% of ESG shareholder proposals related to material ESG issues and 58% to immaterial ESG issues, which initially seemed to suggest that shareholders were not incentivised only by financial objectives when filing a proposal. The actual impact of these

33 J. Grewal, G. Serafeim, & A. Yoon, 'Shareholder Activism on Sustainability Issues.', *Harvard Business School Working Paper* 17-003, July 2016. Retrieved from: https://dash.harvard.edu/bitstream/handle/1/27864360/17-003.pdf?sequence=1 (last accessed 17 June 2019).

34 It is worth mentioning here that the study is focused primarily in the US context, where shareholders generally make *more* use of shareholder proposals as a tool for shareholder activism compared to shareholders in the EU.

35 There was no general standard used for materiality. The standards were developed by means of a standard setting process including multi-stakeholder industry working groups. Appendix I and II of the research paper explain the step by step process. The standards adopted by the Sustainability Accounting Standards Board (SASB) where used to define materiality from an industry level. An example of a material ESG issue was a proposal regarding "Food Safety Concerns" submitted by the shareholders of McDonald's Corporation. SASB identified "Product quality/safety" as a material issue in the Consumption sector (see Appendix IV).

proposals on ESG performance and market valuation, however, is a rather separate issue. The results of the research are summarised below.

	Company performance on focal ESG issue	**Company market valuation (based on Tobin's Q)**
Shareholder proposal on (financially) material ESG issue for the company sector	Increase	Increase
Shareholder proposal on (financially) immaterial ESG issue for the company sector	(Faster) Increase	Decrease

Tobin's Q is determined by the Q ratio. The Q ratio is calculated as the market value of a company divided by the replacement value of its total assets. A low Q (between 0 and 1) means the cost to replace a firm's assets is greater than the market value of all its shares on the market. In this case the company is undervalued. Conversely, a high Q implies that the company is overvalued.

What the research shows, is that the pressure levied against companies by its shareholders to address ESG issues that are not financially material for the firm, but are relevant to other stakeholders, is associated with subsequent decline in market valuation, while market valuation increased for proposals on material issues.[36] The results of the research suggest that firms increase their performance on immaterial issues following shareholder proposals, while in fact it decreases the firms' market valuation subsequently.

In an additional analysis following the results of their research, Grewal, Serafeim and Yoon briefly elaborate on possible explanations for company's behaviour on ESG shareholder proposals. First, the existence of an agency problem and consequently agency costs could lead managers to act in a way that satisfies the shareholders and their reputation. Second, the reputation of the company itself could be a reason to respond to specific shareholder proposals on immaterial issues. Third, the identification of material versus immaterial issues is recognised as an explanation for the behaviour of the company towards ESG shareholder proposals. Companies lack the knowledge on what constitutes materiality for their company in order to act accordingly. Lastly, they suggest that goodwashing – the

36 J. Grewal, G. Serafeim, & A. Yoon, 'Shareholder Activism on Sustainability Issues.', *Harvard Business School Working Paper* 17-003, July 2016. Retrieved from: https://dash.harvard.edu/bitstream/handle/1/27864360/17-003.pdf?sequence=1 (last accessed 17 June 2019).

behaviour of companies to focus on immaterial issues in order to divert attention away from any poor performance on material issues – is a possible explanation for their findings.

8.4.4.2 Shareholders Exercising Forum Rights to Address ESG Issue

Yet another example that substantiates the claim that shareholder activism has a limited impact – at least in the Netherlands and across Europe – comes from recent findings by Van der Elst and Lafarre who investigated the role of shareholders in promoting corporate social responsibility.[37] First, they analysed available data on shareholder proposals submitted to the general meeting of listed companies within the EU. Furthermore, and perhaps more importantly, they analysed the transcripts of the general meetings of Dutch listed companies in order to collect information on shareholders addressing ESG issues by exercising their forum right in the general meeting. The forum right, or the right to ask questions, is in accordance with the right to ask questions laid down in Article 9 of SRD II.

The first part of their research confirmed that, in stark contrast to the US, the tool of shareholder proposals is seldom used in the EU. A further study of the number of shareholder proposals that were submitted in 15 European countries in the period 2013-2017 showed that less than 10% addressed ESG issues. Sweden is the leading country, both in number of shareholder proposals submitted and shareholder proposals addressing ESG issues, with nearly a quarter out of all shareholder proposals concerned ESG related topics. On the other hand, in Austria, Belgium, Finland, Germany, Italy, Luxemburg, The Netherlands, Portugal, and Spain none of the proposals concerned any ESG issues. This means that in the majority of the 15 countries investigated, shareholders did not use their right to submit shareholder proposals to draw attention to ESG issues during the general meetings.[38] This suggests that there is no, or at least very limited, shareholder involvement in this area in the EU. As previously noted, the limited use of the right to file a shareholder proposal does not come as a surprise as it is very uncommon in the EU for shareholders to exercise this right, which begs the question as to why the EU thought that amending the SRD II would drastically change the status quo.

Van der Elst and Lafarre put their finding regarding shareholder proposals into perspective by also analysing the shareholders' forum right. Transcripts of general meetings from Dutch companies in the period of 2004-2017 were used to collect information on the interventions made by shareholders during the general meeting with the aim of addressing ESG related topics. In short, their research found that out of all the interventions

37 *See generally*, A. Lafarre & C. Van der Elst, 'Shareholder Sustainability Activism in the Netherlands', *ECGI Law Working Paper*, No. 396, 2018. Retrieved from: https://ecgi.global/sites/default/files/working_papers/documents/finallafarrevanderelst_0.pdf (last accessed 17 June 2019).

38 A. Lafarre & C. Van der Elst, 'Shareholder Sustainability Activism in the Netherlands', *ECGI Law Working Paper*, No. 396, 2018, p. 8 table A. Retrieved from: https://ecgi.global/sites/default/files/working_papers/documents/finallafarrevanderelst_0.pdf (last accessed 17 June 2019).

during the general meeting, about 10% related to the issue of corporate social responsibility and there was an increasing trend of the addressing of corporate sustainability topics by shareholders in general meetings, at least in The Netherlands.

These findings sound satisfying at first glance, but let us also consider two grounds for challenging the hasty conclusion that there is increased shareholder engagement of CSR issues: First, although voting participation on agenda proposals during the general meeting is high (on average 70%), Vletter-Van Dort has pointed out that attendance of shareholders at the general meeting is generally low.[39] Dutch general meetings are composed for 90% of foreign institutional investors. As stated by Vletter-Van Dort, and also acknowledged by Van der Elst and Lafarre in their research, it is common in The Netherlands for large shareholders such as institutional investor to consult with the board in private meetings rather than during the general meetings. In addition, Van der Elst and Lafarre concluded that although there is an increasing trend of shareholders exercising their forum rights to address ESG issues, the use of forum rights by institutional investors specifically, as the main shareholder type in the general meeting, is still relatively low. Furthermore, research conducted by a special governmental research committee installed to investigate the functioning of public limited liability companies in The Netherlands, found that the general meeting has lost its initial purpose, which was to give opportunities for the shareholders to initiate a dialogue with the company's management.[40]

The low physical participation of shareholders and the influence of institutional investors on the functioning of the general meeting raise a concern of what it effectively means when a question on an ESG related issue is raised during the general meeting. In line with Stout's criticism noted earlier on the presupposed ownership by the shareholders of the company, Vletter-Van Dort is also sceptical about shareholders' attitude to long-termism and argues that long termism does not fit the picture of what institutional investors perceive their responsibilities to be as they may not consider themselves to be the owners of the companies in which they invest in. Although this explains the need for tools committing institutional investors to best practice rules, it also shows that the institutional investors are – at least not yet – living up to society's expectations.[41] This leaves us with some sense of scepticism and questioning whether the measures put forth by the EU are really effective in transforming corporate stakeholders to becoming environmentally conscious actors.

39 H. Vletter-Van Dort, 'De aandeelhoudersvergadering: relikwie of innovatief forum voor dialoog?', *Ondernemingsrecht*, 2017/55.

40 Commissie Vennootschapsrecht, *'Advies NV-recht 15 juli 2013'*. Retrieved from: www.rijksoverheid.nl/documenten/brieven/2013/07/18/advies-nv-recht-15-juli-2013 (last accessed 17 June 2019).

41 H. Vletter-Van Dort, 'De aandeelhouder al hoeksteen van de beursvennootschap', *Ondernemingsrecht*, 2018/45.

8.4.2 *Counterproductive Measures?*

It is indeed possible that pressuring reluctant companies and stakeholders into compliance with the Directives could transform companies into more socially responsible and environmentally conscious entities. Yet, as noted in the previous subsection, a healthy dose of scepticism remains. Perhaps even more alarmingly, there are arguments to suggest that mandating transparency and requiring companies to release more and more information to the public could potentially have adverse and unintended consequences detrimental to various sustainability initiatives. To illustrate this point, this section will discuss: i) the information overload problem and ii) the crowding out problem.

8.4.2.1 Information Overload Problem

One of the concerns with more and more information being disclosed by companies into the market is the information overload problem. It has become quite well known that in the era of fake news and markets being oversaturated with information that investors and other stakeholders are having an increasingly difficult time finding truthful and relevant information. Adding more and more information to this status quo could potentially be counterproductive because the information and choice overload problem can lead us to making careless – and often bad – decisions.[42] "[E]mpirical studies rarely report that disclosures lead disclosees to good decisions,"[43] which is quite a huge concern in and of itself, but there are even more reasons for us to worry, considering the ability – or the inability – of companies to actually disclose accurate and comprehensive information.[44] For example, various companies already have difficulties accurately assessing and determining what their supply chain looks like and what each of the downstream stakeholders are actually doing.[45] This reality is exacerbated by our availability heuristic, which is our general ten-

42 S.S. Iyengar & M.R. Lepper, 'When Choice is Demotivating: Can One Desire Too Much of a Good Thing', *Journal of Personality and Social Psychology*, Vol. 79, No. 6, 2000, p. 996 (arguing that "as complexity of making choices rises, people tend to simplify their decision-making processes by relying on simple heuristics.").

43 O. Ben-Shahar & C.E. Schneider, *More Than You Wanted to Know: The Failure of Mandated Disclosure*, Princeton, Princeton University Press, 2014, p. 7-8. *See also*, C C. Winston, 'The Efficacy of Information Policy: A Review of Archon Fung, Mary Graham, and David Weil's Full Disclosure: The Perils and Promise of Transparency', *Journal of Economic Literature*, Vol. 46, No. 3, 2008, p. 704-717 at p. 713-714 (noting that "federal and state information policies, including but not limited to disclosure policies, suggests that they have not made consumers significantly better informed and safer").

44 U.S. Government Accountability Office, 'SEC Conflict Minerals Rule: Initial Disclosures Indicate Most Companies Were Unable to Determine the Source of Their Conflict Minerals', GAO-15-561, 18 August 2015. Retrieved from: www.gao.gov/assets/680/672051.pdf (last accessed 12 March 2016).

45 *See e.g.*, S. New, 'McDonald's and the Challenges of a Modern Supply Chain', *Harvard Business Review*, February 2015. Retrieved from: https://hbr.org/2015/02/mcdonalds-and-the-challenges-of-a-modern-supply-chain (suggesting that "transparency has paradoxical consequences") (last accessed 29 June 2018). *See also*, S. New, 'The Transparent Supply Chain', *Harvard Business Review*, October 2010. Retrieved from:

dency to give undue weight to more present or salient information over others that are less so.[46] Given the choice overload problem and our cognitive biases and heuristics, Ben-Shahar and Schneider argue the following:

> "[M]andated disclosure is so indiscriminately used with such unrealistic expectations and such unhappy results that it should be presumptively barred. This would spare the world much pointless regulation and might help drive lawmakers – legislatures, administrative agencies, and courts – to search harder for solutions actually tailored to problems."[47]

In short, while the Directives in question show the Commission's willingness to nudge companies to be more sustainable and socially responsible, simply enhancing the powers of shareholders does not significantly impact the role that they can play, even if we assume for the time being that some shareholders actually do care about the ESG metrics. Moreover, simply requiring companies to disclose more and more information so that these supposedly social responsible investors will steer the company in a more socially responsible path is not a guarantee for sustainability, as information overload and the abundance of inaccurate or incomplete information could potentially cause more harm than good.

8.4.2.2 Crowding Out Problem

The second reason as to why the existing EU legislations could potentially be counterproductive to enhancing corporate sustainability initiatives is the crowding out problem. In our context, the crowding out problem occurs when governments and legislatures increase their involvement to address a particular problem, which inadvertently leads to a corresponding decrease in the involvement of other stakeholders.[48] This phenomenon is related to what is known as the *bystander apathy* in the field of social psychology, where we are less likely to act when we see others around us facing the same problem.[49]

---

https://hbr.org/2010/10/the-transparent-supply-chain (pointing to the difficulty of answering the question "where does this stuff come from" and suggesting that technologies like Radio Frequency Identification tags (RFID) could make it easier to trace and track a product and their supply chain) (last accessed 29 June 2018).

46 A. Tversky and D. Kahneman, 'Availability: A Heuristic for Judging Frequency and Probability', *Cognitive Psychology*, Vol. 5, 1973, p. 207-232.

47 O. Ben-Shahar & C.E. Schneider, *More Than You Wanted to Know: The Failure of Mandated Disclosure*, Princeton, Princeton University Press, 2014, p. 183.

48 This term is borrowed from economics and is usually used to describe instances where an increase in government spending, which is financed by increasing their debt, leads to corresponding decrease in private expenditures.

49 *See generally*, R.B. Cialdini, *Influence: The Psychology of Persuasion*, New York, William Morrow and Company, 1993, (using the term to explain the murder of Kitty Genovese, where there were 38 bystanders

The crowding out problem has its roots in the question of why companies – or individual consumers for that matter – choose to behave in a prosocial manner in the first place. One possible theory to answer this question is that prosocial or altruistic behaviour (e.g. being environmentally friendly or spending money to be more socially responsible) is a *costly signal*. Costly signalling theory suggests that "the extra cost of [green] products is a signal of social status and wealth and leads to advantages in social interactions for the signaller."[50] So in return for investing in corporate sustainability initiatives or paying a certain premium for procuring more sustainable components, people's exogenous tendency to want to enhance their status can be satisfied.

Bearing in mind the crowding out problem, bystander apathy, and the role of costly signalling on prosocial behaviours, imagine the following situation: A company – who was happily signalling their market-differentiating sustainability initiatives – loses that competitive advantage because the government has now mandated that every company – even those that did not wish to do so – do the same, thus eliminating the company's competitive advantage. Now from an overall societal perspective, this could potentially be argued as a good thing because now all the companies – at least of a certain size – are required to be sustainable. But it is entirely possible that the signalling company's intrinsic incentive to be sustainable could diminish, as it is no longer a differentiating factor for them. Not only will the power of the signalling essentially vanish, but the government regulation will create a series of compliance issues with companies who cannot – or do not want to – take sustainability issues seriously. Take for example the NFRD (or any other similar legislatives attempts such as the California Transparency in the Supply Chain Act); although many multinational corporations ("MNCs") were already voluntarily disclosing ESG metrics, arguably a manifestation of costly signalling, when the disclosure rules turned their voluntary initiative into something that they are simply expected to do, the dynamic of the voluntarism and what the company can signal has completely changed. In other words, the company's intrinsic incentive to be sustainable or environmentally conscious can be crowded out by extrinsic legislative measures.

It is worth noting, however, that the Directive does keep intact some elements of voluntarism by adopting a *comply or explain* approach.[51] That is to say, the Directive does

that witnessed the victim being attacked, but no one even bothered to call the authorities, thinking that surely someone else had already done so).

50 J. Berger, 'Are Luxury Brand Labels and 'Green' Labels Costly Signals of Social Statues? An Extended Replication', *PLos One*, A. Mesoudi (Ed.), Vol. 12, No. 2, 2017. *See also*, R. Bénabou & J. Tirole, 'Incentives and Prosocial Behavior', *American Economic Review*, Vol. 96, No. 5, 2006, p. 1652-1678.

51 Directive 2014/95/EU of the European Parliament and of the Council of 22 October 2014 amending Directive 2013/34/EU as regards disclosure of non-financial and diversity information by certain large undertakings and groups. Article 1 (1)(e) notes that "[w]here the undertaking does not pursue policies in relation to one or more of those matters, the non-financial statement shall provide a clear and reasoned explanation for not doing so." The 'comply or explain' approach is also the preferred approach of the

give the opportunity for the MNCs not to disclose an integrated report, but if they choose not to, they must explain and justify their refusal.[52] While the comply or explain approach does indeed leave an element of flexibility and voluntarism intact, it has essentially changed the default setting of this previously voluntary initiative from an opt in to an opt out; whereas companies could opt in to a CSR initiative before, they will now have to explicitly opt out of complying with the law. Suffice it to state here that companies opting out of compliance have more stigma attached to them than companies not opting into a voluntary initiative, especially from the perspective of consumers who might deem the company opting out of compliance to be a more socially irresponsible one.[53]

In the end, it is difficult to be critical of the EU's assertion – a belief that is shared by many other stakeholders – that "disclosure of nonfinancial information is vital for managing change towards a sustainable global economy by combining long-term profitability with social justice and environmental protection."[54] It remains to be seen, however, what impact these Directives will have, especially given that even prior to the implementation of the various directives and legislations, a lot of companies were already disclosing ESG metrics and conducting due diligence assessments on their own volition: For example, 95% of the world's 250 largest companies were already producing CSR reports that contained various ESG metrics.[55] That is to say, even in the absence of regulations and legislations, many companies were already adopting these CSR initiatives voluntarily, but now that practically every MNC will have to do so, there is a possibility that the appeal of these CSR initiatives

---

aforementioned proposal to amend the Shareholders' Rights Directive, where the companies that choose not to be transparent will have to explain why.

52 In justifying this particular approach, the European Commission has stated the following: "Most corporate governance is soft law and it is thus essential that the 'comply or explain' approach, whereby a company that chooses to depart from the applicable corporate governance code must give reasons for the departure, works well. This approach offers companies an important degree of flexibility, as it recognizes that, in certain circumstances, non-compliance with some recommendations might correspond better to the company's interest than 100% compliance with the code." *See*, European Commission, 'European Commission proposes to strengthen shareholder engagement and introduce a 'say on pay' for Europe's largest companies', 9 April 2014. Retrieved from: http://europa.eu/rapid/press-release_IP-14-396_en.htm?locale=en (adding that "companies that depart from the applicable corporate governance code often fail to provide appropriate explanations for the departure, which makes it more difficult for investors to take informed investment decisions") (last accessed 14 March 2016).

53 K. Roth, 'What are Human Rights For? Three Personal Reflections' *in* D. Moeckli, S. Shah, & S. Sivakumaran, *International Human Rights Law*, Oxford, Oxford University Press, 2014, p. 8 (doubting the impact of 'comply or explain' or 'naming and shaming' approach because "there can be no shame if the public approves of the conduct in question").

54 Directive 2014/95/EU of the European Parliament and of the Council of 22 October 2014 amending Directive 2013/34/EU as regards disclosure of non-financial and diversity information by certain large undertakings and groups. Preamble 3 (adding that "European Parliament acknowledge[s] the importance of businesses divulging information on sustainability such as social and environmental factors, with a view to identifying sustainability risks and increasing investor and consumer trust").

55 C. Casazza, 'Oversight of Corporate Sustainability Activities' *Director's Handbook Series 2014*, Washington D.C., National Association of Corporate Directors with Ernest & Young LLP, 2014, p. 3.

– as a source of market differentiation and/or competitive advantages – could be reduced. This is all to suggest that together with the information overload problem noted above, there are significant risks with the current conception and manifestation of company law based measures promulgated by the EU.

8.4.3 *Uncertain Measures?*

While mandating integrated reports that disclose more corporate information to shareholders that are more empowered have their potential benefits, there are at least three immediate concerns that emerge: First, in light of the Volkswagen emission scandal, the public must be on alert that there is no guarantee that the companies will always be truthful in their disclosures. Second, even assuming that there are such things as corporate integrity and honesty, just because the companies release more information does not mean that every investor (or any other stakeholder for that matter) will read them and make competent decisions accordingly.[56] On a related final point, some believe that the information that the NFRD requires companies to disclose, are not necessarily the relevant indicators to determine whether a company is truly socially responsible or not. Combining the second and the third concern, some believe that "the steadily growing length of the GRI [Global Reporting Initiative] checklist may have made it more difficult for financial analysts to use these reports effectively."[57]

Moreover, even if a socially responsible investor can get past these three concerns, there is still the concern raised back in Section 4 of this contribution that "shareholders' public interest proxy resolutions seeking changes in the corporate policies and practices are rarely adopted."[58] This reality suggests that even if we assume for the sake of the argument here that there are socially motivated companies willing to disclose honest integrated reports and conscious investors willing to read them and invest/divest accordingly, what

56 D. Vogel, *The Market for Virtue: The Potential and Limits of Corporate Social Responsibility*, Washington D.C., Brookings Institution Press, 2006, p. 65 (noting that only a "relatively small portion of investors" actually that take into account ESG factors in their financial analysis, which "clearly limits the impact of the SRI community on share prices and thus on corporate behavior"). *See also*, World Economic Forum, 'Values and Value: Communicating the Strategic Importance of Corporate Citizenship to Investors', 2003. Retrieved from: https://sites.hks.harvard.edu/m-rcbg/CSRI/publications/other_3_nelson_values_and_value.pdf (noting the limited impact of SRI) (last accessed 28 August 2018).

57 D. Vogel, *The Market for Virtue: The Potential and Limits of Corporate Social Responsibility*, Washington D.C., Brookings Institution Press, 2006, p. 69-70 (adding that not only are there too many factors for analysts to consider, but that "[n]o one has developed a way to calculate [corporate performance on environmental and social impact]").

58 *See generally*, A. Willis, 'The Role of the Global Reporting Initiative's Sustainability Reporting Guidelines in the Social Screening of Investments', *Journal of Business Ethics*, Vol. 43, No. 3, 2003, p. 233-237.

impact they will actually have on saving the planet or any other sustainability related goals remain somewhat uncertain.

So as to provisionally conclude this section, we observe that as things stand: 1) the company law based measures put forth by the EU – while noteworthy – are still insufficient in that they do not deal with the core problem of incentives; 2) simply requiring companies to disclose more information is potentially a counter-productive measure that does not necessarily make companies more sustainable nor socially responsible; and 3) even if the existing company law measures worked as intended with investors reading the non-financial reports and using their enhanced shareholder rights to stir the company down a different path, it does not mean that they can *actually* make companies more sustainable and eco-friendly. This brings us to our next – and penultimate – section on what type of measures could, at least in theory, better tackle the incentives of the stakeholders.

8.5 Modest Suggestions and Considerations

The main reason why we suggested that the existing measures – at least at the EU level – are potentially insufficient, counterproductive, and/or of uncertain impact is primarily because they do not address the fundamental issue of intrinsic incentives. It is our contention here that ultimately, the challenge of making companies and their stakeholders more sustainable and socially conscious cannot be adequately achieved without activating their internal motives. Bearing this thought in mind, this contribution is of the opinion that in its present conception, relying on company law to transform corporations into sustainable and socially responsible entities is akin to hammering a nail with a bunch of bananas. While bananas can be useful in a variety of contexts, when used for purposes beyond their intended capacity, they will most likely fail in achieving those objectives.

Nevertheless, if legislatures insist on using company law in their various attempts to transform companies, it must find ways to pay more reverence to the stakeholders' intrinsic incentives and propose more lofty and holistic measures capable of shifting paradigms, rather than making timid deviations from the status quo. In other words, without actually uprooting some of the prevailing assumption surrounding the issue of company law, grand changes will likely not come about. Accordingly, in this short section, we argue that in order for this idealistic metamorphosis to take place: a) company law has to take the issue of incentives more seriously; b) we must realise that there are existing measures that could make corporations more sustainable entities if only the stakeholders adopted the right incentives; and c) in order to make stakeholders behave more pro-socially and for them to have the right intrinsic incentives, what needs to change more fundamentally is not necessarily company law, but corporate culture.

8.5.1 Incentives Really Do Matter

In an ideal world, a company's voluntary decision to be environmentally sustainable would ensure that it outperforms companies that are not investing in sustainability measures, at least in the long term. In such a world, creating new regulations or other extrinsic incentives would not tamper with intrinsic incentives for corporate stakeholders to behave in pro-social behaviour; but alas, we do not live in that world. If we are to inch closer to that ideal world, we must first grasp the reality that great leaps toward sustainability often do not come about when stakeholders are only compelled to do so by rules and regulations, but only when they internalise such beliefs and the values behind them.

To be clear, this contribution does not intend to dismiss the utility of the measures taken by the European Commission through SDR II and NFRD entirely; however, in order to reach the ambitious goals that these Directives set to achieve, more profound and systematic changes are required. Moreover, we fundamentally question whether company law based measures are really the catalyst necessary for achieving such changes.[59] In order to create real tangible changes in corporate behaviour, simply "ticking the boxes" or adding more tools and information for the stakeholders is not enough. Companies must be shown the long-term benefits of being sustainable and be given the time and space to understand the importance of these sustainability values. Corporate stakeholders have to want to be sustainable for the sake of being sustainable. In other words, there must be a genuine reconsideration of the status quo and of the accepted norms, which cannot be completely overhauled through regulation alone.

8.5.2 Workable Company Law Measures Already Exist

If the incentive problem can somehow be addressed and if we can somehow reach a critical mass of socially responsible and sustainability conscious stakeholders, we posit that there are already enough workable company law based measures that could transform companies into becoming socially responsible catalysts. Here, we offer the examples of: i) benefit corporations and ii) socially conscious exchanges. These measures not only offer companies that are seriously – and intrinsically – motivated to being sustainable, a way to showcase their commitment to sustainability, but it also empowers them through a possible competitive advantage – vis-à-vis companies who only talk the talk – through market differentiation. In addition, these measures provide a "safer" environment where prevailing traditional assumptions of shareholder primacy and short-term profit maximisation are treated on

59 We mean to imply here that the most apt tool – at least in terms of legislative measures – for incentivising sustainability is not necessarily company law, but environmental regulations and public law based measures that set up emission standards, prevent contaminations of water supplies, and so forth.

par with other considerations in a more holistic manner. These company law measures not only allow for differentiation of intrinsic versus extrinsic motivations to manifest – as they are still voluntary measures – but more importantly, it creates a cultural paradigm shift, where sustainability is not only a buzz-word, but can also lead to profitability.

8.5.2.1 Benefit Corporations

One of the workable company law based ideas that is gaining popularity – at least in the US – is for a company to incorporate as a *benefit corporation*.[60] In order for a company to incorporate as a benefit corporation, they must meet several unique requirements: First, not only do their corporate purposes have to explicitly state that they will "operate in a responsible and sustainable manner" but in order to "provide directors, stockholders, and ultimately the courts, some direction, they are also required to identify in their certificate of incorporation a specific public benefit purpose the corporation is obligated to pursue."[61] Directors of benefit corporations are also required to provide an integrated ESG report in addition to all of the other financial documents that they are obligated to report to their shareholders.[62] These requirements add a heightened sense of accountability for the directors, whose fiduciary duty is no longer limited to maximising profits, but they now must put their social and environmental objectives on par with their financial objectives.

The stated objective of a benefit corporation is to "take care of the people, the products, and the profits – in that order,"[63] and they are backing up their claims by incorporating in a very unique manner. The obvious benefit, for the lack of a better word, of incorporating as a benefit corporation is that it: 1) shows the company's serious commitment to social responsibility, 2) increases corporate transparency, and 3) enhances the directors' accountability to the stakeholders and to society at large (not just to their shareholders). There are over 500 registered benefit corporations currently operating in the US and according to a 2012 White Paper written by a group of US practitioners, a benefit corporation "is the most comprehensive yet flexible legal entity devised to address the needs of entrepreneurs and investors and, ultimately, the general public" because benefit corpora-

60 In the US, incorporating as a C corp is the standard way to incorporate, which grants companies limited liability protections amongst other benefits noted back in Chapter 3, whereas S corps has similar benefits to C corps but are given special tax status.

61 J. Markell, 'A New Kind of Corporation to Harness the Power of Private Enterprise for Public Benefit', *The Huffington Post*, 22 July 2013. Retrieved from: www.huffingtonpost.com/gov-jack-markell/public-benefit-corporation_b_3635752.html (last accessed 4 April 2017).

62 B Corporation, *About B* Corps. Available at: www.bcorporation.net/what-are-b-corps (last accessed 29 August 2018) (stating that to be a benefit corporation means that a company will be transparent regarding their social and environmental performance standards and meet higher legal accountability standards so that they can be a sustainable business).

63 B. Horowitz, *The Hard Thing About Hard Things: Building a Business When There Are No Easy Answers*, New York, Harper Collins, 2014, p. 93 (quoting Jim Barksdale and commenting that "taking care of the people is the most difficult of the three by far and if you don't do it, the other two won't matter").

tions "offer clear market differentiation, broad legal protection to directors and officers, expanded shareholder rights, and greater access to capital than current alternative approaches."[64]

While socially conscious stakeholders do not grow on trees, the emergence of the benefit corporation model does suggest that if corporate stakeholders are properly motivated, there are company law measures that would enable and empower them. The key differentiation is that benefit company incorporation preserves the voluntarism and the intrinsic incentives of the corporate stakeholders, unlike with the SRD II and NFRD.

8.5.2.2 Stock Market Listing Requirements

In order for companies to be a publicly listed company on a stock exchange, they must comply with various reporting requirements of that particular stock exchange. Many of the world's stock exchanges currently do not offer guidance on non-financial reporting,[65] but there are some like the New York Stock Exchange, Nasdaq, and the Johannesburg Stock Exchange that explicitly require their listed companies to submit integrated reports in addition to their financials.[66] The incentive for companies to comply or to list in exchanges with such requirements is the same reason why companies choose incorporate as a benefit corporation: Many CEOs and business leaders believe that "embedding sustainability into core business will drive revenue growth and new opportunities."[67] Taking this to heart, companies like Royal Philips Electronic take ESG factors very seriously and

---

64 W.J. Clark & L. Vranka, 'Benefit Corporation White Paper', *Benefit Corporation*. Retrieved from: http://benefitcorp.net/policymakers/benefit-corporation-white-paper (last accessed 18 December 2016). Wide variety of companies including clothing companies such as Patagonia or crowd-funding sites like Kickstarter have re-incorporated as benefit corporations.

65 R.G. Eccles & D. Saltzman, 'Achieving Sustainability Through Integrated Reporting', *Stanford Social Innovation Review* 9, No. 3, Summer 2011, p. 56-61, at p. 57 (noting that "only a handful of the world's top 30 stock exchanges provide guidance on non-financial reporting").

66 *See e.g.* 'NYSE Listed Company Manual'. Johannesburg Stock Exchange, as a matter of fact, was the first stock exchange in the world to require listing companies to submit integrated reports. Other countries' stock exchanges (i.e. Nordic countries such as Denmark and Norway) require reports on environmental impacts of the companies and the UK have been stepping up requirements to include ESG metrics as well under the guise of transparency measures. *See e.g.* R.G. Eccles & D. Saltzman, 'Achieving Sustainability Through Integrated Reporting', *Stanford Social Innovation Review* 9, No. 3, Summer 2011, p. 56-61, at p. 59. *See also*, European Parliament Directorate-General For External Policies (Policy Department), 'New Options for Strengthening Standards on Social and Environmental Responsibilities of Corporations and Their Implementation',EXPO/B/DEVE/FWC/2009-01/Lot5/36 PE 457.138 (2013), at p. 5.

67 The UN Global Compact-Accenture CEO Study on Sustainability 2013: Architects of a Better World. Retrieved from: www.unglobalcompact.org/docs/news_events/8.1/UNGC_Accenture_CEO_Study_2013.pdf (last accessed 4 April 2017), at p. 11. *See also*, R. G. Eccles, I. Ioannou & G. Serafein, 'The Impact of Corporate Sustainability on Organizational Processes and Performance', *Harvard Business School Working Paper Series* 12-035, 2013, (noting that companies that manage their environmental and social performance could "significantly outperform their counterparts over the long-term, both in terms of stock market as well as accounting performance").

consider them as "driver[s] of growth" and an "integral" part of their businesses.[68] In other words, some firms believe that listing on these socially conscious exchanges is yet another way to achieve market differentiation from their competitors that are less environmentally conscious. Again, stock exchanges that impose these listing requirements could be argued as a company law-related measure that can enable companies to be more sustainable if the intrinsic incentive for the corporate stakeholder to do so is already present.

What influences the incentives of companies to list in these exchanges ultimately comes down to the issue of profit versus sustainable impact. Although there are various claims that suggest an almost causal relationship between the implementation of various CSR initiatives (e.g. listing on these exchanges) and long term profitability for the company, this is not necessarily true, at least not in all cases: For example, the London Stock Exchange's subsidiary FTSE Group's FTSE4Good Index and the Dow Jones Sustainability Index, the "two major ethical stock indexes… since its inception… have underperformed the market by 3 per cent and 8 per cent, respectively."[69] This means that if the motivation for companies to engage in sustainability initiatives is primarily for the sake of profit, companies might find that the cost of being sustainable or being socially responsible may not be worth the benefits. Again, this goes to show us that while there are various measures that would enable companies to be more sustainable, whether the companies choose to use them or implement them ultimately comes down to the question of incentives and for relevant stakeholders to see and treat the people and the planet on par with their profit.

8.5.3 *Need for a Cultural Paradigm Shift*

Legally speaking, a company is a legal entity of its own standing, but in reality a company is made up of various stakeholders such as the shareholders, the management, the workers, and so forth. Ultimately, it is the individuals sitting on the board or attending the general meetings that determine the company's culture. Considering that the recently introduced legislation is about "the company" or "the shareholder" having to fulfil certain requirements or having certain responsibilities as a solution to enhancing ESG involvement of companies, the approach is only focusing on the surface of the problem. In other words, it relies on a change in conduct, while what we need is a change in corporate culture and the moral compass of its stakeholders. For this reason, traditional company law might not be the

68 Rudy Provoost, chairman of Philips' Sustainability Board and CEO of Philips Lighting, *Philips Press Release* 18 February 2011, *as cited by* R.G. Eccles & D. Saltzman, 'Achieving Sustainability Through Integrated Reporting', *Stanford Social Innovation Review* 9, No. 3, Summer 2011, p. 56-61, at p. 60.

69 D. Vogel, *The Market for Virtue: The Potential and Limits of Corporate Social Responsibility*, Washington D.C., Brookings Institution Press, 2006, at p. xvi (citing to findings by Stier), *see*, K. Stier, 'Investing in Climate Change', *Ethical Corporation*, 2006.

most suitable tool to advancing various sustainability initiatives. Instead, we have to be creative in looking for alternative solutions that help incentivising stakeholders intrinsically.

In order to actually modify the intrinsic incentives of various corporate stakeholders, what needs to change – above all else – is the corporate culture and some of the fundamental assumptions that linger and permeate around corporations noted back in Section 2. Fundamental change in the status quo is almost impossible without a paradigm shift in corporate culture, but this change – as unattainable as it may seem now – is not impossible. From a business perspective, systems scientist and management expert Peter Senge and his colleagues note that there are several stages in the evolution of a business and its culture.[70] In the earlier stages of the evolution, companies are reluctant to make socially responsible changes if they are costly and the law does not require them to change. They see such changes as unnecessary at least initially, but some gradually start seeing social responsibility as a potential competitive advantage, which evolves them to the "voluntary compliance" stage. Companies at this stage still see social responsibility in a view that is still linked to their bottom line and their hopes that the enhanced brand image/reputation might lead them to higher profits. The truly evolved company, at least according to Senge's framework, is the company that integrates social responsibility into the company's core strategies.[71] The argument that this contribution supports is that a benefit corporation – a corporation that espouses many of the ideas noted in this contribution – that lists on a socially conscious listing exchange with intrinsically motivated stakeholders is the manifestation of the 'truly evolved company'. Where we are at today is that companies are at various stages of this evolutionary framework, with some failing to comply even with the law, while others are going above and beyond what is required by law to incorporate as a benefit corporation. While company law might enable and empower the latter, it will not incentivise the former to transform into the latter in and of itself.

8.6 Conclusion

In sum, company law serves a wide variety of purposes – from empowering shareholders to requiring companies to disclose more and more information to the public – but there are various limitations in terms of what they can achieve given its present conception and manifestation. As this contribution noted, the EU Directives and other similar company

70 *See generally*, P.M. Senge, B. Smith, N. Kruschwitz, J. Laur, & S. Schley, *The Necessary Revolution: How Individuals and Organizations are Working Together to Create a Sustainable World*, New York, Doubleday, 2008.

71 *See generally*, P.M. Senge, B. Smith, N. Kruschwitz, J. Laur, & S. Schley, *The Necessary Revolution: How Individuals and Organizations are Working Together to Create a Sustainable World*, New York: Doubleday, 2008.

law-based measures have failed to address at least two major problems: First lingering concern is whether the shareholders will bother using their enhanced rights afforded to them by the SRD II and whether stakeholders like a perspective investor will actually take the time to comb through the additional information now available to them thanks to the NFRD. Specifically with regards to the latter, even if certain shareholders or investors do decide to read the additional materials, it remains unclear whether they will be able to interpret and decipher the ESG metrics in a competent manner that will actually make companies behave in a more environmentally-friendly manner.[72] As previously noted, simply offering more and more information can not only lead to an information overload problem, but if governments continue to be more and more involved, there is also an increased risk of the crowding out problem.

A more fundamental issue that this contribution raised is the fact that company law does not deal with the issue of intrinsic incentives. In other words, these company law based measures are not necessarily motivating stakeholders to be more environmentally friendly in and of themselves. To the extent that there are environmentally and socially conscious corporate stakeholders, company law can help them to make companies more responsible; however, the argument put forth by this contribution is that company law – as it currently stands – does not stimulate or modify their intrinsic incentives, nor was it ever the primary objective of company law to do so. Akin to hammering a nail with a bunch of bananas, when used for purposes outside of its primary objectives, company law will not achieve the aspirational goal of transforming corporations into more environmentally friendly, socially responsible entities. That is unless, of course, company law itself goes through a radical paradigm shift and reassesses its prevailing assumptions. Otherwise, it's just a bunch of bananas.

72 For example, the Directive on Disclosure of Non-Financial and Diversity Information has not even specified what type of ESG metrics the companies are required to disclose. Article 2 of the Directive states that "[t]he Commission shall publish the guidelines by 6 December 2016," but it can be expected that the Directive will allow some flexibility, not to mention the number of existing instruments such as the UN Global Compact, ISO 26000, OECD Guidelines for Multinational Enterprises or the Global Reporting Initiative already provide guidance. Bear in mind the allegation made earlier that some of these guidelines and the information that they require companies to disclose could actually make matters more confusing for the investors. A. Vaccaro & J. Fontrodona, 'Academic View: The Myth of Corporate Transparency', *The Economist*, 7 September 2010. Retrieved from: www.economist.com/newsbook/2010/09/07/academic-view-the-myth-of-corporate-transparency (noting no amount of transparency laws will save society from "business malpractice and corporate psychopaths") (last accessed 17 June 2019).

9 Sustainability and Optional Regimes

A Legislative Means of Empowering Private Individuals in the Development of Socially Beneficial Activities?

William Bull

9.1 Introduction

As has already been discussed elsewhere in this book, the concepts of the 'sharing economy' and 'sustainable development' are certainly not uncontroversial ones.

First and foremost, the very definition of these notions is disputed. As regards the former, this is the case not only because the term 'sharing economy' has been defined differently by academics, stakeholders, and even EU institutions, but also because the appropriateness of the use of the adjective 'sharing' in this context is disputed, given that many of the businesses and online platforms that operate in this sector of the economy are engaged in for-profit economic activities, which are more concerned with providing access to goods and services than promoting the sharing of these goods and services as such. And as for the latter, apart from the arguably inherent contradiction in the aims of attaining goals of human development whilst at the same time encouraging the sustainable use of natural resources, it has been contested that the idea of using non-renewable resources in a sustainable manner is itself flawed.[1]

Secondly, even if private law as predominantly facilitative law could be used to promote sustainable development goals such as those advanced by the United Nations[2], it is also debatable to what extent the goals of private law should be geared towards facilitating the collaborative economy, as a means in turn of supporting sustainable development. Clearly the onset of the sharing economy gives rise to regulatory challenges that may necessitate a re-evaluation of private law institutions, but what exactly the regulatory response should be to novel business forms based on some form of collaborative activity is far less apparent. Calls for legislative reform in this area have ranged from measures outlawing commercial

1 See for e.g. R.K Turner, 'Sustainability, Resource Conservation and Pollution Control: An Overview', in R.K. Turner (ed.), *Sustainable Environmental Management: Principles and Practice*, (Belhaven Press, 1988), p. 13; S. Hayward et al., 'Environmental Quality 2000: Assessing Michigan and America at the 30th Anniversary of Earth Day', Mackinac Center Report on Facts and Figures on Air and Water Quality, Resource Use, and Other Environmental Indicators, (Mackinac Center for Public Policy, 2000).

2 UN Sustainable Development Goals, as part of the 2030 Agenda for Sustainable Development: https://sustainabledevelopment.un.org/?menu=1300.

sharing practices, to instruments facilitating the expansion of such practices across national borders, to pretty much anything in between. Of course, the kind of regulation one advocates in this respect will depend very much on the general view one takes of the sharing economy, and particularly whether it is seen as an innovative solution to issues of resource management that benefits consumers and the environment alike, or rather as an evolution that contributes little to economic growth while at the same time serving as a vehicle for unfair competition with more traditional business models.

At any rate, there appears to be some consensus surrounding the need to establish new legal frameworks in order to address the challenges posed by the sharing economy, and to "prevent the sharing economy from being curtailed or driven along pre-determined lines".[3] In particular, there is a case for laying down common rules at the EU level, with a view to avoiding inconsistent or even conflicting measures being taken at the national or even the regional level. Indeed this is in line with the argument we have made previously, according to which novel matters should be regulated at the EU level, given the high degree of probability that legislating on 'novelties' will lead to fragmentation if left (solely) to the Member States.[4] Nevertheless, even if this is the case, the question remains what a 21st century private law in the perspective of sustainability and the shared economy *should* look like, not only in terms of the concrete rules applicable to specific collaborative activities, but also in terms of the *form* such rules could take.

In the present contribution, we will seek to tackle the second part of this question, by examining the role optional private law regimes can (and do already) play in facilitating private activities and ventures that also benefit the community or public interest (in the broad sense of the welfare of society as a whole, as opposed to the interests of select individuals within society[5]). Insofar as tools are needed to contribute to the achievement of sustainability goals, optional regimes could feature among these, as legal instruments emanating from the state that empower private parties (be they natural or legal persons) to engage in and develop activities (also) for the public good. In particular, this contribution will consider the possible role of optional instruments of the European Union, such as the European Economic Interest Grouping (EEIG), which can be (and has been) used by both natural and legal persons in different Member States to form temporary (or indeed more permanent) supranational company structures with the aim developing and undertaking

3 P. Goudin, 'The Cost of Non-Europe in the Sharing Economy: Economic, Social and Legal Challenges and Opportunities', European Parliamentary Research Service Study (January 2016), p. 29.

4 See B. Akkermans et al., *Who Does What? On the allocation of regulatory competences in European Private Law*, (Intersentia, 2015), p. 100 ff.

5 On the concept of the public interest see further, for e.g., H. Lok Sang, *Public Policy and the Public Interest*, (Routledge, 2011).

common economic activities across borders.[6] The joint activities in which these persons can cooperate range from research and development programmes in the biofuels sector to the coordination of international transportation and haulage. Furthermore, on top of the area of company law, this contribution will also reflect on potential uses of EU optional instruments in other areas of private law to support commercial activities with a 'social' dimension, and especially in the areas of contract law and intellectual property law, where considerations of sustainability and sharing – and how to balance these with the need to ensure and protect individual freedoms and personal autonomy – are certainly important ones.

9.2 OPTIONAL REGIMES IN GENERAL

Optional regimes[7] are legal regimes that individuals can use as an alternative body of rules of law under which to execute an equivalent legal act (be it forming a recognised company, or making an enforceable contract, or registering an intellectual property right, etc.) in the same jurisdiction. More precisely, optional regimes are legal regimes that private actors who wish to execute a legal act in a certain jurisdiction can choose as an applicable regime, as an alternative to the corresponding legal regime (or possibly regimes[8]) provided by the (pre-existing) domestic law of that jurisdiction. In other words, the aspect of 'optionality' in this context refers to the situation where individuals who elect to perform a given legal act in a certain territory have a choice as to the legal regime under which to do so. Therefore, if an individual in such a territory chooses to execute a legal act under an optional regime instead of under a domestic regime provided by the legal system of the jurisdiction, the optional regime is applicable to that legal act rather than the regime of the national legal system (or at least in the first instance). And, conversely, the applicability of an optional legal regime is excluded in its entirety unless private actors opt for it. It is true that some domestic legal regimes could also be described as optional legal regimes in the sense of 'alternative regimes', insofar as they too could be 'chosen' by private actors as alternatives to legal regimes available in different national jurisdictions. In particular, domestic contract

6 There is also the possibility of legal options being created at national (if not international) level: Indeed, the EEIG itself was modelled on a national legal structure enacted in France, known as the *groupement d'intérêt économique*, which allowed natural and legal persons to undertake joint activities in a company form previously unavailable to them on the French territory. However, the focus of this contribution will be on optional instruments of the EU, given that EU OIs are aimed at facilitating *cross-border* activities of natural and legal persons, which is especially significant as far as regards collaborative efforts towards sharing and sustainability.

7 See further W.A. Bull, *Optional instruments of the European Union: A definitional, normative and explanatory study* (Intersentia, 2016).

8 In some cases a jurisdiction may provide more than one legal regime governing similar subject matter (think, for instance, of different national company forms).

law regimes could be seen as optional regimes on this view, to the extent that they can be chosen as the applicable legal regime by parties contracting between different jurisdictions through so-called 'choice of law' clauses. In addition, national company forms could also be considered as optional regimes in this sense, inasmuch as operators can choose the applicable company law by choosing the state of incorporation. However, domestic legal regimes that can be used via a choice of law are distinguishable from optional legal regimes because, if private actors in a given jurisdiction choose to execute a legal act using the domestic legal regime of another jurisdiction – in which case they at the same time 'choose not to' use the legal regime(s) of the jurisdiction in which they are based to execute that legal act – the applicability of the legal regime(s) of their 'own' jurisdiction is still not necessarily excluded entirely. By contrast, if private actors choose not to use an optional legal regime (either implicitly or explicitly) in preference for the domestic legal regime of a certain jurisdiction, the optional regime is (again in principle) not applicable to their legal act in any way. Therefore, unlike optional legal regimes, domestic legal regimes may be applicable to the legal acts of private actors even if they are not 'chosen'.

9.3 Optional Instruments of the European Union as an Alternative Form of EU law-making

Focusing now on optional instruments of the European Union[9] in particular, these are optional regimes established by European Union legislation. More precisely, European Union Optional Instruments (EU OIs) are optional regimes created by binding 'legal acts of the Union' within the meaning of the Treaty on the Functioning of the European Union (TFEU) that, once adopted, are available for private actors to select. Being established by binding EU legislation, EU OIs are not 'optional' for Member States (or at least not for the Member States that participate in them), but rather are optional because they are applicable to private activities only if they are selected by individuals (who, depending on the EU optional regime in question, may be one or more natural and/or legal persons, based only in the EU or also third countries) in the manner that the legislation prescribes. And, like any optional regime, EU optional regimes are available to private actors as an alternative to existing regimes available within domestic legal orders. Accordingly, EU OIs leave individuals with a choice (or at least an additional choice) between the optional EU regime and corresponding regimes provided by the legal systems of the Member States.

9 Again, see further W.A. Bull, *Optional instruments of the European Union: A definitional, normative and explanatory study*, (Intersentia, 2016). See also J. Basedow, *The Law of Open Societies: Private Ordering and Public Regulation in the Conflict of Laws*, (Brill, 2015), and B. Fauvarque-Cosson & M. Behar-Touchais, 'Implementation of Optional Instruments within European Civil Law', Study for European Parliament Legal Affairs Committee, PE 462.425 (2012).

While EU OIs may (and indeed have) been classified as a form of European 'approximation' (or 'harmonisation'), on the basis that they serve to bring Member State legal systems 'closer together' (or make them 'more consistent'), they actually constitute a distinct form of EU law-making, fundamentally different from 'traditional' EU approximating measures,[10] which typically correspond to binding EU legislation that seeks to engender convergence between Member State legal systems by replacing and/or amending divergent national rules of law with uniform (or at least more uniform) European rules or standards.[11] Unlike EU approximating legislation, EU OIs do not in principle require any amendment to or replacement of existing provisions within the legal orders of the Member States, but rather introduce new, alternative legal regimes into national law. And unlike EU OIs, EU approximating measures do not create alternative legal regimes that are only applicable when selected by private individuals. On the contrary, the applicability of the domestic rules modified by EU approximating measures is not (or at least not necessarily) subject to any requirement for individuals to first opt into them. In this sense, EU legislation establishing OIs may be considered as a kind of 'soft hard law', because although it is binding on the Member States in the same way as traditional 'hard law' approximating measures, it leaves Member States free to maintain their own legal regimes, and private actors with the choice as to whether to become subject to its application or not.

Thus, in themselves, optional instruments amount to an alternative form of EU law-making, which aims to bring Member State legal systems closer together in a very different way to traditional approximating legislation. It is not a question of the content of substantive norms of European origin, so much as one of the legislative form these norms take, and the effect this has on the legal orders of the Member States. EU legislation establishing OIs affiliates the Member State legal systems to the same 'European' legal regime, which takes effect within – and is therefore recognised in unison by – each of these systems. This has the consequence that a new legal form (or right, or title, etc., as the case may be) is introduced into each of the Member States in addition to the pre-existing domestic regimes of those States – and each of these new legal forms is connected with one another, under the umbrella of the European regime. In the context of the discussion surrounding a 21st century private law in the perspective of sustainability and the sharing economy, the question is specifically what form any common European rules intended to address the challenges posed by the sharing economy and to achieve sustainability goals should take. In other words, could optional instruments of the European Union serve to facilitate cross-

10 Approximating legislation is characterised here as 'traditional' simply on the ground that the European legislator has frequently and consistently enacted legislation of this kind ever since the creation of the European Economic Community (EEC).

11 Of course, depending on the EU approximating legislation in question, the degree of uniformity aimed at can and does vary, and in any event total uniformity is not realistic.

border collaborative activities and sustainable development as an alternative vehicle for achieving legal solutions?

In what follows, we will seek to provide an answer to this question by examining certain specific EU OIs, or areas of European law in which optional instruments have been adopted and/or proposed, and how these may (or indeed already do) facilitate private ventures that also benefit the community or public interest. We will begin by looking at the aforementioned European Economic Interest Grouping in the area of European company law, before moving to explore other areas of private law, notably intellectual property law and contract law.

9.4 The European Economic Interest Grouping (EEIG)

The EEIG was actually the very first optional instrument to be adopted at European-level, enacted by means of a Regulation on 25 July 1985.[12] This legislation created a new Community-wide form of corporate legal entity, to be added to the list of existing national company forms available to private actors in each of the Member States. As a result, natural and legal persons would now have an additional possibility of forming and operating an EEIG. Provided that there are at least two natural persons who carry on their principal activities in different Member States and/or legal persons (i.e. companies, firms and other legal entities of any size governed by public or private law) that have their central administrations in different Member States in the grouping, an EEIG can be formed by these persons in accordance with the Regulation.

In general terms, the purpose of the EEIG is to allow for effective economic cooperation between its members across borders within the Common Market. It is akin to a partnership/ business association/ joint venture, insofar as any profit or loss generated by an EEIG is attributed to its members and, moreover, the purpose of its activity must be 'to facilitate or develop the economic activities of its members and to improve or increase the results of those activities', rather than making profits for itself.[13] In other words, the EEIG is a vehicle that is ancillary to its members. This is in contrast to the purpose of a company (sensu stricto), which operates autonomously from its members, and seeks to make profits 'only part of which would be distributed, the rest being retained for its own purposes in the form of reserves, provision for depreciation etc.'[14] On the other hand, though, the EEIG does have other features which are shared by more permanent forms of cooperation. Most importantly, an EEIG has full and autonomous legal capacity, meaning it has 'the capacity,

12 Council Regulation 2137/85 of 25 July 1985 on the European Economic Interest Grouping (EEIG).
13 EEIG Regulation, Art. 3(1).
14 Proposal for a regulation of the Council on the European cooperation grouping (ECG), COM(73) 2046 (submitted to the Council by the Commission on 21 December 1973), p. 19-20.

in its own name, to have rights and obligations of all kinds, to make contracts or accomplish other legal acts, and to sue and be sued'[15], in accordance with the provisions that are generally applicable to company structures.

So the EEIG Regulation introduced an instrument of cooperation that allows private individuals to undertake joint commercial activities across borders for a limited or unlimited period within a legal framework that was previously unavailable to them. The list of activities that could be undertaken within this framework is long, ranging from common research and development programmes and the joint provision of goods or services to the creation of consortia for participation in public tenders (to name but a few);[16] and these could be in a wide array of sectors, including agriculture, finance, transport, the liberal professions, etc.[17] It is true that these activities do not have to be aimed at achieving goals connected with resource management and sustainable development, but it is equally true that they can be. For example, as the Commission notes, one EEIG has been set up by small and medium-sized enterprises (SMEs) to develop common activities of research and development in the field of biofuels.[18] This is a particularly noteworthy example in the context of the present discussion, as biofuels constitute a renewable alternative to fossil fuels in the EU's transport sector. Provided biofuels are produced in a sustainable manner, they can thereby help to lower greenhouse gas emissions and increase the EU's security of energy supply without adversely affecting the environment. But there are also various other examples of EEIGs whose activities are geared towards sustainability goals. For instance, ICE EEIG, based in Brussels, is a grouping of six consultancy firms that takes part in technical assistance funded projects and aims (among other things) at the establishment of consultation frameworks to support sustainable economic development.[19] Another EEIG registered in Ireland is IGROW EEIG, which is active in the field of integrated technologies and services for sustainable growth in different areas, including the economy, water, energy and the environment.[20] And the legal management organisation of BONUS, a joint research and development programme initiated by national research funding institutions in eight EU Member States around the Baltic Sea in support of sustainable development and ecosystem based management of the region, was formed as an EEIG.[21]

15 EEIG Regulation, Art. 1(2).

16 See A. Santa Maria, *European Economic Law*, (Kluwer, 2009), p. 175.

17 See J. de Bruycker, 'EC Company Law-The European Company v. The European Economic Interest Grouping and the Harmonization of the National Company Laws', 21 *Georgia Journal of International and Comparative Law* 2 (1991), 191, 197, and also (referring to) European Commission, 'The European Economic Interest Grouping (EEIG): A New Instrument for Economic Cooperation in the Community', The European File 3 (1989).

18 See European Commission, 'The EEIG: an instrument for transnational cooperation: A practical handbook for SMEs', p. 11 ff. (also for numerous other examples of EEIGs).

19 International Consulting Expertise (ICE) EEIG: www.ice-org.eu.

20 Integrated Technologies and Services for Sustainable Growth (IGROW) EEIG: www.igrow-eeig.com.

21 Baltic Organisations' Network for Funding Science EEIG: www.bonusportal.org.

It therefore seems fair to say that the optional European legal structure that is the EEIG is playing a significant role in promoting social entrepreneurship and sustainability-driven economic activities across borders in the EU, particularly in terms of research and development on a transnational scale (even if the total number of EEIG formations in the EU is not particularly large[22]).

9.5 The Community Plant Variety Right (CPVR)

Another area of European law in which optional instruments that may also serve the community interest have been adopted is intellectual property law.

To begin with plant variety rights (also known as plant breeders' rights), a Regulation on Community plant variety rights was adopted in 1994.[23] The purpose of this Regulation was to create a Community-level plant variety title that would enable plant breeders 'to acquire, upon a single application and through a single decision, direct and uniform protection throughout the Community for varieties of all botanical taxa and hybrids of taxa.'[24] Accordingly, with the introduction of the Community plant variety right (CPVR), breeders (who again may be natural or legal persons) would be liberated from the need to obtain plant variety protection in individual Member States on the basis of separate applications, as they would now have the option to seek protection on a Community scale through an intellectual property right equally valid and operative in the territory of all of the Member States.[25]

Plant variety rights are perhaps best understood as a special title of protection of intellectual property positioned in the vicinity, and available in lieu of, a general patent regime. The intellectual property in question consists of new and distinct varieties of plants that are capable of cultivation,[26] created by breeders in the agricultural or horticultural market. These innovative varieties will usually offer benefits such as greater yields or stronger resistance to pests and disease.[27] Breeders therefore acquire plant variety rights in order to ensure a return on their investment in developing a new variety of a botanical genus or species, as these exclusive rights allow them to prevent others from freely propa-

22 According to Libertas European EEIG Information Centre, as of the end of 2017 a total of 2,547 EEIGs have been formed since the Regulation became applicable on 1 July 1989, most of which have been formed in Belgium, France, Germany and the Netherlands: See LIBERTAS – European Institute GmbH, EEIG Statistics from the European EEIG Information Centre, available at: www.libertas-institut.com.

23 Council Regulation 2100/94 of 27 July 1994 on Community plant variety rights (CPVR).

24 Proposal for a Regulation on Community plant variety rights, COM(90) 347 final, p. 3.

25 See CPVR Regulation, Art. 2.

26 As follows from the legal definition of the term 'variety' provided in the International Convention for the Protection of New Varieties of Plants ('UPOV Convention') 1961 (Art. 2(2)).

27 See T. Millett, 'The Community system of plant variety rights', 24 *European Law Review* 3 [1999], p. 231.

gating it for a certain period of time.[28] In other words, plant variety rights provide breeders with an incentive to develop novel plant groupings, which in many cases can benefit the public interest, on top of the breeders themselves. Apart from the adverse health effects that pesticides cause, particularly in developing countries, pesticide use gives rise to a number of environmental concerns, including soil contamination and water pollution as well as a diminution of biodiversity. Hence innovative crop strains that are more resistant to pests and therefore reduce the need for pesticides can be of benefit both to public health and to the environment. Similarly, novel plant varieties that deliver greater yields and resistance to disease are beneficial in terms of sustainable production, which aims at "doing more and better with less."[29] That is, they can serve to improve responsible production and efficiency in the use of land and agricultural resources. Of course, as with any intellectual property right, it is true that the availability of exclusive plant variety rights may conversely have the effect of hindering the propagation of new strains of plants, inasmuch as other plant breeders will be prevented from commercialising those strains, again for a certain period anyway.[30] However, there is also the possibility of compulsory exploitation licences being granted on grounds of public interest in certain circumstances, if for example the right holder is unable to meet demand, in order to assure public access to protected varieties. This possibility is enshrined in the CPVR Regulation as well, Article 29 of which provides for a compulsory exploitation right. Therefore, in this way, IP systems can also assure a form of sharing, by curtailing over-protection of individual interests in favour of community interests.

Thus, with the adoption of the CPVR Regulation, plant breeders can obtain a unitary plant variety right that is recognised by all EU Member States as one and the same, thereby entitling them to plant variety protection throughout the territory of the EU on the strength of a single title. Unlike the EEIG (or indeed various other EU OIs), there is not actually a formal cross-border requirement for obtaining a CPVR, although if the breeder "sees a market for a new variety in more than two Member States the Community option is the logical choice."[31] Breeders can submit an application for plant variety protection in any of the official languages of the European Union,[32] either directly to the Community Plant Variety Office (CPVO, based in Angers, France)[33] or via a national agency of a Member

28 *Ibid.*

29 See United Nations Sustainable Development Goals, and specifically Goal 12: Ensure sustainable consumption and production patterns; www.un.org/sustainabledevelopment/sustainable-consumption-production/.

30 In the case of the CPVR this period is 25 years – or, when it comes to varieties of vine and tree species, 30 years – following the year of grant; see CPVR Regulation, Art. 19.

31 B. Kiewiet, 'Plant variety protection in the European Community', 27 *World Patent Information* 319 (2005), p. 321.

32 Cf. CPVR Regulation, Art. 34.

33 CPVR Regulation, Art. 4.

State.[34] The CPVO, which was established by the same Regulation, is accorded the exclusive competence to examine CPVR applications and ultimately to grant Community plant variety rights. This examination is conducted on the basis of uniform criteria, again laid down in the Regulation itself.[35] Given that prior to the introduction of the CPVR it was necessary for plant breeders to seek protection separately in each Member State by obtaining national plant variety rights, this means that the CPVR Regulation has served to strengthen the protection available in the EU for new plant varieties. According to the most recent figures published by the CPVO at the end of 2017,[36] a total of 47,638 CPVRs have been granted since the Community plant variety protection system started operating in 1995, and a total of 61,513 applications have been received during this period. As for the annual number of applications for CPVRs, this has evolved from a total of 1,394 in 1996 to a peak of 3,626 in 2014.[37] The largest number of applications in 2014 (by far) were filed in the Netherlands (1,324 applications), followed by France (463), the United States (462) and Germany (376) – though CPVRs have also been filed in other EU Member States and third countries.[38] On the basis of these figures, the CPVO asserts that the CPVR system "has been a success story from the start"[39] – and certainly many would agree. In the opinion of Llewelyn and Adcock, for example, the figures produced by the CPVO "indicate the success of the system."[40]

9.6 The European Patent with Unitary Effect (UP)

Moving on to patent law (more generally), at the end of 2012 another OI was adopted to provide for unitary patent protection in the EU, namely the European patent with unitary effect (or 'Unitary Patent', UP).[41] The Regulation introducing this OI was passed by means of the enhanced cooperation procedure (for only the second time in the procedure's history)

34 CPVR Regulation, Art. 49.

35 As elaborated in test guidelines adopted by the Administrative Council of the CPVO.

36 Community Plant Variety Office statistics of 31st December 2017, available at: www.cpvo.europa.eu/main/en/home/about-the-cpvo/statistics.

37 See Community Plant Variety Office Annual Report 2015, available at: www.cpvo.europa.eu/main/en/home/documents-and-publications/annual-reports.

38 See Community Plant Variety Office Annual Report 2014, available at: www.cpvo.europa.eu/main/en/home/documents-and-publications/annual-reports.

39 Community Plant Variety Office Annual Report 2014, at p. 8. See also B. Kiewiet, 'Plant variety protection in the European Community', 27 *World Patent Information* 319 (2005), p. 321, 324. Kiewiet points out that the number of applications received by the CPVO by 2004 (over 20,000) was "higher than the sum of the national applications received by the national PVR authorities within the European Community over the same time period...".

40 M. Llewelyn & M. Adcock, *European Plant Intellectual Property*, (Hart, 2006), p. 241.

41 Regulation 1257/2012 of the European Parliament and of the Council of 17 December 2012 implementing enhanced cooperation in the area of the creation of unitary patent protection.

with the involvement of all of the EU Member States minus Italy and Spain (which objected to the proposed translation arrangements for the Unitary Patent, since Italian and Spanish is not included in the list of official languages in which UPs can be filed).[42]

In fact, the possibility for private actors to obtain protection for their patentable inventions covering multiple European countries via a single registration procedure in accordance with a single set of criteria already existed, since the entry into force of the European Patent Convention (EPC) in 1977. The EPC, which is an international treaty to which EU Member States as well as a number of other European countries are party, established a centralised patent registration system, administered by an international body created for this purpose, namely the European Patent Office (EPO),[43] which enables private actors to obtain, through a single procedure and subject to common registration criteria, a so-called 'European patent'. However, this European patent actually consists of a 'bundle' of individual national patent rights, one for each of the countries that applicants designate in their applications, as opposed to a single right that is valid throughout the European Union (as is the case with the CPVR). This means that the rights granted under a European patent must still be maintained and enforced in each of the relevant jurisdictions individually, in the same way as national patents granted pursuant to national registration procedures.[44] Hence, the main aim of the Unitary Patent Regulation is to accord European patents granted by the EPO unitary effect vis-à-vis EU Member States. In other words, the UP Regulation is intended to build on the EPC, by creating the possibility of obtaining a European patent *with unitary effect*, the main feature of which 'should be its unitary character, i.e. providing uniform protection and having equal effect in all the participating Member States.'[45] This way, as in the case of the CPVR, private actors would only need to obtain, maintain and enforce a single right in order to protect their intellectual property in the European Union (or, when it comes to the Unitary Patent, 'the participating EU Member States'), rather than a portfolio of national patent rights.

Yet, the UP Regulation is (at the time of writing) yet to become applicable, even though it was adopted by enhanced cooperation already some time ago, because its applicability is dependent on a parallel initiative to create a pan-European specialised patent court, known as the Unified Patent Court (UPC),[46] which is to have exclusive jurisdiction over actions relating to the validity and infringement of UPs (as well as European patents

---

42 Italy is now participating in enhanced cooperation in the area of the creation of unitary patent protection, however. This was confirmed at the end of September 2015, by Commission Decision (EU) 2015/1753.

43 In fact, the EPO is just one organ of the international organisation whose task it is to grant European patents (i.e. the European Patent Organisation); the other organ being the Administrative Council. See European Patent Convention, Art. 4.

44 Cf. H. Ullrich 'Select from within the system: The European patent with unitary effect', *Max Planck Institute for Intellectual Property and Competition Law Research Paper*, No. 12-11 (2012), p. 14.

45 UP Regulation, Preamble, Recital 7.

46 See UP Regulation, Art. 18(2).

without unitary effect within the EU), in place of existing national court systems. This newly-established European-level court is provided for in a separate intergovernmental agreement,[47] outside of the framework of the EU, which was signed at the beginning of 2013 and is currently in the process of being ratified by the signatory EU Member States (i.e. all of the EU Member States except for Spain and Poland, which decided not to participate, at least for the time being, as well as Croatia, which has not submitted a request to join the UP package, at least not yet).[48] And in the UP Regulation the EU legislator maintains that the establishment of 'a Unified Patent Court to hear cases concerning the European patent with unitary effect is essential in order to ensure the proper functioning of the patent, consistency of case-law and hence legal certainty…'[49] Therefore the UP will only start operating once the UPC agreement has come into effect.

Similarly to plant variety rights, patents provide inventors with a financial and proprietary incentive to innovate, as patent holders are entitled to prevent third parties from free use of the patented inventions for a certain period. And these inventions can certainly be of benefit to the public interest as well, be it in terms of public health or the environment. Whether it is for pharmaceutical products and medical processes, or climate change mitigation technologies such as renewable energy production and storage (i.e. so-called 'green patents', for which the EPO has established a new classification scheme[50]), patented inventions can patently serve to advance the state of the art of sustainability-friendly technology. This ties in with a number of the UN's sustainable development goals, including those of ensuring healthy lives and promoting well-being for all at all ages; ensuring access to affordable, reliable, sustainable and modern energy for all; and taking urgent action to combat climate change and its impacts.[51]

So, once it becomes operational, the UP Regulation will provide natural and legal persons with the possibility to obtain a European patent that benefits from unitary protection in all of the EU Member States save for Spain, as well as Croatia and Poland.[52] Just like European patents without unitary effect, European patents with unitary effect will be available for any inventions, in all fields of technology, provided that they satisfy the criteria for patentability required for European patents under the European Patent Convention

47 Agreement on a Unified Patent Court, 16351/12 (Brussels, 11 January 2013).

48 At the time of writing 15 signatory Member States have ratified the Agreement on a Unified Patent Court. In order for the agreement to enter into force a total of at least 13 states including France, Germany and the United Kingdom must accede to it and, of these latter Member States, currently only France has completed its ratification of the agreement.

49 UP Regulation, Preamble, Recital 25.

50 As stated on the EPO's website: www.epo.org/news-issues/issues/classification/classification.html.

51 I.e. United Nations Sustainable Development Goals 3, 7 and 13, respectively: www.un.org/sustainabledevelopment/sustainable-development-goals/.

52 This is because the UP cannot take effect in Poland as long as it does not participate in the UPC agreement, even though Poland did participate in the enhanced cooperation that led to the adoption of the UP Regulation.

(and particularly the requirements of novelty, inventive step and industrial application).[53] Like the CPVR, the possibility of obtaining a UP will not be subject to a cross-border requirement, although once again it will realistically only be an option worth considering for those who are seeking protection in a plurality of Member States. Such persons will be able to file an application for unitary patent protection to the EPO in English, French or German, and have any disputes concerning their UPs adjudicated upon by the UPC (in collaboration with the Court of Justice of the European Union via the preliminary ruling procedure[54]). And given that the Unitary Patent also offers an IP right with uniform protection across the EU (albeit in most rather than all Member States), it too will serve to strengthen the protection available in the EU when it finally comes into being. This is not to say that there are no points of concern surrounding the unitary patent package, but the general idea of creating unitary IP rights certainly seems to be a sound one, which is strongly supported by interested individuals.

On the other hand, it should again be pointed out that the reinforcement of the protection offered to inventors by IP systems in order to enable them to better realise the profits from their creations may also have the effect of hindering the development and adoption of more sustainable technologies. By inhibiting knowledge sharing and prolonging the lifespan of existing technologies for a certain period, intellectual property can lead to slower innovation cycles and uptake of sustainable alternatives in certain economic sectors. Still, as in the case of plant variety rights, there exists the possibility of compulsory licensing in patent law[55] as a way of balancing the interests of right holders in being able to exercise their rights with those of the public in seeing the emergence of new products. That is, in view of the need to ensure that refusals to licence do not unjustifiably prevent consumer demand being met 'on reasonable terms', patentees can be forced to share their patented technology with third parties, notwithstanding their exclusive rights under the patent. Admittedly, unlike the CPVR Regulation, the UP Regulation does not regulate the matter of compulsory licences for UPs, declaring instead that this is to be 'governed by the laws of the participating Member States as regards their respective territories.'[56] But most, if not all, EU Member States have exercised their right under Article 5(A) of the Paris Convention to pass legislation providing for compulsory licensing in the public interest.[57] Naturally, this does not mean to say that the possibility of compulsory licensing 'resolves'

53 See European Patent Convention, Art. 52 ff.

54 See Agreement on a Unified Patent Court, Art. 21.

55 Cf. Article 5(A) of the Paris Convention for the Protection of Industrial Property of 1883, subsection 2 of which guarantees the right of each State Party 'to take legislative measures providing for the grant of compulsory licenses to prevent the abuses which might result from the exercise of the exclusive rights conferred by the patent…'.

56 UP Regulation, Preamble, Recital 10.

57 See for example UK Patents Act 1977 (as amended), s. 48, Danish Patent Act, §47, etc.

the issue of IP rights being exercised in such a way as to restrict industrial development; in fact, the importance of the rules on compulsory licensing (certainly relative to rules on competition law) is debatable.[58] However, the existence of national rules on compulsory licensing does at least serve as an indication that in patent law efforts have been taken to avoid over-protection of individual interests.

9.7 European Contract Law

The last EU Optional Instrument of especial significance for this contribution is the 2011 proposal for a Regulation on a Common European Sales Law (CESL),[59] in the field of European contract law. Admittedly, this proposal has since been withdrawn (at the end of 2014),[60] but it nevertheless represents a significant initiative in the overall context of European private law, and one that may well be revisited in the future.[61]

The idea behind the CESL proposal was to create an optional contract law instrument that could be chosen (through agreement) by contracting parties as the applicable legal regime, which would govern various aspects of their contract, from its formation to its interpretation and the remedies that could be claimed in the event of its infringement. More precisely, had it been adopted as proposed, the Regulation would have made available this legal regime to contracting parties 'for cross-border transactions for the sale of goods, for the supply of digital content and for related services'.[62] The parties in question could be businesses and consumers or businesses alone, although in the latter case the scope of the proposed Regulation was limited to contracts between large parties on the one hand and SMEs on the other.[63] The aim of the CESL was therefore to enable these private actors

58 On this see for example, and further, C.S. Petersen *et al.*, 'The Unified Patent Court (UPC), Compulsory Licensing and Competition Law', 4 *Nordiskt Immaterieelt Rättskydd* (2014).

59 Proposal for a Regulation of the European Parliament and of the Council on a Common European Sales Law, COM(2011) 635 final.

60 See Annex to the Communication from the Commission to the European Parliament, the Council, the European Economic and Social Committee and the Committee of the Regions 'Commission Work Programme 2015: A New Start', COM(2014) 910 final, Annex 2, item 60 (p. 12).

61 On this possibility see for example H. Schulte-Nölke, 'Now More Than Ever: A Plea for an Optional EU Contact (sic.) and Consumer Code Forming an "EU Bill of Customer Rights"', 15 *Law of Business and Finance* (2017), p. 171.

62 COM(2011) 635 final, Art. 1(1). Under Article 4 of the proposed Regulation, cross-border transactions were defined (essentially) as contracts between parties in different countries, of which at least one is a Member State. This also means that the CESL could eventually have been opted into by contracting parties in third countries, although it would not have been available in situations where none of the contracting parties were based in a Member State.

63 That is, according to Article 7(1) of the proposed Regulation, the CESL could be used only if the seller of goods or the supplier of digital content is a trader. If all the parties to the contract were traders, the CESL could have been used as long as at least one of those parties was an SME.

to bypass differences in national contract laws in Europe by making available to them a 'self-standing uniform set of contract law rules' in all of the Member States.[64] That is, the Commission envisaged that the enactment of an optional sales contract law regime that is common to each of the Member States would allow market actors (particularly traders) to select this regime as the law (primarily) governing their various transactions within the European Union, 'instead of having to adapt to different national contract laws, provided that the other party to the contract agrees.'[65]

In fact, it is already possible for parties contracting between different jurisdictions to select the contract law regime of another jurisdiction as the regime governing their transactions, through a 'choice-of-law' clause. In the European Union, this possibility is (now) enshrined in the 'Rome I' Regulation,[66] Article 3(1) of which affirms that '[a] contract shall be governed by the law chosen by the parties. The choice shall be made expressly or clearly demonstrated by the terms of the contract or the circumstances of the case...'. This entails that, in situations involving a conflict of laws,[67] contracting parties (whether business-to-business or business-to-consumer) are free to choose the law applicable to the contract, be it the law of a Member State or a third country. However, as Article 6(2) of the same Regulation makes clear, when it comes to consumer contracts a choice of law made by the parties in accordance with Article 3 cannot 'have the result of depriving the consumer of the protection afforded to him by provisions that cannot be derogated by agreement by virtue of the law which, in the absence of choice, would have been applicable...' That is to say, the mandatory consumer protection rules of the law of the country where the consumer has his/her habitual residence[68] remain applicable to B2C contracts in which a choice for the law of another country has been made, to the extent that those rules offer greater protection than the law of that other country. Hence the reason why the Commission refers to the continued need for cross-border traders to 'adapt' their contracts particularly in relation to B2C transactions, for it is in the case of such transactions that, even with the possibility of choosing the applicable law, it can still be necessary for businesses to adapt to different (mandatory) national contract law rules.

Thus, as far as regards B2C contracts, it was envisaged that the creation of a European sales law providing also its own set of rules of consumer protection – which would be made available as a second contract law regime in each of the Member States[69] – would enable traders to make use of a common contract law regime to govern their dealings with con-

64 COM(2011) 635 final, p. 4.
65 COM(2011) 635 final, p. 4.
66 Regulation 593/2008 of the European Parliament and of the Council of 17 June 2008 on the law applicable to contractual obligations (Rome I).
67 See Rome I Regulation, Art. 1(1).
68 See Rome I Regulation, Art. 6(1).
69 See COM(2011) 635 final, p. 8.

sumers throughout Europe, while at the same time avoiding the residual application of national mandatory rules pursuant to Article 6(2) of the Rome I Regulation – since that Regulation only applies to choices of 'foreign' law, and not 'second national' regimes.[70] At the same time, a high level of protection for consumers would have nevertheless been guaranteed (at least according to the Commission) by virtue of the consumer protection rules provided in the CESL.[71] In other words, consumers across the EU who would have agreed to contracts governed by the CESL would have benefited from the same mandatory consumer rights as prescribed in the instrument, which in the case of most of the Member States would have been more protective than the rights provided under domestic law. It is true that a choice for the CESL would inevitably have led to 'some loss of protection on at least some subjects';[72] however, the instrument (at least as proposed) was nevertheless widely considered to provide a level of protection that was 'about as high under the CESL as it is under any national law'.[73] Indeed, this is in line with the legal basis chosen by the Commission for the CESL proposal, i.e. Article 114 TFEU, the third paragraph of which requires the Commission to 'take as a base a high level of protection'. And, more generally, this reflects the need that also exists in contract law to balance the personal autonomy and individual freedom with social concerns; and specifically in this case social justice for weaker parties.[74]

Accordingly, it was envisaged that the CESL would enhance consumer confidence 'and thus provide consumers with an incentive to enter into cross-border contracts on that basis.'[75] In this sense (if not also in others), therefore, it is arguable that the CESL could also have contributed to the achievement of sustainable goals, by instilling into consumers in the EU greater confidence to enter into contracts with traders and suppliers, who for their part would have been encouraged to offer their goods and services in Member States other than the State in which they are based. Taking the example of contracts for the supply of energy (as a typical example of a contract concluded at a distance), for instance, it is possible that the existence of a higher level of protection for the consumer under the contract would have empowered more consumers to consider alternative options for their

70 On this see further G. Low, 'Unitas via Diversitas: Can the Common European Sales Law Harmonise through Diversity?', 19 *Maastricht Journal of European and Comparative Law* 1 (2012), p. 132; M. Fornasier, '"28." versus "2. Regime" – Kollisionsrechtliche Aspekte eines optionalen europäischen Vertragsrechts', 76 *Rabels Zeitschrift für ausländisches und internationales Privatrecht* 2 (2012), p. 401.

71 See COM(2011) 635 final, Recital 11.

72 M.W. Hesselink, 'An Optional Instrument on EU Contract Law: Could it Increase Legal Certainty and Foster Cross-Border Trade?', Study for European Parliament Legal Affairs Committee, PE 425.642 (European Parliament, 2010), p. 16.

73 H. Beale, 'A Common European Sales Law (CESL) for Business-to-Business Contracts: Pros and Cons', 53 *Annales Universitatis Scientiarum Budapestinensis de Rolando* 133 (2012), p. 134-135.

74 On this see further, for e.g., Study Group on Social Justice in European private Law, 'Social Justice in European Contract Law: a Manifesto', *European Law Journal* 10 (2004).

75 COM(2011) 635 final, Recital 11.

energy supply and eventually to switch to providers offering, say, energy obtained from wholly renewable sources. Admittedly, whether or not the CESL would have proved a 'success' with businesses (not to mention consumers[76]) is a matter of some debate, although two Eurobarometer surveys of 2011 (one regarding business-to-business transactions and the other consumer transactions) did find that the proposal to introduce a single EU contract law for cross-border transactions 'was strongly favoured by the surveyed enterprises.'[77] At any rate, what does seem clear is that, in order to really facilitate cross-border trade, the CESL would have needed to attract parties to opt in.

9.8 CONCLUSION

In short, then, we have seen that European Union optional instruments may indeed serve to promote cross-border activities related to sustainable development – in fact, to one extent or another, they already do play a role in supporting sustainable activities within the EU. Whether it be in the area of company law, IP law or even contract law, optional instruments have been adopted or at least proposed by the European legislator that facilitate (or could facilitate) private ventures which can also be of benefit to the community and not only the individual. For example, sustainability-driven companies operating in the energy sector could set up a European Economic Interest Grouping together with a view to developing joint research and development activities; or obtain a Community Plant Variety Right over a novel strain of crop propagated for the production of a first-generation biofuel; or, once it comes into effect, apply for Unitary Patent protection to protect newly-developed technology for the storage of renewable energy. And, as an alternative form of common European rules, EU OIs offer important advantages over more traditional forms of EU private law-making in the strive to achieve sustainability goals. Most notably, EU OIs can enable private actors to transcend not only the disparate rules but also the territorial boundaries of Member State legal systems, by establishing regimes that are recognised in unison by all (or if not all then at least most) Member States. In contrast, regardless of the extent to which they are approximated, the domestic legal regimes of the Member States remain separate from each other and, for the most part, territorially limited. This means that, when it comes to many cross-border private activities, Optional Instruments of the European Union actually deliver something that EU approximating measures cannot.

76 The focus on businesses here can be explained by the fact that it would have essentially been up to businesses in the first place to determine whether or not to offer consumer contracts governed by the CESL; and only then would consumers have had the possibility to opt into the instrument.

77 Commission, Flash Eurobarometer 320, European contract law in business-to-business transactions, Analytical Report (2011) and Commission, Flash Eurobarometer 321, European contract law in consumer transactions, Analytical Report (2011), p. 7.

Accordingly, there are good reasons to conclude that, as a legislative tool of private law, such optional regimes can and do play an important role in empowering private individuals to develop initiatives that are also of benefit to society, insofar as they contribute to the implementation of sustainable solutions by private parties themselves, which in turn support the achievement of sustainable development goals. This claim could and should no doubt be tested further, however, particularly through empirical research that seeks to measure in more precise terms the influence existing optional instruments like those discussed in this contribution have on the facilitation of private sustainability-driven activities.

10 Conclusion: Private Law on Sustainability

Gijs van Dijck and Bram Akkermans

10.1 Private Law's Purpose

The lack of attention of private law scholars for sustainability issues[1] raises the important question whether private law has any role to play when it comes to sustainability. Private law's purpose, especially in terms of the facilitation of markets and the granting of autonomy to private parties to organise themselves and reach their own solutions, can be used both to advocate promoting sustainability as well as raising objections to do so.

In this book, Jaap Hage poses the question whether the law should aim to enhance sustainability. He warns not to jump to finding solutions in the law, but to also keep in mind the more general question whether the law has a role in the first place. The answer to this question may seem less obvious than one initially may expect.

Hage distinguishes between procedural justifications and substantive justifications for upholding 'sustainability laws', choosing substantive justifications over procedural ones (although they may overlap). He ultimately argues that happiness should be the measure to determine whether sustainability goals should be created and upheld. In this respect, it is argued that only the happiness matters of those who are capable of providing sufficient thought to the question whether they want to continue living.

From the contributions we of course cannot infer who is or feels capable of giving sufficient thought to whether they want to continue living. However, it is possible to obtain an idea of whether the authors, and the legal community they refer to, believe sustainability should play a role, plays a role, and how it plays a role when evaluating or designing private law.

Agustin Parise refers to a wealth of literature that signals a paradigm shift from a liberal model of individual protection to a more ecological model with more responsibility for the property holder as to secure sustainability. From this, it can be inferred that the ecological considerations regarding sustainability have already been taking place.

1 See, exceptional to this, U. Mattei and A. Quarta, *The Turning Point in Private Law*, Northampton (Edward Elgar, 2018).

Bram Akkermans and Jill Robbie both seem to presuppose the importance of sustainability. They argue in favour of a modified property law in which sustainability goals have a central role. In this respect, Robbie, in her analysis of the reform of property rights regarding water, private water rights in particular, challenges the division between public law and private law (pointing out environmental protection and regulations that interact with existing property rules), the individual ownership paradigm, the national focus, and the monodisciplinary approach that have been characterising property law. The same elements are mentioned by Akkermans, who adds, among other things, that human flourishing should be the theoretical foundation that underlies property law and that regulators should take action in order the safeguard or enhance sustainability.

The contributions of Michael Faure and Yayun Shen and Gijs van Dijck depart from a different starting point. They do not take position on whether sustainability should be pursued. Their contributions predominantly focus on what private law, environmental law and liability law in particular, can or should do *if* sustainability goals are to be promoted. In this respect, Van Dijck examines how tort law can be made more suitable to address environmental harm, whereas Faure and Shen more generally discuss the instruments within environmental law that can contribute to achieving more sustainability, while stressing the interplay between public and private regulation as well as the need for an multidisciplinary approach.

Kim Berg and Mark Kawakami address the question of the role of company law in curbing environmental harms if they are or would be required to do so, while not explicitly taking position in favour of or against enhancing sustainability. Bull, in turn, explores the use of optional instruments after identifying a need for regulation of the sharing economy. He explains it is not only important to analyse how private law can respond substantively to developments in the field of the sharing economy, but that it is also necessary to investigate in which form regulation should take place.

10.2 Sustainability and Private Law

According to Parise, a paradigm shift can be sensed when an established assumption is replaced, which is often illustrated by an event that affects at least one of the sources of law. We can observe such a possible replacement in multiple contributions.

Parise, who concentrates on whether a paradigm shift has taken place or is taking place in the field of property law, finds signs of such a shift. Parise's analysis suggests that the nineteenth century's liberal paradigm of ownership is being replaced by one where the social and ecological function of ownership is more prominent, with more room for state intervention and more responsibility for the property holder to use the object to the benefit of society. In fact, Parise claims that "never before has environment occupied the paramount position within the paradigms of ownership". Pivotal in the emerging paradigm is the duty to secure sustainability.

Akkermans' contribution seconds Parise's findings on this crucial point. Akkermans points to the role of private law, referring to principles such as freedom of ownership, free circulation of goods, and the freedom of contract as the core principles that are being challenged. He refers to a division in the literature, with the difference essentially boiling down to whether or not to consider well-being and equality in addition to the traditional view. In the traditional view the right of ownership is seen as an individual right for which increase in personal wealth and individual welfare are the underlying principles and purposes. Akkermans points to several signs of a possible paradigm shift, such as an increase in popularity of commons (right of ownership is shared by a large group). The platform economy and the circular economy can also be seen as examples of the paradigm shift.

Akkermans himself contributes to the paradigm shift by developing a property law that internalises the concept of sustainability while not abandoning (traditional) property law and while not moving towards a communal system. His analysis leads to his algorithm for the creation of sustainable property law, which consists of 12 foundations that may serve as the guiding principles for a property law aimed at enhancing sustainability. Signs for the same paradigm shift can also be observed in Robbie's contribution, who points to the Scottish Government setting a target of an increase of 100% of electricity generated through renewable sources by 2020, and to the UK, which has set targets for the year 2020 for energy need to be generated by renewables. Through her focus on private water rights, she illustrates how property law can be reformed in the light of sustainability. She also shows how we must move beyond the current boundaries of property law, such as the difference between private law and public law and the idea of individual ownership. With that Robbie sees the role of property law in helping us preserve the use of the world's resources also for future generations.

The ecological paradigm, or the challenge to move to such a paradigm, also becomes visible in the field of environmental law. Faure and Shen point out that environmental regulation does not necessarily restrict companies' profits. The Porter Hypothesis predicts that it in fact can result in higher profitability. Two versions of this hypothesis exist. The first version entails that stricter environmental regulation leads to more innovation. The second version is that stricter regulation enhances business performance. The empirical evidence for the first version is strong, but mixed for the second version.

Faure and Shen then turn to the requirements liability rules must meet in order to provide proper incentives for preventing environmental harm: strict liability is preferred over negligence, solvency guarantees should exist, no statutory limit (caps) should be imposed, and liability should be attributed to all who caused the harm. The issue, however, is that private law remedies available to individual victims may not be compatible with environmental harm redress. The damage may be too low for an individual victim for him to have a proper incentive to initiate legal action, issues of causation or latency are to be expected, and collective redress may prove too costly.

Some of the liability issues are further explored by Van Dijck. Taking the Urgenda case as an example, he discusses the loss and causality requirements, also in relation to an injunction. The Urgenda case most notably demonstrates that the interpretation of the loss criterion in terms of a 'possibility of a loss' rather than an actual loss, the burden of proof on the plaintiff can be alleviated. Requesting and ordering an injunction further alleviates this burden, as it results in the claimant not having to prove a loss, and as a result, not having to prove causality between the injustice and the loss, at least under Dutch law, although causality may still become an issue when wrapped in a 'sufficient interest' coat. Regardless, the main takeaway is that courts have substantial leeway as to whether they want to give way for sustainability arguments. This can be achieved by reinterpreting tort law norms and concepts rather than abandoning them. Whether courts do may ultimately boil down to how sympathetic the court is regarding the environmental claim at stake.

Faure and Shen discuss another way of how private actors can enhance sustainable development: through corporate social responsibility (CSR), a form of self-regulation where stakeholders themselves take on engagements that go beyond government regulation. Advantages of CSR types of regulation include the expertise of the stakeholders involved, low organisational and administrative costs, and a large willingness to apply norms and standards that stakeholders created themselves, which altogether leads to a higher intrinsic motivation of the stakeholders to comply. However, CSR also comes with limitations, for instance free-riding and the voluntary nature to adhere to and comply with CSR standards, causing compliance and enforcement to be weak.

CSR forms the starting point of the contribution by Berg and Kawakami. They analyse how to preserve the intrinsic motivations stakeholders already have and how to differentiate socially responsible companies from those that are not in order to incentivise the latter to change. Regarding a paradigm shift, Berg and Kawakami argue that a culture paradigm shift needs to take place in order to enhance sustainability, and they explore how such a shift could take place. Berg and Kawakami observe that profit maximisation currently is still the dominant perspective, yet identify cracks in this primacy, which can be illustrated by the introduction of the Directive on Disclosure of Non-Financial and Diversity Information, as it requires certain companies to disclose environmental and social information in their annual reports. The incentive of such rules is, however, not straightforward. Empirical findings suggest that the tool of shareholder proposals is rarely used in the EU, that sustainability issues are addressed in a minority of instances, and that 'firms increase their performance on immaterial issues following shareholder proposals, while in fact it decreases the firms' market valuation subsequently'. Moreover, companies may not truthfully disclose, regardless of whether and how sustainability-related disclosure is regulated, investors may not pay attention to these matters, and regulation may not address relevant issues that require disclosure. Shareholder activism may therefore have a limited impact, or even have counterproductive effects when it comes to enhancing sustainability. Berg and Kawakami conclude that the activation of internal motives is ultimately required to make companies and their stakeholders more sustainable and socially conscious, and that what needs to change 'is not necessarily company law, but corporate culture'.

Bull, finally, explores the use and applicability of optional instruments, which can be described as the practice where private actors wishing to execute a legal act in a certain jurisdiction choose the applicable regime. Bull shows how optional instruments can assist in empowering private parties to work towards their own sustainable solutions. The role of private law, in Bull's perspective, can be to facilitate sustainability initiatives rather than to regulate them. This analysis places the role of private law in a yet unexplored perspective when exploring the effect of sustainability. The need for private parties to contribute towards a sustainable society is part of many international agreements. For these private parties to be able to do so, rules of private law must enable them to do so. As Bull shows, European optional instruments may serve to promote cross-border activities relating to sustainable development.

10.3 The Future of Sustainability Research in Private Law

We make at least three important observations for setting a research agenda on sustainability in private law. A first observation is one of delineation. Most authors do not define the concept of sustainability. Of course the Brundtland definition on sustainable development provides some general insight, yet it does not make very specific which aspects are to be included and which not. Most authors seem to assume that sustainability refers to ecological sustainability, but the concept of sustainability is wider than that. It also includes aspects of democracy and governance, which may make the concept too broad and eclectic for research purposes. This begs the question what sustainability means in a legal context, in a private law context in particular, and whether it should be defined as broad as others have done or more narrow in order to prevent the term from losing its innovativeness, since other concepts such as democracy and governance already exist and have been studied within and outside of private law.

Second, the contributions show that there is a role for private law to play, in different areas (property law, liability law, company law) as well as in different ways (substantively, procedurally). At the same time, the question can be posed whether private law, law in general, or even regulation has a role. Regulation may even reach counterproductive results. Although both positions (role, no role) cannot be true at the same time, they do point to a new avenue of research: When and where the law or regulation has a role, and perhaps more interesting, when and where does it not?

Third, there is the element of incommensurability. Working on sustainability often results in a financial burden that needs to be allocated. Working to eradicate poverty, or on income equality may be detrimental to economic growth. Protecting forests or water may even result in additional costs that will also reduce the rate of economic growth. The tension between the achievement of these sustainability objectives is likely to be irreconcilable, as it involves values originating from fundamentally different value domains (monetary, capacity, collectiveness) for which no measure is available to determine which value is to be preferred. How to deal with such incommensurability deserves attention.

These aspects discussed in this conclusion give rise to a research agenda for the near future. As the pressure to change our way of living grows and we begin speaking of climate crisis instead of climate change, and the energy transition towards leaving fossil fuels behind is in full progress, private law will have to determine its place.[2] By enabling private parties, as well as companies, to factor in sustainability into their decision making processes, private law can contribute to fulfilling one of the most important objectives of the UN SDGs: we can and must all contribute – at every level of scale – towards changing the way in which we live. More work, therefore, remains to be done to further explore the contributions of private law. This requires a commitment to investigate not only the role private law can play, but also what specific – sustainable – solutions private law can offer.

2 See, e.g. www.theguardian.com/environment/2019/may/17/why-the-guardian-is-changing-the-language-it-uses-about-the-environment.

About the authors

Bram Akkermans is associate professor of European Property Law and Sustainability at Maastricht University. He is also associate director of the Maastricht European Private Law Institute (MEPLI).

Kim Berg is a PhD candidate at ICGI (Institute for Corporate Law, Governance and Innovation Policies), connected to the Private Law department of the Faculty of Law in Maastricht.

William Bull is assistant professor of private law at Maastricht University and coordinator of the European Private Law Maastricht Project.

Gijs van Dijck is professor of Private Law at Maastricht University, director of the Maastricht European Private Law Institute (MEPLI), coordinator of the Maastricht Law and Tech Lab, and Principal Investigator at the Brightlands Institute for Smart Society (BISS).

Michael Faure is professor of Comparative and International Environmental Law at Maastricht University. Michael Faure is also professor of Comparative Private Law and Economics and Managing Director of the European Doctorate in Law and Economics at the Erasmus University School of Law. He is academic director of the Ius Commune Research School and the Maastricht European institute for Transnational Legal Research (METRO).

Jaap Hage is professor of Jurisprudence at Maastricht University.

Mark Kawakami is an assistant professor of private law at Maastricht University and the coordinator of the Maastricht Mediation Clinic and the Maastricht Neuroeconomics, Mindfulness, and Law Network.

Agustín Parise is associate professor of law at Maastricht University. He is also director of scientific studies of the International Association of Legal Science.

Jill Robbie is a lecturer in Private Law at the University of Glasgow.

Yayun Shen is a researcher in Environmental Law and Economics at the Rotterdam Institute of Law and Economics (RILE), Erasmus University Rotterdam.

Maastricht Law Series

The Maastricht Law Series is created in 2018 by Boom juridisch and Eleven International Publishing in association with the Maastricht University Faculty of Law. The Maastricht Law Series publishes books on comparative, European and International law. The series builds upon the tradition of excellence in research at the Maastricht Faculty of Law, its research centers and the Ius Commune Research School. The Maastricht Law Series is a peer reviewed book series that allows researchers an excellent opportunity to showcase their work.

Published in this series:

Volume 1: Reinhard Zimmermann, Does the Law of Succession Reflect Cultural Differences?, ISBN 978-94-6236-856-9
Volume 2: Anna Berlee, Access to personal data in public land registers, ISBN 978-94-6236-841-5
Volume 3: Marcus Meyer, The Position of Dutch Works Councils in Multinational Corporations, ISBN 978-94-6236-848-4
Volume 4: Jaap Hage, Foundations and Building Blocks of Law, ISBN 978-94-6236-860-6
Volume 5: Bastiaan van Zelst, The End of Justice(s)?, ISBN 978-94-6236-881-1
Volume 6: Lars van Vliet & Agustin Parise (eds.), Re- De- Co-dification? New Insights on the Codification of Private Law, ISBN 978-94-6236-900-9
Volume 7: Caroline Rupp, Rafael Ibarra Garza & Bram Akkermans, Property Law Perspectives VI, ISBN 978-94-6236-904-7
Volume 8: Aalt Willem Heringa, Europees Nederlands Staatsrecht, ISBN 978-94-6290-604-4
Volume 9: Symeon C. Symeonides, The "Private" in Private International Law, ISBN 978-94-6236-949-8
Volume 10: Jaap Hage, European Integration, ISBN 978-94-6236-981-8

Volume 11: Jan M. Smits, Five Uneasy Pieces. Essays on Law and Evolution, ISBN 978-94-6236-982-5
Volume 12: Hannah Brodersen, Vincent Glerum, & André Klip, The European Arrest Warrant and In Absentia Judgements, ISBN 978-94-6236-985-6
Volume 13: Bram Akkermans & Gijs van Dijck, Sustainability and Private Law, ISBN 978-94-6236-986-3
Volume 14: Antonia Waltermann, David Roef, Jaap Hage & Marko Jelicic, Law, Science, Rationality, ISBN 978-94-6236-989-4

9 789462 369863

Printed by Libri Plureos GmbH in Hamburg,
Germany